FILM ART PHENOMENA

Nicky Hamlyn

 Publishing

This edition first published in 2003 by the
British Film Institute
21 Stephen Street
London W1T 1LN

The British Film Institute promotes greater understanding and appreciation of, and access
to, film and moving image culture in the UK.

Cover design: ketchup
Cover illustration: *On and Off/Monitor* (2002) by Simon Payne

Set by: Wyvern 21 Ltd, Bath
Printed in the United Kingdom by Cromwell Press, Trowbridge, Wiltshire

British Library Cataloguing-in-Publication Data

A catalogue record for this book is available from the British Library
ISBN 0 85170 972 9 (pbk)
ISBN 0 85170 971 0 (hbk)

Contents

For Claire and Felix

Acknowledgments

I would like to thank A. L. Rees for encouraging me to undertake this project in the first place. The Photography and Moving Image Research Group at Kent Institute of Art and Design contributed to my expenses and to the cost of colour reproductions. Ben Cook and Mike Sperlinger at the Lux Holding Company and David Curtis at the British Artists' Film and Video Study Collection at Central St Martins College of Art and Design have been unfailingly kind and helpful. The following have also helped in various ways: Nick Collins, William English, David Humphrey, Greg Kurcewicz, Karen Mirza, Professor Peter Mobbs, Annabel Nicolson, Simon Payne, William Raban and Guy Sherwin. I would also like to thank the BFI library and my editor Rob White for getting me to think properly about the structure and purpose of the book. I thank especially all the film- and video-makers for providing information, images and support.

Parts of Chapters 1, 2 and 6 appeared originally as 'Film, Video, TV' in the journal *Coil*, issue 9–10 (London: Proboscis, 2000). Parts of Chapter 6 appeared as 'Michael Snow Retrospective at Arnolfini Gallery', in *Film Waves* no. 15 (London: Obraz Publications, 2001). Parts of Chapters 6 and 10 appeared as 'John Smith's Local Locations' in *John Smith Film and Video Work 1972–2002* (Bristol: Watershed/Picture This Publications, 2002). Parts of Chapter 7 appeared as 'Andy Warhol Films at Tate Modern' in *Film Waves 16* (London: Obraz Publications, 2001). The second part of Chapter 8 is an expanded version of a catalogue essay written for *Strange Attachments*, a programme I curated for the Pandaemonium festival held at the Lux Centre, London, in 2000.

Introduction

It is only shallow people who do not judge by appearances. The mystery of the World is the visible, not the invisible.[1]

Does the spectator ever succeed in exhausting the objects he contemplates?[2]

This book offers some ways of thinking about aspects of artists' film and video. To this end I have drawn as much on my own experiences as a film-maker as I have from critical thinking and writing in the area. I have identified a number of constituents and issues in the practice, and each chapter is devoted to one of these, in relation to which a small selection of works is discussed. However, the topics announced in the chapter headings are, as often as not, a starting point for a train of thought which takes in other issues. This means that there is some overlap between chapters, and recurrence of works discussed.

I have endeavoured to confine myself to work which takes on the challenge facing an interrogative film and video culture: how can media designed to represent the world as effortlessly as possible (viz. the triumph of the camcorder) be used to question the adequacy, desirability and givenness of those representations? In other words, how can those media be turned against themselves? This question has guided the choice of work that I have made for discussion. Nevertheless there are eligible films and videotapes which are not included. Their absence reflects only the fact that the book is not intended to be compendious.

My background as a Fine Art student has crucially informed my attitude to film, art and cinema. My relation to the first two has been enthusiastic, whereas I have always had a profound ambivalence towards the latter. Youthful exposure to films like *Tom Thumb* and *In Search of the Castaways*, as well as early episodes of *Dr Who*, made me vaguely aware of the emotional power of the moving image, but I remember, as a teenager, coming home after a visit to see Zeffirelli's *Romeo and Juliet* (1968), conscious that I had been emotionally manipulated and that this was in the nature of the form, and not so much a product of the play itself, moving though it is. On the other hand, seeing Robert Morris's felt pieces at the Tate Gallery, at the age of fourteen, left me baffled but intrigued, and this was a much more productive and positive experience for me. My formation really began there, with Morris, Mondrian, and Warhol's silver cushions.

As a painting student at Reading University, fresh from Art A level, I was plunged into an alien but dynamic environment where muscular post-painterly abstraction, performance and installation jostled together. I abandoned painting, having fallen fortuitously into film after successfully participating in a project run by my part-time tutor, Ron Haselden, who had trained as a sculptor but was for several years a film-maker and subsequently a maker of mixed-media, multi-screen projections – Expanded Cinema – sculptural installations and, latterly, light-works. Some of this work is discussed in the book. I was also taught by a diversity of visiting lecturers who supplemented Ron's part-time post, a number of whom were crucial in my education: Peter Gidal, Stuart Brisley, Malcolm Le Grice, Marc Chaimowicz, Mary Kelly and others. Gidal and Le Grice's films obviously have had a big impact on my own film-making, and their theorising and polemics have informed the theoretical assumptions of this book. Specifically, Gidal's critique of academic film studies, which is a critique of retrospective theorising which fails to engage with its effects on the spectator, has been important.

A crucial event, referred to several times, was the Festival of Expanded Cinema, held at the ICA, London, in January 1976. I was in my final year as a student and had been encouraged to participate in the organisation of the event by Ron Haselden, who was also on the selection panel. This was a kind of coming of age for me (the festival began on my twenty-second birthday) because it included a number of my peers who were all slightly too young to have been involved in the London Film-makers' Co-op in its structural materialist heyday: Rob Gawthrop, Bob Fearns, Steve Farrer, Roger Hewins. The festival was notable for the wide variety of multi-screen and mixed-media work, not only by established film-makers, but also by a number of artists from outside the Co-op ambit: Carolee Schneeman, Rosalind Schneider, Derek Jarman, Peter Logan and others.

In the decade when I was a student, art was frequently discussed in relation to politics, and the politics of form became an important and central issue in these debates. (A flavour of those times was afforded by the *Live in Your Head* exhibition, held at the Whitechapel Gallery, London, in 2000.) I hope I have kept some of that debate going here. In doing so I have inevitably returned to work from the 70s, but I have also looked at recent material which, in continuing the exploratory and scep-tical tradition of structural materialist film, runs counter to the Faustian euphoria surrounding digital media and virtual reality.

Inevitably, perhaps, a film versus video theme runs through parts of the book. This reflects my own anxieties and preoccupations as a film-maker trying to decide how to deal with the threat to my medium posed by the proliferation of digital systems and the gradually decreasing use of 16mm film. For despite film's buoyant profile within the artists' film community and, increasingly, within the art world via Tacita Dean, Stan Douglas and others, this is a commercial medium and as commercial use declines, so too will the availability of film stock and facilities: many of the labs in London no longer print 16mm film, because 98 per cent of the negative they process is transferred straight to video. When 16mm negative can no longer compete with tape or disc as an originating medium, negative processing too will no doubt cease, even though, at the time of writing, medium-sized labs like Todd-AO are processing about 1 million feet of colour negative per month. None of the foregoing should be taken as constituting an anti-video stance, however. Some of the best new work is video so, far from pitching film against tape, I have tried to show how the work of Guy Sherwin and Simon Payne, for example, plays to the strengths of those respective media.

A lot of thought has been devoted to form and structure, because they are a fundamental issue for makers of non-narrative film and video. In narrative movies, form is to a major extent predetermined by a combination of the demands of the screenplay, genre and grammatical conventions. Film and video artists do not have this convenience (which in any case they would see as a hindrance). They must create from scratch, and thus these forms or structures often become the principal feature of a lot of this kind of work, hence the importance of *structural film*.

For parts of the book I have cannibalised earlier essays and reviews, so some of the material may be familiar to readers of small magazines and, occasionally, books. Hopefully, however, these recycled sections will also find a new readership who in any case would have difficulties in tracking down the originals. The bulk of the writing, though, is new. I have tried to discuss work which is available, if not familiar, to the reader. Much of it is in distribution in the UK and elsewhere, and is at least occasionally screened. For a modest fee, private viewings can usually be arranged both at the Lux Holding Company and the British Film Institute. Failing that, there is nothing to stop students clubbing together and hiring films, as my own students have done.

Notes

1. Lord Henry Wotton, in *The Picture of Dorian Gray* (1891) by Oscar Wilde, quoted in Susan Sontag, *Against Interpretation* (New York: Delta Books, 1966), p. 3. This oft-quoted passage is also recited by the narrator in Patrick Keiller's film *Robinson in Space* (1997), BFI/Connoisseur Video.
2. Siegfried Kracauer, *Theory of Film* (Princeton, NJ: Princeton University Press, 1997), p. 165.

I

MEDIA

I

Film and Video

Film's similarity to photography – its form as a string of photographs – has affected the way film-makers have thought about it. Equally, film precedes video, and its terminology is widely used in video's: people talk about 'filming' and 'films' when they actually mean 'recording' and 'videotapes'. In the 1980s, when arguments about media specificity were perhaps more essentialist than now, or at least were thought to be so in some quarters, there was a rather self-conscious effort to tighten up these sloppy usages, by video artists who sought to distinguish themselves from film-makers by describing themselves as 'tape makers'.[1] One can see numerous precedents to the history and thinking about these media in the history of technology: the earliest cars looked like horse-drawn carriages without the horses, but after a while their appearance changed, as designers realised that they were designing the former, not the latter.

Over the last two decades there have been arguments, more or less interesting, about the respective merits of video and film. For writers like Peter Wollen the relevance of these debates has long been eclipsed by the widespread presence of hybrid forms – videos shot on film, films cut on tape – a tendency he noted in his introduction to the Arrows of Desire show held at the ICA, London, in 1992.[2] (It is worth noting that the now ubiquitous production path of film to video via digital editing reflects more than anything else the fact that most moving image production is destined for TV or corporate/AV presentation.) At the same time though, Wollen has protested loudly at plans by the BFI to distribute on video films that were hitherto available as 16mm prints. Wollen's stance epitomises the state of the debate: on the one hand film, video and digital are all current moving image media, all equally viable and in some respects interchangeable. On the other hand, it is important to respect the integrity of a work's original medium: there are still significant differences between these media in terms of how they are experienced. Top quality video projection, with added digital grain and flicker (an utterly pointless development), may yet appear indistinguishable from the 16mm equivalent. On the other hand, a gallery full of projectors running film loops could not be more different from a multi-monitor video installation. Film projectors in galleries inevitably draw attention to themselves. The best work made for this format plays on the contrast between the sculptural/mechanical presence of the projector, the filmstrip, and the projected image itself. Video projectors are relatively self-effacing machines, whose noiseless operation facilitates the direction of the viewer's attention to the image.[3]

The dramatic differences in costs and working practices at different stages in the production process have affected the way the different media are approached. Guy Sherwin has made an explicit commitment to film, arguing for its strong ontological links to the profilmic. The cheapness and mutability of video have allowed David Larcher to assemble large-scale, improvisatory works that would be considered extravagant, not to say impossible, had they been created on film.

Video: TV

After the *Seven TV Pieces* (discussed in Chapter 6) David Hall made a group of films with Tony Sinden which took an analytical approach to questions such as the picture plane (*This Surface*, 1972–3); to depth, foreshortening and framing (*Edge*, 1972–3); acting (*Actor*, 1972–3); the projection event (*Between*, 1972–3); and abstraction/ambiguity through framing (*View*, 1972–3). *Between* is one of the most media-specific of Hall's works. A cameraman walks backwards and forwards along the cone of light thrown by a film projector, capturing his shadow as he walks towards the screen, and the light coming from the projector as he returns. At every turn we see a copy of the previous section, then a copy of the copy and so on, until the image has broken down into high-contrast grain patterns.

This technique was used again in the videotape *This is a Television Receiver*, which was broadcast unannounced at the opening of BBC2's *Arena* programme on 10 March 1976. Richard Baker, then well known as a newsreader, recites a didactic text describing the physical features of a typical TV set. He goes on to explain that what looks like a man is not actually a man but the image of a man, and what sounds like a man's voice is in fact 'vibrations on a cone'. The two played together create the impression of a man talking, 'but it is not a man'. At the completion of Baker's speech we see a copy of it, made by reshooting the original from the TV screen. This is followed by a copy of the copy and so on for three repeats.

Describing the work in this manner may make it sound banal and mechanical, but within the context of broadcast TV the work is subversive in a number of ways. Although they often become celebrities, newsreaders rarely draw attention to themselves, much less their function, in the way Richard Baker does here. TV personalities almost never discuss the medium in a manner that calls into question its nature and raison d'être: such debates, on programmes like *Points of View*, are usually over the content, costumes or performances in a programme, or concern allegations of bias or imbalance within a programme or the institution as a whole. The unannounced insertion of an event like *This is a Television Receiver* throws into relief the character of most TV programming, hopefully giving the viewer pause for thought.

This is a Television Receiver, David Hall

By the time we reach the final repeat the image and sound have deteriorated dramatically. The grossly distorted face appears now as a smear of coloured lines, which pulsate around the hard edges of the screen. Landscape-like spaces can be read into what has become a mesmerising, ethereal image. The pleasure thus derived is in itself subversive, since it substitutes an anti-TV aesthetic of 'useless' pleasure for the dull instrumentalism of most output. Furthermore one can contemplate, in its unfolding, the widening gap between what one 'knows' one is watching and what is actually unfolding before the eyes: at a certain point one is obliged to recognise that the 'image of a man' can really no longer be so described, even though it is derived from that original image. The virtual space initially occupied by the talking head has been displaced by an abstract surface, whose rippling immateriality emphasises the constraining boxiness of the TV set.

The process of making a copy of the copy uses a visible, material process to expose the nature of the video image, magnifying the stream of electronic pulses, RGB gun-firings and brief phosphor-glowings that create the illusion of an image.[4] The noise in the (analogue) system which causes the deterioration from generation to generation increasingly becomes the subject of the work. This too is part of its subversiveness: the idea that an unwanted by-product of data transfer might displace the carefully engineered products of broadcast television to give the viewer something just as interesting, if not more so, to watch.

Video

This approach – by which unwanted, intrusive or negative phenomena are positively embraced – is deployed (digitally) by David Larcher in his tape *Videovøid* (1993), some of whose imagery is conjured from tape 'dropout'. The images spring out of a negative paradox, tape dropout being the trace of an absence, in this case of magnetic coating from the tape's base material, resulting in the horizontal white lines familiar to viewers of rented videos.

Larcher has long been interested in the trace, a phenomenon that can be distinguished from the indexical sign by its immateriality. A footprint stands as evidence of a substantial event with lasting, palpable consequences: the foot can be reconstructed as a plaster cast, for example. The trace, by contrast, exists only fleetingly, as a record of an event such as the passing of a bird, that might leave no more evidence than a momentary disturbance in the movement of the air. Some such phenomena, or epiphenomena, will only be caught, if at all, as a moving image.

Before he began working in video, Larcher made very long films – *Mare's Tail* (1969, 2½ hours), *Monkey's Birthday* (1973–5, 6 hours) – which are notable for the extensive, laborious reworking that took place on the camera footage using an optical printer. Clearly video, with its flexibility and ease of use in post-production, is a far more suitable medium for someone like Larcher, who made immediate and effective use of it in *EETC* in 1986.

EETC is a transitional, hybrid work that was shot on a mixture of film and tape. Post-production began on film, with optical printing at the London Film-makers' Co-op, and was completed on tape: 'off off off lined at London Video Arts'. Larcher's earlier films were assembled from accumulated quantities of footage gathered while travelling with his family in their Mercedes lorry around various parts of the world. *EETC* continues this trend of diary/home-movie making, except that now the footage is continuously reworked, re-examined according to the unifying idea of the 'trace'. The recurring image of a flock of birds flying in an E-shaped formation is eventually accompanied by the words spoken on the soundtrack by the French painter Tal Coat: 'a flight is also nothing but a trace. A flight of birds ... you see the flight ... you no longer see the bird. When is the bird, when is the flight, when is the trace?'

After a protracted 'title sequence' *EETC* opens in a manner that looks backwards to film even as it simultaneously introduces a live matting and luma-key performance. The camera points at a portable cinema screen set up in the landscape. Larcher enters the frame to put on a handclap sync-mark, a common practice amongst documentary film-makers when it is impractical to use a clapper-board. At about the same time, a rectangular matte is superimposed on the screen, in such a way that when Larcher walks into shot he sometimes appears within the matted area, and sometimes without. There follows a series of variations on this set-up, during which he sprays the screen black, white, then black again, establishing a set of screens within screens, which eventually are all sprayed black. This blackening of the screen renders it useless for projecting onto, but perfect for luma-keying.

The sequence establishes a number of things. First, we are posited as an audience, about to see a projection (fiction) on a screen which is bordered by the real world (which also has its own off-screen audience who are heard but not seen). But this distinction between fictive and real is broken down, as soon as it is established, by the matting of new background images in place of the opening ones. The constant swapping around of foreground and background breaks down the initially naturalistic space, replacing it with collaged images whose spatial relationships are unfixed or contradictory. The images contained within one or other of the rectangular mattes periodically bleed through into adjacent rectangles. When this happens the spatial recession implied by the array of frames within frames is undermined.

Semantic relationships are also created, for example between grain reticulation seen in close-up (the microstructure of the image) and its macro effect (the background landscape) and between grain and flower petals (both organic materials).

In technological terms this sequence is the most interesting in the whole work. The manual creation of what are usually electronic procedures – sync-marks, mattes, luma-key backgrounds (similar to the more familiar 'blue screen' background used in special effects sequences) implies neither an anachronistic distrust of impersonal new technologies, nor a sentimental attachment to the craft ethos of film. Rather it should be seen as a way of taking control of those video processes which normally come with predefined engineering parameters which inevitably bring their own look to TV work. Larcher's actions serve to demystify these production processes, which are commonly used, but which are usually either concealed or are, by their electronic nature, invisible.

At the end of this sequence, edge fogging intrudes from the left-hand side of the screen, adding yet another layer to the process, reminding the viewer that for all the elaborate and quite concrete-seeming on-screen activity of handclapping and spray painting, this is still in the end only a flimsy image born out of a highly refined controlling and channelling of light: 'the sky is everywhere' as Tal Coat says on the soundtrack.

At the end of *EETC* the screen-within-a-screen template remains, but we have left the hybrid, organic world behind and arrived at a wholly electronic space filled with skewed video colours and slow-motion scan lines.

Cookery

Throughout the work analogies are drawn between the trace, film-making and cooking as processes. (It's fitting, in this regard, that the Austrian film-maker Peter Kubelka was a professor of film-making and cooking at the Frankfurt Academy of Fine Arts.) This association between film-making and cooking bespeaks the gulf between the old and new media. The old media were hands-on, the technology transparent and craft-based. We see film of Larcher hand-processing film in a Morse tank, while on the soundtrack, a voice describes the way that gelatine, the medium containing the light-sensitive silver halide crystals, is produced. We also see film cans being opened and closed and 16mm film being hung out to dry in a garden. We hear the 'music' of film rolls flapping round on a Steenbeck editing table, and in a scene where logs are thrown from one spot to another, the raw sound of the logs clonking against each other is sampled and 'cooked' into a set of musical phrases. This process precisely

prefigures the major processes of *Ich Tank* (discussed in Chapter 2) whereby naturalistic sources are transformed into highly synthetic sequences. The
multi-dimensional spatialities of *Ich Tank* are also prefigured in *EETC*, except here
it is time that is so treated. When the 16mm film is hung out to dry in the garden, we
see an image in the present of an event from the past, which itself contains images
of events from further back in time. The 16mm film constitutes a future to that past
image in that it will be seen – printed and projected, perhaps incorporated into *EETC*
– at some future date. Near the end of *EETC*, we see a screen within a screen within
a screen of Larcher watching himself watching himself knocking a hole in a wall,
except that in the innermost screen – the hole knocking – the film is running backwards. Thus a void is being filled with a sledge hammer, and the time of the innermost
screen is running backwards towards that of the outer ones.

As *EETC* progresses the pace increases: photographs, movie footage and mattes
are churned into an electronic flux of grain, colour, distortion and vestigial images.
The representations of processes seen earlier in the work are themselves processed
and incorporated into ever more complex collages. The difficulty of describing the
work in conventional terms – there are no shots or scenes in the usual sense – is a
function of its state of flux. Our language is based around a division of the world into

EETC, David Larcher

objects which are located in a determinate time and space. *EETC* breaks this structure down, questioning its adequacy to describe phenomena which are by their nature ongoing, mutable. This is a process eminently suited to video. Unlike film, video-camera footage can be effortlessly reused, so that any event can be endlessly reworked, opening up the idea of an inexhaustible reality. And the video image itself exists only as a dot traced horizontally, line by line, down the screen, fast enough so that the retina can retain the sum of the information as an image. Therefore the image does not exist in a determinate moment of time but is always being continuously updated.

The constantly evolving, unpredictable processes of *EETC* are given a verbal expression near the end of the work where we hear again the voice of Tal Coat: '(Frans Hals) tried to do exactly what he saw but couldn't conceive of ... and that is the great thing ... no longer to conceive of things ... to limit oneself to one's perceptions ... but in such a way it implies the "never seen".' The 'never seen' is precisely the promise that video, as opposed to film, can deliver. Film's strength, or its weakness in this context, is its ties to the real. Digital media hold out the possibility of quite new and unimaginable images, synthetic images, in the same way that the birth of electronic music in the 1950s offered the prospect of completely new kinds of sound-world.

Film

Guy Sherwin's films demonstrate just as distinctively the importance of film for its indexical ties to the real. In a programme note to a screening of his films at the Lux Centre in London, Sherwin wrote:

> whatever advantages digital technology might have over film, its ontological link to the objective image-source is weaker than in film. In other words, digital imagery always appears synthetic in comparison to film, even if the image depicted has more detail.

> My black and white, silent, grainy films have a stronger sense of fidelity or connectedness to the reality 'out there' than their high-definition digital counterpart – and that film is the medium with the strongest link to its referent.[5]

It is important that Sherwin's argument rests not on the 'superior' picture quality of film but on the fundamental differences between the way film and video images are formed[6]. These differences may be summarised as follows: film's image, like photography (with which it is identical in this respect), is formed directly by light falling on the film, whereas video images – or, strictly speaking, signals, since they are at any one moment almost entirely incomplete – are electronically reconstituted from a stream of voltages.

In a recent film, *Tree Reflection* from the Short Film Series (B&W, silent, 3 minutes, 1998, series begun 1975), a single, three-minute shot of a tree-lined river is subjected to a simple procedure at the printing stage whereby the trees and their reflection in the river swap places. This is achieved by printing the film the right way up, then printing it again onto the same roll of print-stock, upside down. This means that the upside-down superimposition also runs backwards. A consequence of this is that the film has a double palindrome – or mirror – structure. The resulting work asks us to reflect on how much an object can change before it becomes a different thing: at what point on a sliding scale does the changeover occur? Where, in other words, are the grey areas in our taxonomy of the world, and what do those areas tell us about that taxonomy's limitations?

The film is experimental in the sense that a number of effects are created which could not easily have been anticipated. The ripples in the water appear to move in a downward sweep, but at the midpoint of the film, where there is 50/50 trees/reflection in both halves of the picture, this movement appears as a continuous flow from the top of the screen down through the frame, not in contrary motion from the middle as one might expect. A coot which passes backwards through the frame towards the end of the film appears the right way up, even though one understands that it is really the reflection that is the right way up.

It is important to the film's ethic that the procedure by which it is made is a visible one which is allowed to run its predetermined course. The same effect could be

Tree Reflection, Guy Sherwin

achieved using video/non-linear editing, but this would involve a rendering process in which the two shots are mixed together through a process of electronic reconstitution. Such a process, however, would break the causal chain by which the work was produced and thereby go against its raison d'être. The work's impact comes from the dramatic gap between means – fixed, mechanical, predictable – and the visible results – unpredictable images and shifting perceptions which conflict with understanding.

Flight (1998) is a four-minute work made from a tiny fragment of film of pigeons, semi-silhouetted in trees, shot with a long lens. The imagery has been slowed down and sometimes stopped, using an optical printer to rework the original fragment. The effect of this is that a bird, frozen in the act of taking off from a branch, disappears. This is nothing to do with camouflage, but is a function of the way a frozen blur of a bird effectively becomes part of the surrounding foliage: what appears are alterations to the foliage, not a frozen bird against a frozen background. As movement is returned it is still unclear whether that is the bird's flapping wings or the wind in the trees. Thus we are invited to consider how the visual field may be full of such disappearances and ambiguities, spurious phenomena to which we are generally blind because our world is held together by an intuitive sense of the continuity and completeness of the visible world.

Flight, Guy Sherwin

As before, it is important for the efficacy of the work that the problematic to which the film gives rise is generated from reordered as opposed to manipulated frames: the integrity of the original imagery is clearly intact. If the work had been made in video and edited digitally, it is possible that the questions raised by the film version would not arise, because the viewer can assume they are witnessing sleights of hand attributable to digital trickery. (This relates to what is behind the underwhelming quality of so much special FX work in recent feature films.[7])

Like the above two works, *Night Train* (B&W, optical sound, 2 minutes, 1979) may be seen as continuing the Vertovian tradition of employing film to reveal phenomena not normally visible to the naked eye. *Night Train* was shot from a moving train at night, using time exposures

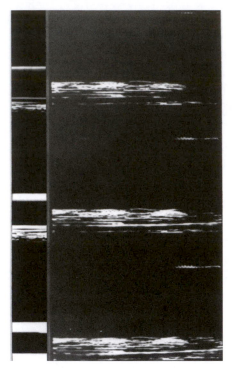

Night Train, Guy Sherwin

of half a second per frame. The camera records passing lights as traces, so the nearer the objects to the train, the longer the trace. This results from the familiar travel experience whereby we appear to pass nearer objects faster than distant ones. It translates into a black screen with abstract horizontal white lines, distant light sources tracing short faint lines, near ones long bright lines. The judder of the train also affects the quality of the trace, imparting a zigzag which makes it resemble an ECG scan. The train draws itself across the light sources, but because the camera is fixed relative to the train, it is the lights that appear to draw themselves across the train window and onto the celluloid, making lines in the same way that a glacier acquires striations from the rocks it passes. The soundtrack is created by extending the image into the optical sound area at the edge of the film. The continuous flow pauses once or twice when the train stops at a station and a naturalistic image abruptly forms. The striking contrast between these two kinds of image forces us to rethink our experience of night travel. We conceive of the distant lights and the railway stations as roughly the same kinds of thing, yet the visual trace of these presents us with images so distinct as to seem almost mutually exclusive beyond the common denominator of light.

There is a precise technical sense in which this work could not have been made on video, that is in regard to time exposure: while it is possible to increase the shutter speed of a video camera, it cannot be decreased to below one 25th of a second. But such technical distinctions between video and film cannot by themselves provide the basis for arguing for a medium-specific use of film, video and TV. It is probably more useful to compare the decision to work with film, as opposed to video, or vice versa, with the decision painters make to use gouache or oil or watercolour paints. One develops a practice within the specifics of one's chosen medium, and the work, which is the product of an engagement with those various media which is sensitive to the differences between them, is the outcome of that engagement. An oil painting cannot be made to look like a watercolour, but even if it could (as has happened with digital editing software designed to make video look like film), what would be the point, unless one's work specifically addressed such precise issues of illusionism? (The paintings of Glen Brown, in which broad deKooningesque brushstrokes are replicated photorealistically with a super-fine brush, spring to mind.) The fact that film and video are commercial media, within which context they are understood instrumentally as ideally interchangeable 'originating' media, has tainted the debate about the distinctions made by artists who chose one over the other. Their reasonings have been traduced as essentialist or old hat, which in the context of painting they never would be, except perhaps by those for whom painting is finished anyway.[8]

With video there is frame-to-frame stability, whence, partly, the quality of unmediated presence – nowness – typical of the medium. But this stability is achieved at the cost of an apparent mismatch between the microstructure of the image and the fixed array of RGB guns used to generate it. Film grain seems to hold out the promise of more detail at a greater level of magnification in a way that video does not. With the latter one reaches a bedrock of the three pure colours generated from a more or less visible grid, beyond which nothing visible exists. This should not be taken to imply that there is significance somehow beyond the grain in film, or at a greater degree of magnification. But because the spectator's eye cannot keep up with the speed of the grain's movement, there is a constant sense of things ungrasped within the image, things slipping by, even when there is very little movement in the profilmic.

Texture is not necessarily to do with the presence of grain, but is also a product of the resolving power of a given medium. Video recording is biased to the green and blue parts of the spectrum, the parts to which humans are most sensitive. This means that reddish images, such as faces, are less well recorded and hence less well textured. This lack of texture means a lack of differentiation within the image, which manifests as weaker three-dimensional modelling and hence flatter-looking imagery. The importance of texture in the creation of convincing three-dimensional images is evidenced in the ubiquitous and often excessive use of texture mapping in 3D computer modelling.

Video's tonal range, too, is only a fraction of film's and the consequent lack of contrast within an image contributes to its lack of depth and dynamism. (See note 6.) One has only to think of strong chiaroscuro painting to appreciate this. None of these remarks, however, should be seen as value laden: flat paintings can be just as exciting as ones which exhibit depth, and video, with its own potentialities, can offer experiences as rich as film's.

The works discussed here are all effective advocates for the media with which they were made because all of them have expanded the aesthetic language of those media in exciting and distinctive ways. They are the result of ideas developed by practitioners through a sustained engagement with a particular medium or, in Hall's case, with a set of institutional norms. This marks them out from many artists today who entrust the fabrication of their work to others, or whose use of film, video and TV is casual or occasional.

Film bears the marks of its own physical history. This has been exploited explicitly in works like Ian Kerr and Lis Rhodes' *C/CU/CUT OFF/FF/F* (1976) in which two 100-foot-long film loops, one black, the other clear, were projected in a gallery at the ICA, so that they gradually disintegrated through contact with the projector and floor. This process of degradation of the film, its reduction to its own material history, is the subject of the work. David Larcher carried this practice over into video with his hybrid film and analogue video work: *EETC*. Here dropout, time-base errors and other features are exploited. But it is hard to see how a similar approach will be possible with DVD, which will replace tape. DVD is a kind of revenge of technocracy on creative approaches which examine the specificity of the medium.

The democratisation of moving image technology is achieved at a high price: the idiot-proofing of all aspects of production, resulting in cameras which effortlessly, relentlessly generate perfectly focused, exposed and colour-balanced images, stands as a metaphor for the increasingly administered and conformist world in which we live, wherein harmless protest is encouraged but true dissenters are demonised or ridiculed.

In experimental film-making, exigencies like misty eyepieces are a formative part of the material reality of the process. This is in contrast to the commercial cinema, where the material support is effaced so that they don't disturb the unity of the world of the movie. Digital air-brushing has facilitated this tendency, manifestly in films like *Titanic* (1997) and *The Lord of the Rings: The Fellowship of the Ring* (2001), where computer-generated material is seamlessly integrated with filmed components.

Notes

1. See essays and reviews by Nick Houghton in various issues of *Independent Media.*
2. Peter Wollen, catalogue essay, *Arrows of Desire* (London: ICA, 1992), pp. 6–16.
3. Anthony McCall's *Line Describing a Cone* (1973, 30 minutes) and Dryden Goodwin's *1996 Frames* (1996, indefinite) both make effective use of the contrast between the film image and the technology generating it. McCall's is a fixed-duration 67-gallery (or cinema-space) work, incorporating the projector, the beam of light (enhanced with smoke) and a slowly evolving image. The image, the gradual 'drawing' of a white circle on a black background, simultaneously manifests as a growing arc of light in the beam. When the circle is complete the arc has become a palpable cone into which the spectator can move his head. Goodwin's film is a loop of 1,998 frames, each one having a different image of a car on it. The film is 'driven' through the projector; the cars are driven under the bridge from which they were filmed. The filmstrip moves through the projector; but the images of the cars are still images: non-sequential single frames.

   The slight up and down movement of the film image – caused by each successive frame being inaccurately thrown onto the place of its predecessor – grain movement, the rattle of the projector and the visibility of its beam all contribute to the medium's imposing presence. By contrast, Bill Viola's installation *The Passing* (1991) would not work on film. The hushed ambience within which the image of the submerged man floats holographically in space is very much the product of video technology used in the most self-effacing possible way: noiseless, concealed projector, dim beam, stable image etc. Because the image is so dim, the relative contrast between it and the darkness of the room within which it is presented is slight. This helps to draw attention away from the image's source, contributing to the sense of it being detached and immaterial, like an apparition. (Many of James Turrell's light installations similarly efface their means by avoiding any strong or obviously directional light sources.)

4. The process of copying the copy is found in a number of art and sound works from around this time, including Steve Reich's *Come Out* (1966), Alvin Lucier's *I Am Sitting in a Room* (1970) and Art and Language's *Xerox Book* (1969).

5. Guy Sherwin, *Chronology and Some Reasoning*, programme notes to a screening of his work at the Lux Centre, London, 30 January 1998.

6. For an appraisal of the relative quality of film and video see Thomas G. Wallis (a technical director at Kodak), 'Film vs Video', *Film Waves*, no. 8, Summer 1999, p. 28.

7. For a discussion of the disappointments engendered by FX-laden movies, see Jonathon Romney, 'The Return of the Shadow', *The Guardian G2*, 22 September 1999, p. 16. Romney praises the horror film *Cat People* (Jacques Tourneur, 1942) for its subtle understatedness and castigates Jan de Bont for replacing shadowy, suggestive *mise en scène* with computer-generated monstrosities in his crass 1999 remake of the original 1963 version of *The Haunting* by Robert Wise.

8. At the time of writing the defunct Lux Centre's processing and printing machines are in storage and at least one London laboratory no longer prints 16mm film, although large quantities of negative continue to be developed. Telecine has replaced the answer print since most work nowadays is destined for TV or video. The decline in commercial demand for 16mm prints therefore may eventually have a direct effect on the activities of film-makers. Artists working with commercial media in a rapidly changing environment are in a precarious position given that their chosen medium may only be available for as long as there is a commercial demand for it, unless facilities houses make a special effort to continue to provide services which in themselves may not be cost effective, or can cross-subsidise these services like Hendersons, the black-and-white-only lab in Norwood. Hendersons provide an excellent service from 16mm neg development through to show-prints, but their bread and butter is in archival printing and, ironically, in the printing of 35mm optical soundtracks for use in the production of DVD transfers of old movies.

2

Digital Media

The difference between analogue video and digital media is at least as great as the difference between film and video. Malcolm Le Grice discusses some of these differences and the consequences for long-cherished notions like medium-specificity in his book *Experimental Cinema in the Digital Age*. In the computer, all input is converted into digital data, regardless of its original analogue form. For Le Grice the translatability of digital data into almost any output form, for example picture data output as sound or text, threatens the very idea of medium-specificity and indexicality.[1] Writers like Timothy Binckley argue similarly that, unlike in other media, digital processing and the final form of the work – video images, music, text – are quite distinct things.[2] It is this separation between the analogue realms (the camera imagery and its output as TV pictures) and the digital domain, where processing takes place, which facilitates what was impossible with analogue video: the synthesis of completely new images, or the reworking of existing ones, in principle at least, at the level of individual pixels. Added to this is the possibility of 'lossless' copying in the digital domain, so that, in principle, an image may be copied or modified an infinite number of times, allowing multiple layering and collaging, without the picture degeneration and instability common to analogue videotape systems.

What this means is that a new kind of imaging has emerged, which exploits these possibilities and which could be said to be specific to digital media, to the extent that it could not have been made with the older technologies. Unsurprisingly, this kind of imaging is typically characterised, particularly in the commercial world, by extensive treatment: 'morphing', collaging, layering, anamorphism, filtering etc. In fact one way of tracing the development of new software is by watching TV adverts and movies, where some of the above effects will be heavily in evidence for a few weeks. This was most spectacularly the case with morphing, one of the first digital effects. Morphing was deployed in everything from shampoo adverts to *Terminator 2* (1991) and *Star Trek 6* (1992). On the other hand, a number of artists have produced distinctive works which use this technology to explore the moving image.

'Few if any significant works of digital media art have been made using off the shelf software,' according to the media theorist Sean Cubitt.[3] In order to make significant digital works, artists have either to explore the implications for representation of the possibilities of modelling or manipulating photographically representational images, or they have to write software for themselves in order to take control of the micro-level processes which if left to themselves tend to produce predictable results. The endless streams of abstract colour imagery concocted by 'VJs' in clubs represent the lazy end of digital video work. In them the software can clearly be seen acting in a formulaic manner on a given shape, twisting and rotating it into fractal-like patterns, creating a maelstrom of swirling, multi-coloured porridge. The lack of friction in the work, the lack of hesitancy or surprise, the quick realisation that a predictable inter-play of sequencings is being mechanically played out, is what makes the work rapidly become boring, the brilliant colour oppressive.

Arbitrary Logic

For his live colour abstract video *Arbitrary Logic* (1988) Malcolm Le Grice used two Atari computers for which he wrote software which defined a set of parameters for the manipulation of a grid-like field of coloured rectangles (see PLATE 2).

It is appropriate that Le Grice collaborated with Keith Rowe, of the free impro-vising group AMM, who created a live soundtrack for the work, because both image and sound have the quality of unfolding in a moment-to-moment exploration. In free improvised music the player is constantly on guard against settling into a repetitive pattern of sounds, or over-relying on familiar combinations of sounds: anything, in fact, that allows the work to become predictable. At the same time it must not become incoherent, and so the player has to have an end point in mind, in order to give the piece an overall coherence and trajectory. It has been said that in improvised music the player goes on a journey with a compass, but not a map. A map would give them the easy option of following the roads, rather than cutting across country. Roads here are the equivalent of 'off the shelf software'.

Because Le Grice's piece arises out of an interaction between a set of parameters and human physical motion – the moving of the computer mouse to influence the colour array – it exhibits the qualities of hesitancy and unpredictability that distin-guish it from the type of rave graphics described above. If anything, it has more in common with the kind of analogue light shows that Mark Boyle created in the 1960s, because these were also created live by manipulating hand-made materials; oil- and water-based media, pigments, colour filters etc., held in glass slides which reacted to heat and manual procedures.[4]

Ich Tank

The ambition to create the 'never seen' announced at the end of David Larcher's *EETC* is taken much further in his video *Ich Tank* (1997). Where *EETC* was organic, funky and anthropocentric, *Ich Tank* is crystalline, hi-tech and other-worldly, despite the periodic presence of fish, birds and Larcher himself. The work opens with a slow-motion view through the bottom of a goldfish bowl which Larcher peers into and manipulates. This shot is distinguished from the rest of the work by its distortions and motion being manually created in a kind of bio-feedback performance for camera. Eventually the image changes abruptly to a scene on a boat at sea. This shot is 'tiled' (multiple copies forced into a flat rectangular form) and these tiles are then reassembled into tunnel-like structures reminiscent of computer-game environments. This sets the tone for the rest of the tape.

No sooner does a naturalistic image appear than it is replicated and repositioned to become a piece in a geometric construction. This construction may itself then form an element in a yet more complex construction. The work reaches a high point at the moment at which a 3D 'object', formed out of a shot of water, traces an upward spiral, leaving a continuous wake. The spiral flattens into a rectangle and a new spiral forms around the flattened one. This whole then tips through 90 degrees to form the frame for an image of a bird tapping on a window.

The layering process – screens within screens – initiated in *EETC* (discussed in Chapter 1) are taken to the nth degree in *Ich Tank*. Images are the raw material out of which fractal-like multidimensional structures are compounded. Larcher goes about as far as possible in creating a rococo world of evolving, abstract kinetic shapes (see PLATE 1). Although abstracted from nature, the bits of reality from which these

Ich Tank, David Larcher

forms were derived survive only as texture or microscopic movements which animate the surfaces of the forms. Perhaps what is most fascinating then in *Ich Tank* is the way it eventually reverses the process whereby digital images are compounded. Larcher's original filmed images are multiplied and reduced to the point where they appear to turn into atomistic particles. Thus instead of creating iconic images from digital data, the work creates abstract particles from iconic images. Nevertheless, the images gain much of their efficacy from being occasionally intercut with shots of birds or fish, which, after the giddy complexity of the synthesised sequences, are startling in their concreteness.

In pushing the imagery to extreme levels of intricacy, Larcher dramatises both the strengths and potential weaknesses inherent in a system in which 'anything' is possible. When images can be conjured out of nothingness, disconnected from the real world, they can all too easily degenerate into disinterested play. In its insistence on a process of metamorphic fragmentation without end, *Ich Tank* also foregrounds the disconcerting sensation occasioned by a medium which is so apparently immaterial. There is no physical effect in the way there is most strongly with music, painting, film or even analogue video, where noise and dropout constitute a base level which evidences the material history of an artefact and tracks the passage of time as the medium passes through its playback device, so that even during pauses – musical 'silences', dust and pinholes in film, or dropout in videotape – there is a level of presence. With digital media these spaces are more like hiatuses. The sensation is akin to that of the inky black silence described by listeners when listening to CDs for the first time, after years of vinyl.

Film-makers have often exploited grain movement to animate the surfaces and edges of static shapes, and for the way it can interact with textured surfaces. This fascination with image quality *per se* has sometimes led to work which fetishises the surface, but it has also served, in certain artists' films, to actively problematise the relationship between image and support, to borrow a phrase from painting. Andy Warhol's films productively divide attention between grain structure and image, whereas in the work of Peter Gidal grain presence serves to foreground the processes whereby images come into being: the constructedness of the image. In Paul Sharits' films, discussed in Chapter 5, complex optical/physiological interactions between grain structure and the texture of filmed surfaces are explored.

Video artists, by contrast, have tended not to dwell on the surface qualities of the image. This has been partly because they have brought a different, often less precious attitude to image production, using the camera to 'gather' large quantities of footage which can then be edited and extensively treated at the editing stage, but also because the video image usually has little texture of its own in the way film does or, rather, the texture it has arises from the grid-like raster display by which the image is presented. Additionally, there may be lines and 'noise' generated by the signal processing circuits.

The surface in digital video

In his video *Black and White* (2002) Simon Payne embraces these unwanted effects, the noises in the system, using them to render ambiguous a sequence of minimal surfaces, some of which have apparent texture and some not, while in *On and Off/ Monitor* (2002), discussed below, he challenges the uniform indifference of the raster grid to shifting nuances in the microstructure of the image, by showing how there is a subtle interplay between image and raster.

In the first shot of *Black and White* (reminiscent of an early Brice Marden painting) we see a grey area which occupies about two-thirds of the frame, the remaining third being white. The vertical dividing line is soft, the overall image textureless, but slightly mobile. In the second shot the line shifts to left of centre and sharpens, and the image stabilises. What is the first image? The grey area recedes from the white, and the slight movement suggests that the shot was made from a wonky tripod, or perhaps even hand-held, but there is no way of knowing. It could just as well be an electronically generated matte, and the second shot seems to invite us to conclude thus, because this stable version is less ambiguous. Yet how can we know that the softness of the line in the first shot was not also electronically generated? The apparent black line which runs to the left of the dividing line could be a shadow, or an optical phenomenon called a Mach band, in which the contrast between two differently toned areas is enhanced by processes in the eye.[5]

Alternatively the phenomenon could be a 'spurious artefact' generated by the image-processing circuitry. The darker area appears to be more textured than the white, but this too could be for a number of reasons. It may be that the white area has been lit absolutely evenly, to eliminate any texture-creating micro-shadows. Or it could simply be an absolutely flat surface with no inherent texture. It could equally be an electronically generated white matte, while the darker area could also be an electronically generated surface which we are invited to read as real because it has texture. But that texture could be a product of the TV raster, generating grey from

Black and White, Simon Payne

the RGB guns, or it could be because the gain control on the camera has been turned up. The white, by contrast, as a pure tone could appear to be less textured.

In the next shot there is a much more pronounced shadow and penumbra, seemingly less ambiguous. Because this shadow is at the edge of the screen, however, we cannot see whether it is being generated by an off-screen object, or is being cast by

the white area, which occupies 90 per cent of the frame. This shadow abruptly snaps into focus, simultaneously revealing the white area to be randomly textured, and therefore almost certainly a real surface, while the black area now appears as a receding plane. In other words, there probably was no shadow, merely the convincing appearance of one, a pure product of the shot being out of focus. As if to confirm this, the shot pops out of focus again, but this time the black/shadow area occupies nearly half the frame, and the shadow has spread, so that there is now a gradient from white to black. Is this a function of zooming in on the shadow area and defocusing, or just defocusing more than before?

The next shot is the reverse of the opener, except that the dividing line between black and white is sharp, and only about 10 per cent of the frame is white, as opposed to about 40 per cent in the first shot. This has the effect of making the white area look not like a surface, as it did in the first shot, but like a deep space which is admitting light into the scene. The piece continues in this vein for several shots until we see motes of dust drifting down into the grey area. It now looks as if we are seeing filmed images, not electronically generated ones, but we still cannot read the image. What is the white area? It must be a surface, but it has no apparent texture, and where is it in relation to the grey space?

Over the next few shots it becomes clear that we are looking at real surfaces and spaces, but their interrelationships are profoundly ambiguous. The shots continue to alternate between implied deep space and absolute flatness, modulated only by blurred edges which sometimes imply recession, sometimes not.

The piece then moves into a phase in which the screen space, now a solid black, is broken by a solid white polygon which intrudes from one side. We seem to be look-

ing up through a skylight, but this supposition is confounded when the same shape reappears in a different orientation. Suddenly it again seems as if we might be looking at mattes, rather than real spaces, but both impressions are contradicted when the edge of the white polygon is defocused, revealing it to be the surface of a flat object with shallow depth. This is subsequently shown to be a door, but the framing of the door makes explicit how framing, in and of itself, can render ambiguous or abstract even recognisable objects.

On and Off/Monitor

In *On and Off/Monitor* (2002) there is a more assertive polemic around first, second and third generations of the same image and the allied implications of that for texture, focus and resolution. The work is busier than *Black and White*, the cutting faster, and the rapid pace makes the piece hard to follow, for it is very complex. Overall, the work has a mirror form, in that from the mid-point the first half runs backwards:

> The orientation of each shot is horizontally flipped in the last half too. In this sense I wanted to present not the stability of a kind of representation or concept of a monitor in its surroundings but deal more or less with the subject of the piece in (its) compositional arrangement.[6]

The mirror structure is there not so much for formal reasons than as a way of saying that the piece can be run backwards and laterally inverted and this will not matter because it is not about naturalistic composition, or composition for its own sake, except insofar as cropping a scene in various ways can introduce ambiguities that challenge the viewer's tendency to situate representational images spatially, to imagine them in a determinate space (see PLATE 5).

The images we see are immediately established as representational, because the image of a window sill appears on screen next to the same image shot off a TV monitor (shot A), which is recognisable as such because we see the work's maker fleetingly reflected in it. The motes of dust that appeared later on in *Black and White* appear here in the fifth shot (B), after only six seconds, reinforcing our understanding that the images are filmed, not generated. A thick black vertical band divides the two halves of the screen. This line is the side of TV box, but because of the way the shot is cropped it looks as if the montage could have been done electronically: the TV is not naturalistically situated in a space, hence there is no naturalistic depth in the

Shot A   Shot B

image, no apparent space between the TV image and the filmed image. There are, however, cues to read depth into one or other half of the image. In the first few shots the sill and its off-TV twin are both square-on to the camera. At a certain point, however, the TV image is angled, inviting us to see it as receding into depth (C), but the imposition of the vertical stripe, combined with the square-on window sill, counteracts this reading, so that it can be read as both receding and alternately flat.

Further into the work are close-up shots of the TV raster. The orientation and the degree of focus of this pattern is crucial in cueing specific responses to the images. In one shot the window sill, on the right half of the screen, is square to the camera and close-up. On the left we see a near-exact continuation of that image (D), in the same orientation, on the monitor, but the raster pattern, which should rightfully appear as a square-on rectilinear array, fans out in increasingly curved lines towards the centre of the screen, as if the monitor had been shot at an acute angle. (There are echoes here of Malcolm Le Grice's 1970 film *Berlin Horse*.) Again the vertical black line of the TV set reinforces the ambiguities. If the TV has been shot at an angle, why can't we see the side of it receding into depth, assuming that this shot,

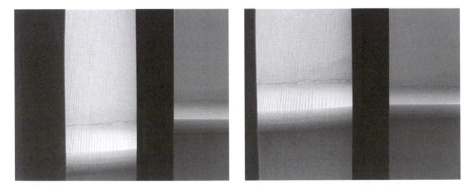

Shot C   Shot D

like the others, has been made in situ, and not collaged electronically? The answer must lie in a number of factors to do with the precise positioning of the camera to the TV so that the vertical band – the side of the TV box – does not spread into deep space, while at the same time being sufficiently off square to generate the curved lines. In fact a quite small deviation from the rectilinear will produce pronounced curved lines, partly also depending on the lens used; it's just that such lines only become noticeable in a work like this, where all the other features in the image are precisely controlled – where they function, in fact, like the 'control' in a scientific experiment.

Monitor also makes some very filmic points about the relationship between focus and surface. In out-of-focus film shots, grain structure (and hence surface) is foregrounded. Payne does something similar here with video, except whereas in film, grain and surface are synonymous – on the same plane – in video the issue is more complicated. The glass screen off which reflections are cast and the surface where the image is formed are on different planes. The source whence the image is generated is several inches behind these, at the back of the vacuum tube. This is brought out in one sequence where the screen is split into three (E), with first, second and third generations of the same image aligned. The images begin in focus, and are then defocused, which pulls the raster into focus. This effect is produced by a combination of pulling focus in the original shot, then pulling focus again when shooting off the TV monitor screen. This allows the whole image to be out of focus, or the raster to be in focus but the image out, or the whole image to be in focus. Within each of these possible combinations, different degrees of in and out of focusness are possible.

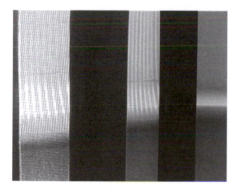

Shot E

After this, there are some cuts, where the only thing that changes in the image is the maker's arm, reflected in the black stripe of the TV box. But curiously, at every cut, with every jump of arm position, the image of the raster grid also shifts subtly, as if the changes in the arm reflection recorded by the camera are indirectly disturbing the simultaneous recording of the raster display. In order to get rid of all traces of raster grid and reflection, the image must be slightly defocused. In such shots the only difference between the image and its off-screen twin is the colour balance, since the TV image is always bluer than the original.

Apart from ideas about real and constructed spatial depth and angle of view, *Monitor* explores a range of interactions between representation, raster grid, the front glass of the TV and its reflections. These relationships are permutated through focus pulls which shift the interaction between image and raster screen in unexpected and often dramatic ways. The results of these interactions are never predictable. Sometimes, for example, a focus pull will produce a grid image of the raster, but at other times a set of diagonally striped blocks or zebra stripes will appear. The foregoing rather dry and laborious account is in contrast to the work itself which is subtle, concise and complex.

Arguably this work could not have been made with analogue video, for the minute shifts in the constitution of the image on which the work depends would be mostly lost in the process of tape-to-tape transfer from camera original to edit suite, to master and viewing copy. At the same time Payne employs the classic analogue technique of shooting off the screen to bring out specific aspects of the relationship between the monitor and the image it bears. This carefully calculated combination of digital and analogue procedures is evident in the precision with which the work has been conceived and executed.

Digital multiplication

Gerhard Omsted's *Lamp Light* (2001) is a good example of the intelligent use of a digital editing program, in this case Adobe Premiere, to produce something which would be practically impossible to make with either film or analogue video. The piece has a simple developmental structure lasting ten minutes. We see at first the image of a malfunctioning sodium street lamp, spasmodically flickering. The work then develops in a manner akin to cell division, as the image doubles, then quadruples and so on, until the individual images are so numerous and small that they cease to be distinguishable, but are visible as an unstable field of pulsating points of light (see PLATE 3). By the end of the tape each image has been reduced to something approaching the size of a pixel, suggesting that the electron firing/phosphor glow – the light of the image – has become identical with the miniaturised image of the lamp. It is as if the image maps onto the raster array which generates it. Thus the work moves from the image of a light emitting lamp to a field of light. The pulsation could be the flickering of the tiny images, but perhaps it could also be the interference created by the pixels having to generate an image that is about the same size and shape as themselves. This is, at least, an idea at work in the tape.

Like *Lamp Light*, Joe Read's nine-monitor *Brighton* (2001) also divides the screen into a mosaic of constituent images. Read filmed areas of the Palace Pier in Brighton (now called 'Brighton Pier') in Super 8. This footage was transferred to mini DV, then digitised for editing. On each monitor the image of, for example, a funfair ride is composed of nine contiguous fragments of the same looped, hand-held, shot. The editing structure is such that the images on one monitor regularly spread onto adjacent monitors, displacing the image on those monitors in a wavelike movement.

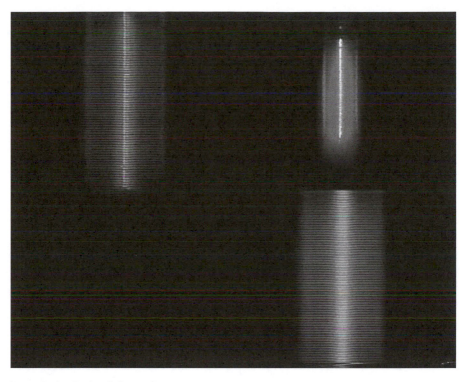

Lamp Light, Gerhard Omsted

In *Heavens* (2001) there are six monitors in a row. This time each monitor bears a single composite image made from eighty-one fragments, each of which is one eighty-first of the whole original Super 8 shot. The single image is thus reconstituted from itself, except that each eighty-first of the composite image, although spatially contiguous, is temporally out of sync with its neighbours. However, because the loops are in a fixed relationship to each other, the synchronisation does not drift as it would in a six-projector equivalent. Although the structural system is identical for all six monitors, the effect is different in each. In a shot looking longways through the iron struts under the pier, zooms in and out were made in the original shot. This creates an effect of rectilinear grids of various dimensions, meshing and interacting in the final form of the piece. In a similar sequence, the view up from below the pier through the boardwalk is animated by the interactions between the silhouettes of pedestrians and the slats over which they walk. In a shot of a 'Waltzer' roundabout, the rotations of the Waltzer itself are jumpy and disrupted, while the bulk of the image area, which is blanker and more static, is contrastingly stable (see PLATE 4). Here, areas of colour appear as abstract, rectangular mosaic patterns. The image is in a constant, but regular, cyclical state of formation/dissolution. It is mobile and animated, both in terms of the intrinsic motion within the profilmic, and as a product of the

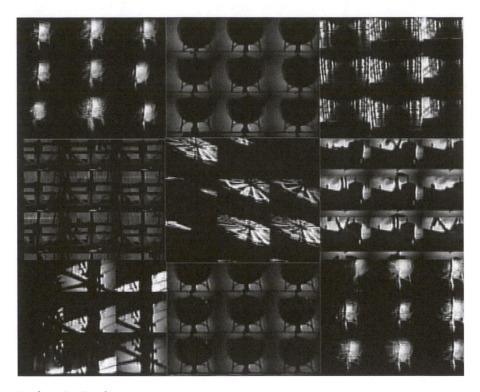

Brighton, Joe Read

editing/construction system. The constituent images are all representational, yet the compound effect is abstract. The nearest comparison would be with 'joiner' type photo-assemblages, made famous (but not invented) by David Hockney. But where Hockney's approach deliberately, artily, varies camera angle and position to introduce overlaps and distortions, Read's methods are rigorously systematic in terms of camera placement and editing structures. The phenomena produced by the work are not engineered or contrived, but arise organically out of the process.

Both these works extend the notion of editing into a total structuring process, in that an editing program is used not simply to join shots together, but to construct the whole work, since, especially in *Lamp Light*, the role of the initial image is increasingly subsumed in a structure whereby the shot is reduced to a multitude of pinpoints. In both cases, Premiere is used in horizontal and vertical axes, expanding on the mono-linearity of most time-based work, and creating structures which really are non-linear. In his essay 'Art in the Land of Hydra Media' Malcolm Le Grice identifies the ability of a computer to resequence material originally shot in a linear (fixed) fashion as evidence of the non-linear potentials of digital moving image art.[7] Read's and Omsted's work is non-linear not so much by virtue of its original material having being resequenced (although Read's has been), but in the fact that it is spatially expanded: it moves vertically as well as horizontally in time and space. Furthermore Read's piece can be read any number of ways. There are abstract movements through and across the different monitors, but there are also local interactions which occur vertically, horizontally and diagonally. Both works turn the screen into a grid, every part of which is equally significant, at any moment. In this respect it recalls the non-hierarchical serial structures of minimalist painting and sculpture (Eva Hesse, Carl Andre, Sol LeWit). Insofar as they obey a raster, as opposed to a vector, modality of image-making, they are analogous to the medium of video, with its grid and its flying spot, tracing the image onto the screen in a constant updating process.

Read's and Omsted's tapes also demonstrate how it is possible to exploit a particular feature of a software program to produce work which is not overdetermined by that feature – 'technology led'. In fact it is precisely the flexible and non-determining nature of the particular feature in question – the facility to generate large numbers of extra video channels – that gives the artist the space to use it intelligently. The more intractable a software function, the less room there is for its creative manipulation, and therefore the more its use will seem gratuitous. Typical examples are texture filters or animation functions which interpolate movements between first and last key frames. Such rigidly defined functions tend to imprint their own identity most heavily on the work.

Notes

1. Malcolm Le Grice, *Experimental Cinema in the Digital Age* (London: BFI, 2001).
2. Timothy Binckley, 'The Wizard of Ethereal Pictures and Virtual Places', *LEONARDO*, Computer Art in Context supplemental issue, 1989, pp. 13–20.
3. Sean Cubitt in the introduction to Malcolm Le Grice, *Experimental Cinema in the Digital Age* (London: BFI, 2001), p. x.
4. *Arbitrary Logic* is discussed again in Chapter 11 in relation to interactivity.
5. 'Mach bands refer to the light and dark bands that can be seen flanking the boundaries between the luminance ramp (or edge). A dark band is visible on the darker side of the ramp and a light band on the lighter side, despite the absence of such differences in the pattern when measured with a light meter.' Nicholas J. Wade and Michael T. Swanston, 'Light in the Eye', in *Visual Perception*, 2nd edn (Hove: Psychology Press, 2001), p. 123.
6. Simon Payne, letter to the author.
7. Malcolm Le Grice, 'Art in the Land of Hydra Media', *Experimental Cinema in the Digital Age* (London: BFI, 2001), p. 305.

3

Expanded Technologies

Moving image technologies can be modified or subverted. Parts of the apparatus, the film camera for example, can be omitted, production stages bypassed. Technical protocols and procedures can be offended in the interest of expanding the languages of film, and for questioning existing ones. The fact that this has happened and continues to happen in experimental work contradicts the critique of the formalist avant-garde's supposed obsession with sprocket holes and frame lines as essentialist. In its ongoing expansion of the means of image-making, experimental film- and video-makers are doing the opposite. Furthermore such work constitutes an implicit critique of the status quo. There is an important democratising impulse here, in which artists wrest a commercial technology that has been imposed on society, and modify it for their own ends. Thus, for example, a TV set may become a special kind of light source instead of a bearer of images.

A list of typical works would include: Man Ray's cameraless 'Rayogram' film *Return to Reason* (1923) as well as the hand-made films of Len Lye, Stan Brakhage, Lis Rhodes and others; Paul Sharits' films for shutterless projector, and his presentation of *Ray Gun Virus* (1966) sandwiched between two sheets of plexiglass; pinhole camera films; negative films; David Hall's *A Situation Envisaged: The Rite II* (1988–90) in which a bank of TV sets showing broadcast material are turned to the wall; and the 'films' of the French artist Ahmet Kut, which took the form of unprojectable sculptures made by joining short lengths of 16mm film together at right angles.

Coincidentally, almost all the work discussed in this half of the chapter deals with light, or makes light explicit. Film depends on light. It illuminates and models objects, gives life to an image, but precisely because, like air, it is a *sine qua non*, it tends to go unnoticed, unless it suddenly dies. Once an image is destabilised, defocused, blurred or reduced to a stream of passing colour, its light comes to the fore. By the same token Stan Brakhage's 1974 film *Text of Light* (discussed in Chapter 7) is as much about light, about the production of luminosity and colour, as it is about the way the handling of the camera is crucial to the production of light effects.

A discussion of Steve Farrer's films – made with a rotating, shutterless 35mm projector/camera – looks forward to Chapter 8, which focuses on innovative camera mountings: supplementary technical inventions in other words, through which conventional camera–subject relations are disrupted, and thereby personified points of view are rejected. As much as the work discussed there extends the creative possibilities of the media, it also constitutes an implicit critique of the apparatus and the viewer's place within it.

The projector

At the Festival of Expanded Cinema, held at the ICA in London in 1976, Rob Gawthrop presented a three-projector live event: *Eye of the Projector*. The same roll of film, including found footage of an ICI schools film about water, among other things, runs simultaneously through all three projectors, whose beams are sometimes aligned in a row, sometimes superimposed on top of each other. As part of the performance Gawthrop manipulated the projector, removing and hand-holding the lens, and slipping the film on and off the claw. The piece explores a number of issues and dichotomies. It actualises what is most of the time only potential – that is, the fact that all the moments of time in the film are simultaneously present, but only momentarily visible. This is similar to the image/material substrate dichotomy, in which a distinction is made between the physical medium – celluloid – and the image that appears when light is shone through it. By reducing the image to the flashes of coloured light which it is, Gawthrop's piece dissolves that distinction: the imagery really is the material substrate, is identical to it, but we can only really see that when the image is destabilised, when the apparatus which serves it reclaims it from its superior position.

The shifting between stable image and stream of light, achieved by slipping the film on and off the projector's claw, dramatises the continuous/intermittent motion dichotomy, and the in-frame/out-of-frame dichotomy, as well as the substrate/image dichotomy. But the work also raises an important question about all photographic images: is an image that slips by in a stream of colour still an image? This is not the same as the *Stargate* sequence in *2001*, where we travel through a tunnel of blurred light, for here we are seeing a stable image of blurring light, which is just as dependent on the claw mechanism as a stable image of a stable object.

In 2000 Simon Popper made a simple piece, *Soubresauts*, which takes Gawthrop's privileging of the projection event to a logical conclusion by getting rid of film altogether. There are two lenses in a projector, the first to diffuse the light from the lamp, the second to focus the image. In *Soubresauts* a projector, from which the first (condenser) lens has been removed, thereby projects the image of the filament of its own lamp onto a wall. This work represents one kind of opposite to cinema, in which the projector is an invisible, silent tool. Not only is the projector proclaimed as a sculptural feature of the work, but its image is also both self-proclamatory, self-describing and paradoxical even, in that it reveals a silhouette of something that is usually obscured by its own luminosity. It has the same ontology as a shadow puppet, or, indeed, a film.[1] Although the piece clearly is what it is, it is tempting nevertheless to think of it as a film experience. This impression is partly prompted by the fact that the projector's shutter creates a stronger flicker than it would were there film running through it.

Against TV

David Hall has made a number of works in which TV is destroyed, mocked or turned against itself. This has sometimes taken the form of literal destruction, as in the burning of a wooden television cabinet in the first of the *Seven TV Pieces* (1971), but he has also made work in which TVs negate themselves or are otherwise denied their function. In 1972 he collaborated with Tony Sinden on *Sixty TV Sets*, which was reprised in an expanded form at the Serpentine Gallery in 1975 as *One Hundred and One TVs*. In the earlier version the TVs were dispersed around rooms in Gallery House, Kensington:

> they kept blowing fuses in the gallery. And they were all receiving off-air signals, but then
> because they wouldn't work properly, the dealer from Shepherds Bush who'd provided
> these old sets came almost every day to adjust them. He was trying to get a perfect picture.[2]

In the enlarged version the sets were arranged in banks around the walls of the gallery. Each was tuned in to a broadcast, creating a storm of sounds and pictures that made it almost impossible to watch TV in the usual way. Nevertheless, visitors to the gallery were drawn by the images of a football match to the point where, although the image quality was poor and the sound cacophonous, 'they were actually trying to watch the football'.[3]

One Hundred and One TVs, David Hall

In one sense it might seem as if the project had failed. In the first version, a white-coated technician and his assistant unwittingly sabotage the work by earnestly trying to eliminate the fuzz and stabilise the vertical roll of the picture (at the same time turning it into a kind of performance piece for TVs and technicians). In the second, the audience's persistence in reading the work in conformity with habit, by trying to 'watch TV', appears to defeat the artist's intentions, overcoming his attempt to mount a critique of TV by turning it from a ubiquitous source of naturalistic sound and image into a semi-abstract sculptural installation. But these two similar audience responses prove the truth of Hall's motive for making the work, which was to recognise the hypnotic power of television and so try to subvert it.

In 1989 Hall participated in the Video Positive Festival in Liverpool. A group of artists were invited to make a piece of work for a 'video wall', a sophisticated, multi-monitor precursor/alternative to video projection, designed for presenting large-scale images at conferences. The idea was to make a splash with some cutting-edge technology at what was the first edition of the festival. Most of the other artists used the programmability of the system to create complex multi-channel works, in which one or more images could be made to occupy anything from one to all of the screens in any configuration. Hall, by contrast, presented *A Situation Envisaged: The Rite II* (1988–90) which consisted of a block of fifteen monitors, arranged in a video-wall-like configuration, but not programmed, and set away from the main group of video-wall pieces:

> The only screen to be viewed is a central monitor. The image is of the moon panning from one side to the other, and is a facsimile black and white 30 vertical-line construction similar to the earliest transmissions of the 1930s. The other monitors face a wall and are not seen, but reflected light from them on the wall forms a moving 'aurora' around the stack. The sound is an 'overdose' – a loud conglomeration deriving from the multiple broadcast channels, and a composed musical score.[4]

Both *One Hundred and One TVs* and *A Situation Envisaged* express disquiet and scepticism about the value of broadcast television. The former celebrates the riotous beauty of bad reception; snow, bar-lines, vertical roll, white noise, fractured image and fuzzy sound – as it simultaneously denies stable sound and image. The latter is contrastingly cool, refusing to employ state-of-the-art technology in the manner for which it was intended. The TVs turned to the wall both deny the spectator the pull of the broadcast image and, by bathing them in their own reflected light (see PLATE 6), draw attention to the fact that TV, in its obsession with scheduling, stranding and 'spoiling' – broadcasting a popular programme to clash with another on a rival channel – is as neurotically self-regarding and defensive as it is confident and outgoing. In the flickering coloured glow that emanates from around the edge of the block of monitors, the work offers something far more beautiful, something both monumental and ephemeral, colourful yet austere.

The work is a celebration of the simple, pale beauty of the low-tech image of the moon, a broadcast image reclaimed for art. This move is not motivated by nostalgia, for Hall has embraced new technology and was one of the first film-makers to move into video, the better to engage with issues around the relationship between video art and broadcast TV. Yet the image of the moon is offered as an alternative to the frenetic, relentlessly manipulated imagery that pours out of the box in adverts, trailers and stings.

Yellow

Arran Crabbe, although not taught by David Hall, was a student on the Time Based Media course at Kent Institute of Art and Design in Maidstone, which Hall set up in 1970. If there can be said to be a reductiveness in Hall's conscious rejection of the hi-tech, this is taken a stage further in Crabbe's videotape *Yellow* (1996), a kind of installation piece which highlights a self-evident aspect of the television's manner of functioning by removing the image. TV sets are emitters of light, but because the light is usually in the form of an image this simple fact is overlooked. In *Yellow* the TV emits only a pulse of light of varying density, which flashes in sync with the verse recited on the soundtrack. In a darkened room the whole space becomes filled with fluctuating yellow light, so that we enter the yellow world of the poet, for the time it takes him to elaborate his obsession with things yellow: 'Yellow's my favourite colour/everything I like is yellow.' While the piece is running in the darkened room, yellow is the only thing. We have a completely immersive experience whose trance-inducing potential is countered by the dry humour and inanity of the verses.

Printer manipulations

In *Slides* (1971) Annabel Nicolson printed the film herself by hand-feeding the original material as it was running through the Debrie contact printer at the London Film-makers' Co-op: 'I saw it as a chance to see/create, by movement, a kind of dance between the printer and myself.'[5] The Debrie is a slow-running machine which runs frame by frame, in a manner akin to that of the cine camera and projector. It is a printer with relatively slack tolerances: a similar model is used by the National Film Archive for copying shrunken and distorted film that a modern high-speed printer would reject. This makes it a good tool for creative/experimental printing, hence its importance for the London Film-makers' Co-op at times when film-makers have wanted to explore and control those processes normally undertaken by commercial laboratories.

The material of *Slides* consists of 35mm slides of a number of Nicolson's paintings, cut into narrow strips and joined together into lengths. There are also some short sections and still frames from an earlier film *Anju* and some pieces of celluloid, sewn with a dark coloured thread, anticipating the later performance piece *Reel Time* (1973) in which Nicolson, illuminated by the projector beam, sews the looped film in a (empty) sewing machine as it passes on its way to the projector. The imagery consists of landscape footage, still images, abstract colour bands and brush strokes and a sequence of a face which has been cut out from one film and inserted into the material of another. Sprocket holes appear regularly and frequently swap sides as the original film is flipped or alternated (see PLATE 8). As the Debrie printer pulls the 'raw' (unexposed) print stock through the printer at a steady rate of sixteen frames per second, Nicolson moved the negative backwards and forwards across the printer light, responding to what she could see through the tiny window in the front of the machine:

> It was very loud, having to watch it as it was being printed. I had a long strip in my hands which I moved up and down, looking at certain parts, taking time over some sequences which I liked. It was an exploration of the things I liked about film, the light, colour, intensity. A chance to look at it all in depth.[6]

A kind of tug-of-war ensues in which at one moment the printer pulls the negative with it at approximately the same rate as the raw stock, resulting in moments of image stability, while the rest of the time Nicolson pulls the negative against the direction of the raw stock. This simple toing and froing generates a range of complex effects, depending on the speed of movement of the film and the degree of abstraction of the image, among other things.

The content and nature of the image directly affects the forcefulness of the tug-of-war effect. Where the image is minimal, as in for example, the stretches of solid colour, the effect diminishes, whereas in the more strongly iconic sections it is at its most pronounced. At certain points, however, these more representational sections spin out of their representational mode and become kinetic, returning the work to the quasi-abstract state that it exists in for most of its eight minutes.

The behaviour of the sprocket holes, which might constitute a kind of key as to what is happening to the film, fails to do so most of the time. The holes often generate a wagon-wheel effect, where things that are moving forward appear to be moving backwards and vice versa. At other moments the position of each hole changes from frame to frame so that sprocket holes are superimposed on the retina in different positions, making it impossible to see how they are moving. A powerful contrast is established between this sprocket hole behaviour and sections of representational image to which they are attached. Even when they are jumping around, the sprocket holes assert a powerfully graphic regularity, compared to which the individual frames of image appear extremely tentative and fragile. Although the film is not behaving conventionally here, the contrast between the holes and the image makes visible the purpose of sprocket holes: to stabilise and hold each successive frame in the same place, against which the incremental shifts in the image from one frame to the next can be measured, without which there would be no movement. This visualisation also emphasises how in film everything within the frame becomes part of the image, regardless of its normal function – hence, partly, the richness of the surface in which light-deflecting scratches, splices and dust form part of the (unique) history of every film, indeed of every copy of every film. (This kind of history is peculiar to analogue media.)

Super 8 pinhole camera films

Jennifer Nightingale has made a series of films in which either aspects of the process have been omitted, as in her *Film No. 1* (2001) which is in black and white negative, or in which the normal camera has been bypassed, as in *Films No. 2, 3* and *4*, which form a series of short Super 8 pinhole camera films.

Film No. 1 is consistently out of focus, but, like Peter Gidal's *Condition of Illusion*, not so out of focus that it is ever so divorced from its subject that an illusory deep space can be read. In fact its being in negative makes it nearly impossible to read depth into the image at all. Even when a momentarily recognisable human figure passes through the space, it fails to articulate that space as such, but is enveloped by black shapes which appear to be on the same plane. Once or twice, Nightingale rotates the camera through 180 degrees, suggesting to us that we are seeing a real space, but it is impossible to tell whether we have gone from right way up to upside down or vice versa, or simply rotated an upward-looking shot. She films what must be lights, and this generates a curious experience. That we are able to see these images as out-of-focus lights and not as unidentifiable black things depends on an ability to identify them on the basis of their form, overriding the difficulties created by their being in negative, whereas in looking at the space as a whole, the reversal into negative makes it almost impossible to read spatiality. Therefore our ability to form gestalts of certain objects or phenomena, and thus recognise them, is more powerful than other complicating factors, such as the image being in negative, whereas for spatial arrays and illusory depth, the negativising of the image creates profound difficulties.

For her next three films, Nightingale purchased Super 8 cartridges, which have their own aperture and a pressure plate to hold the film flat in the camera as it is exposed. She made a simple tube-like assembly with a flat front with a pinhole in it, which was fitted over the aperture. The film was cranked by hand through the camera using a hair grip. Because there is no shutter in this form of film-making, images are rendered as continuous streams of light, except when the film is stationary and a single stable frame is recorded. Thus the rhythmic interplay between light stream and stable form is dependent on the way the film-maker controls the movement of the

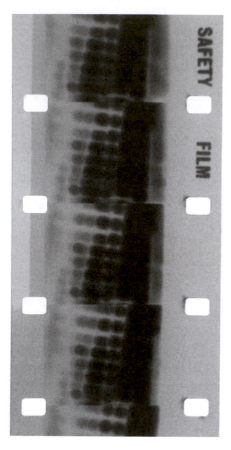

Film No. 1, Jennifer Nightingale

film through the cartridge. This method of working dramatises the dichotomy between film as continuous strip and film as intermittent image sequence. *Film No. 2* (2001) is dominated by a vertical band of blue on the left of the screen, interspersed by the pulsating blue shield shape which gives rise to the vertical band, but which forms only when the film was stationary in the cartridge. The shield shape is frequently perceptible as a white light, and thus no longer as an object (see PLATE 7). This object/light dichotomy forms a second dynamic in the work.

On the right-hand side of the screen are some smaller shapes which appear only when the shield form is white. These presumably are too faint to register when the film is being cranked, and only appear at all when it is stationary, and thereby exposed for a longer period of time. Thus the image field, although uniformly subjected to the same processes, is not consistent, but varies according to the level of illumination of objects in the scene. In *3* and *4* (2002) the dichotomy between light stream and fixed image breaks down, because a frame-by-frame cranking has been attempted. Thus the image is registered as a series of semi-static shapes, but because there is no claw or registration pin to align each frame consistently, they are in a different place each time on the frame, resulting in a stream of shapes whose superimposition is the product of the persistence of vision.

Unsplit Standard 8

Super 8 continues to be a viable format, mainly because it has been used in TV advertising in recent years. It appears to be valued for its coarse grain (which looks nothing like digital grain) and of course it is very cheap compared to 16mm. My own film *Rhythm 1* (1974) was produced using a now (almost) obsolete film format: Standard 8, the precursor of Super 8. Standard 8 comes in 25-foot lengths, 16mm wide. Like audiocassette tapes, it is exposed down one side, then turned over, reloaded and exposed on the other side. After processing, the film is split lengthways and the two pieces joined together to make one 8mm wide, 50-foot length.

Rhythm 1 was shot with a Standard 8 camera with a cardboard propellor in front of the lens which was spun during filming. Four subjects – a man, a woman, a street and an alleyway – and two camera states were permutated in the following way: moving camera with moving subject, moving camera with static subject, static camera with moving subject, static camera with static subject. Each half of the film was exposed twice. The propellor was spun by hand, so that each frame on each half could potentially have no image, or one or other of two of the images, or both images in the form of a double exposure. After processing the film was left unsplit and shown in 16mm form, so that four Standard 8 frames are visible on screen. The film was the

product of a number of influences, primarily an unsplit Standard 8 film by David Crosswaite which I had recently seen. I was also influenced by systems art, having attended a talk by the English artist Malcolm Hughes, who used complex number systems to calculate the forms of his white reliefs. It also reflects a personal urge to categorise, which perhaps stems from having studied biology, which is heavily concerned with classifying and naming. I was interested in the fact that the conceptually hard categories of moving and static had, as images, inherent ambiguities in that two of the shots had both moving and static details in them, and the interaction of these with the erratic rhythm of the propellor. This interest in interaction stems from the importance of process art at the time, as exemplified in work like Robert Morris' *Continuous Project Altered Daily* (1969), perhaps the most polemical of pieces in its prioritising of process over object, meaning or form. The interactive process should produce unforeseen results, and this unforeseeability is at the heart of the art-making process, the means by which art – and artists' film –

Rhythm 1, Nicky Hamlyn

establishes and elaborates its own true discourse, as opposed to being a vehicle for other kinds of discourse, as happens most obviously in TV current affairs or sports programmes. There, video is used as a transparent recording medium. Of course, TV imposes its own stamp on live coverage of a football match, creating an experience which is utterly different from being at the game, but its operations are determined by the movement of the game, not by any autonomous explorations of, for example, the conjunction of video camera, stadium and players, where the players might be treated as mobile elements in a 'performance' held in the semi-open oval space of the stadium.

The machine

A radical and far-reaching rethinking of the cinematic apparatus has been undertaken by Steve Farrer, who has made a series of films with and for a modified 35mm rotating camera/projector, in which the film travels horizontally through the machine (in the manner of VistaVision) while the machine itself rotates. The rotation of the machine and the movement of film through the camera gate are mechanically linked, so that if the former speeds up, so does the latter. The use of the same machine to film and project the image further recalls the practice of early itinerant documentarists, who used the same machine to film, print and project images.

Farrer's first work for the machine, *Against the Steady Stare*, was presented at the Diorama in Regent's Park, London, in 1988.[7] A selection of 360-degree shots made at various locations was presented on a circular screen which surrounded the audience. The rotating projector, placed in the centre, lays the images onto the screen so as to reproduce, in three dimensions, the layout of the profilmic space, the events taking place within them and the camera's point of view within the scene. In other words, the image travels around the screen at the same speed as the camera rotated at the profilmic event, requiring the audience to turn constantly if they are to follow every moment of the film. Although the image is framed, there are no frames – there is no shutter in the machine – and no illusion of movement in the usual way (see PLATE 12). Thus time is not chopped up into brief, discontinuous slices, but is preserved as a continuous still image, up to 1,000 feet/ten minutes in length, running along the length of the film. The image is updated as the changes that occur in each part of the scene are recorded as the camera passes them every couple of seconds.

This is a constantly moving, as opposed to intermittently moving, film yet its subject is preserved as a still image. The film travels continuously through the projector and that is what we see, not a series of still frames flashed onto a screen. Because the projector is travelling at the same rate as the film, there is no relative movement between these two, and hence the image within the frame is static. The spectator has two main options. By staring at one portion of the screen they can register changes which have taken place at each momentary pass of the image. Alternatively they can rotate with the projector so as to witness the continuous image. Both involve difficulty. In the former, changes in objects become increasingly imperceptible the further away from the camera they were, a problem compounded by the fact that the frame sweeps past at some speed. Rotating with the camera is dizzying and mitigates against following the profilmic events. On the other hand the filmstrip itself is a true and unbroken record of those events and their recording onto film. In this respect it is opposite to every other film in existence.

In most movies there is an evident disjunction between the frames on the filmstrip, whose images are often blurred and spatially overlapping or multiple, and their appearance when projected: for the most part sharp, contiguous, singular. Even films like *Ray Gun Virus*, whose filmstrip's structure as a series of discrete frames corresponds exactly to their projected form, are experienced differently in those two forms.[8] But *Against the Steady Stare*, notwithstanding the difficulties of keeping up with the rotating image, dissolves this notorious dichotomy, because what one sees on the screen corresponds precisely to the appearance of the filmstrip.[9]

Notes

1. For a discussion of the ontology of the projected film image, see G. E. Moore, *The Commonplace Book 1919–53* (Bristol: Keytexts Thoemmes Press, 1993), p. 139.
2. David Hall, interviewed by Steve Partridge in *Transcript* vol. 3 no.3, p. 35.
3. Ibid.
4. David Hall, 'Video Positive '89', Merseyside Moviola, 1989, programme notes, p. 23.
5. Annabel Nicolson, letter to the author.
6. Ibid.
7. The original Diorama was developed in Paris by Louis Daguerre and Charles Bouton. The Regents Park Diorama was designed by Pugin and opened in September 1823.

     'Daguerre's aim was to produce naturalistic illusion for the public. Huge pictures, 70 x 45 feet in size, were painted on translucent material . . . By elaborate lighting – the front picture could be seen by direct reflected light, while varied amounts and colours of light transmitted from the back revealed parts of the rear painting – the picture could "imitate aspects of nature as presented to our sight with all the changes brought by time, wind, light, atmosphere".

     'By light manipulation on and through a flat surface the spectators could be convinced they were seeing a life-size three dimensional scene changing with time – in part a painter's 3D cinema. To display such dioramas with the various contrivances required to control the direction and colour of the light from many high windows and skylights, as well as a rotating amphitheatre holding up to 360 people, a large specialist building was required.' R. Derek Wood, 'The Diorama in Great Britain in the 1820s', *History of Photography* vol. 17 no. 3, Autumn 1993, pp. 284–95.

8.   *Ray Gun Virus* and *Post Office Tower Retowered*, a film which dramatises these
     disjunctions, are discussed in Chapter 5.

9.   The writer Rod Stoneman notes a change in the nature of the experience which occurs
     when the mechanism speeds up: 'The change in . . . speeds transforms the gentle sweep
     of a lighthouse beam circling in a slow arc to the pervasive presence of a flickering
     whirl. As these parameters vary the illusion of the image changes: a moving frame
     carrying a static picture becomes a moving window on a fixed landscape "outside" in
     Rod Stoneman, '360 Degrees', *Artscribe*, no. 11, Summer 1989.

4

Installation and its Audience

The proliferation of multi-screen gallery installations by younger artists in recent years has been striking: at the 11th Kassel Documenta, held in 2002, it was estimated that it would take a full week to view all the moving image work that was on show. But there is a relatively unknown historical precedent for this kind of work in the form of Expanded Cinema, which has enjoyed a recent resurgence, partly through the revival of interest in historical work from the 1960s and 1970s occasioned by two major surveys of work from that period. *Live in Your Head* was held at the Whitechapel Gallery in London in 2001, where David Hall's *TV Interruptions* were shown in the gallery alongside conceptual and sociopolitical work from the period, and the multi-screen films of Filmaktion (Malcolm Le Grice, Gill Eatherley, William Raban and Annabel Nicolson) were presented by the film-makers over two days. *Shoot Shoot Shoot*, a comprehensive survey of work from the London Film-makers' Co-op from 1966 to 1976, was held at Tate Modern in 2002, prior to a world tour.

Expanded Cinema is characterised by a concern with the nature of the projection (as) event: the space and the audience's placement within it, the projector, light beam and image. The work characteristically aims to change the spectator's relationship to the image, not just conceptually, but also physically, as in Anthony McCall's *Line Describing a Cone* (1973), where the spectator is expected to walk through and peer into the projector beam, or Tony Hill's *Floor Film* (1975), in which images are projected onto the floor on which he/she stands. This tradition has been sustained by artists like Neil Henderson and Simon Popper, whose practice is evidence of a resurgence, if not continuity, of activity by younger artists who have been taught by older film-makers in those art schools where a tradition of semi-formal teaching of experimental film-making has survived. In its characteristic concerns Expanded Cinema has been more sophisticated and effective compared to recent gallery installations, where the problems of presenting time-based work in galleries have often been fudged, or avoided altogether by constructing an entirely conventional cinema space within the white cube.

Typical in this regard is Tacita Dean. Although her 16mm films are shown in art galleries, they are in many ways akin to straightforward cinema films, since the specificities of the space or the sculptural implications of the projection process are not

explicitly addressed. The loop machines which allow the shorter pieces to run continuously are enclosed in order to minimise their presence, while the longer films are
shown from specially constructed projection boxes. In this respect the work also
conforms to the common practice of video artists of using silent, digital video projectors mounted high above the spectator.[1]

The multi-screen work of artists like Sam Taylor-Wood and Stan Douglas has
exhibited a more engaged relationship with the viewing space, but in so doing it has
often merely resurrected issues which were dealt with explicitly by makers of Expanded
Cinema works. For example Stan Douglas' double-sided screen film/video *Der
Sandmann* (1999) reprises some of the formal innovations made in the 1960s and 1970s,
without engaging at any level with the implications of the latter. The work appropri-
ates the forms which emerged from those radically analytical films and uses them to
serve a narrative conceit, negating their original purpose. The fact that such work is
hailed as innovative merely betrays the ignorance of many critics in their consideration
of contemporary video work.[2] It also points to the gulf, both ideological and institutional, between the traditions and practices of experimental film and video, and
work by artists who insist on the gallery as their rightful arena, or who, like Sharon
Lockhart and Matthew Barney, strictly control the conditions under which their films
are screened, in order to safeguard their value as limited edition commodities.

Castle One

In 1966, Malcolm Le Grice made his film event *Castle One*, an emblematic attack on
audience passivity. The film is composed from found footage, mostly of mass meet-
ings, demonstrations and political speeches: situations in which coercive rhetoric
combines with mass psychology to overwhelm individual critical voices – an evoca-
tion of administered modern society and the oppressiveness of consensus politics. A
light bulb hanging by the screen flashes on and off periodically, partially obliterating
the film and illuminating the audience, so that they become self-spectators, obliged
to consider the nature of their situation. The effect of the light bulb is not only to
break the spell of cinema, but potentially to offer the audience an alternative experience. Just as John Cage sought to break down the distinction between music and
noise, so the light bulb – the 'noise' in *Castle One* – can become the source of an
aesthetic experience. The audience, meanwhile, silhouetted or half-lit, become part
of an audiovisual experience in which they are participant-observers. *Castle One*, in
making the audience's relationship to the film/screen the subject of the work, thereby
constituted the symbolic beginning of Expanded Cinema.

The Festival of Expanded Cinema, held at the ICA in London in January 1976,
was an important event for the exhibition of a range of this kind of work. It celebrated
the consolidation of a number of related areas of work; fixed duration, multi-screen
films, film installations and events with elements of sculpture and/or performance.[3]

The aim of the festival was to produce 'a shift in the role of the spectator, a shift in the complacent expectations of the audience'.[4] The critical criteria for the work that was selected 'centred on the creative use of the projection event … the selected pieces tend to emphasise either the physical, spatial or temporal aspects of these creative possibilities to facilitate such a perceptual shift'.[5] In his introductory catalogue essay, Deke Dusinberre summarised the 'didactic function' of the festival as being the cultivation of 'An awareness of the physicality of cinematic image production in space and time'.[6]

The festival brought together work by older makers from the London Film-makers' Co-op: Malcolm Le Grice, William Raban and Ron Haselden; a younger generation of experimental film students: Rob Gawthrop, Steve Farrer, Lis Rhodes, myself and others; and artists from outside the Co-op ambit; Derek Jarman, Peter Logan, Jeff Keen, Carolee Schneeman, Pierre Rovere.[7] Le Grice was by then a grand old man of structural film, with ten years of work behind him, and was already beginning to move out of multi-screen projection events into single-screen experimental narrative. He showed a bridging work, the four-screen, sixty-minute *After Manet*, which is discussed in Chapter 8.

Sculptural concerns

Ron Haselden trained and practised as a sculptor before turning to film-making in the mid-1970s. His work is concerned with three-dimensional space, in which the aspect of time as a structuring element is equally important. Throughout the 1970s and early 1980s he made a number of single-screen and expanded films, and multi-media installations in which his sculptural interests came increasingly to the fore until film eventually dropped out of the work in the mid-1980s.

Many of Haselden's early films, like the two multi-screen pieces shown at the ICA festival, *MFV Maureen* and *Lady Dog* (both 1975), were evolving presentations, in which, respectively, footage was reworked over a period of days, or which took the form of a short film or loops projected onto a screen to which was added photographs

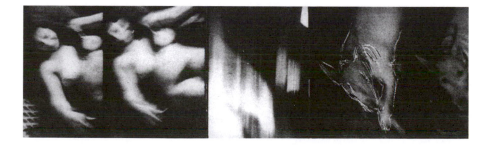

Lady Dog, Ron Haselden

of frames from the film (*MFV Maureen* also exists as a six-screen loop work). In *Lady Dog* Haselden filmed:

> the actions of a dog and a naked woman in my living room. The camera records the event from a position overhead and in the projection the film footage will be subjected to a time and spatial transition. Using a montage of stills from the brief sequence filmed, the action is performed as a part static and part animated structure while the projection is directly integrated with the stills.[8]

At the ICA Haselden projected the looped film in a dark space. As it ran he attached photographs to parts of the screen, gradually building up a sequence which traced the cine camera's original trajectory. A timer switched on lights at regular intervals so the audience could see the developments.

There are two opposed forces in these films, both of which emerge from Haselden's background as a sculptor. On the one hand the sculptural concern has been translated into the decision to represent the spatial disposition of the frames in the film, repositioning them on the screen such that they trace the path of the camera as it cuts through space. The representation of a film as a sequence of photos perhaps reflects the desire to arrest and spatialise the camera's movements, to turn time into space so that the spectator can contemplate what is otherwise a transitory experience.[9] Sculpture is not only spatial and actual – a real object in the real world – but it is also more strongly temporal than painting, because the experience of having to move around a sculpture reminds the spectator, through the bodily effort required to take in the object, that time is passing, that the experience is temporal. The duration of this is in the spectator's hands, whereas in fixating, immobile, on a painting which can be taken in from one position, the sensation of temporality is held in abeyance. Haselden's strategy restores to the spectator something of the temporal experience of sculpture. On the one hand the momentary is held indefinitely; on the other the spectator is obliged, in order to trace the path of the photographs, at least to turn the head and move the eyes, and eventually, when the photo piece is large enough, move bodily.

Haselden has long been interested in dance and has made several other pieces of dance-related work, some of which were filmed from overhead. This practice of filming the subject from above flattens it out, Busby Berkeley style, emphasising movement as pattern and de-emphasising the bodily. The strangeness of Busby Berkeley routines stems mainly from the fact that our attention shifts off the individual bodies when they form part of a larger pattern. However, the exact overhead view is also an important component here. This is partly because we are unaccustomed to seeing bodies directly from above, but even if we were, we would still only see a one-dimensional, hat-shaped head- and shoulders-plan, which conceals almost everything underneath it for most of the time. The flattening out which occurs in Haselden's film may be seen as a way of reordering sculptural imperatives so as to incorporate the specificities of the moving image. Since the work cannot be three-dimensional, that aspect is translated into time, while the illusory spatiality of the photo is suppressed, and its flatness emphasised. It is interesting to com- pare David Hall's route to video from sculpture. As the elements in the sculpture were reduced, it became flatter until in 1970 he made *Displacement*, an installation in which a shape was sanded into the floor of the ICA gallery in London. From this position of negativity, of making work by removing rather than adding, Hall moved into time-based work, but a number of his video pieces, both single-screen and installation – such as, respectively, the third of the *Seven TV Pieces* and *A Situation Envisaged: The Rite 2*, play on the contrast between the monitor as image bearer and as physical object. The precise placement of monitors in the space has always been an important part of Hall's aesthetic, reflecting the influence of his former discipline.[10] Most of Michael Snow's most notable films, *Wavelength* (1967), *Back and Forth* (1969) and *La Région centrale* (1970), also reflect his concerns as a sculptor. As in Haselden's work, all three films involve the flattening of deep space through particular camera strategies.

Haselden's other ICA presentation was *MFV Maureen*. This is composed of six loops, each of which was was shot from the centre of a Scottish fishing vessel as it worked off the coast of Eyemouth, near the border with Northumberland. The six screens make up a putative panoramic view of about 160 degrees, but a number of factors prevent the images from ever coalescing into a unified view. In each shot the

camera makes shallow, back-and-forth pans of about 40 degrees. Each was filmed individually and all overlap to some extent, so that even if all six were aligned there would be some duplication of parts of the image. As it is, in the process of viewing the work, these overlaps form key moments which allow the spectator briefly to get his bearings. Because the camera is on a tripod it is held vertically in relation to the angle of the boat, which means the angle of the horizon seesaws constantly. There is a complex interaction between the chaotic pitching and rolling movement of the sea and the steady panning of the camera. Thus the horizon, as the most persistent presence in the image, forms a constant behind the other, more occasional appearances of wheel house, winch etc. At the same time the horizon never lines up, stressing the discontinuous and ever-changing nature of the filming situation. The activities of the fishermen are another imponderable. Their movements help to disturb what could otherwise be a dry mechanical record. The film, then, is the product of a number of forces: the unpredictable movement of the sea, the habitual activities of the fishermen and the planned camera movements.

What is striking about the viewing process is the way one is tempted ceaselessly to shift attention across the screens, searching for the moment of synchronisation that never comes. The movement within each screen is steady and predictable, but as a whole the piece is highly active and complex, which makes it hard to follow one screen alone. It is very much a composite work, as much about the interaction of movements between sea and camera as it is about individual framings or even the documenting of life on a fishing boat, although the fishermen's activities are an important part of the work's dynamic. The linear presentation format is critical here, as the eye tends to be drawn along the row of screens, for which the panning of the cameras is a key factor. In *After Manet* and Sam Taylor-Wood's seven-screen loop film *Third Party* (1999) it is possible to concentrate more on individual screens, since each has a relative autonomy. In the former, diverse framings, degrees of close-up and the fact that the cameras are hand-held by four individuals means that each screen has a life of its own which can be followed as such. In *Third Party* the screens are separated in space as well as being disposed around four walls, which obviously necessitates their being watched individually.

Haselden's interest in boats and dogs led to several more innovative multi-screen films, many of which incorporated photographic images derived from the cine film. *Sticks for the Dog* was presented at the Acme Gallery, Covent Garden, in 1976. The work consisted of three short film loops back-projected onto a screen to which individual frames, printed onto transparent film, were attached over a period of several days. The three moving images – of a hand throwing a stick, the stick turning in mid-air, and a dog scrabbling for it on the ground – were positioned so as to reproduce the camera's original arc. The frame enlargements were placed in the same way as in *Lady Dog*.

Sticks for the Dog foregrounds a linked, double tension: first an extrinsic one between the spatial and temporal continuity of the profilmic event and its presentation as a trio of spatially disconnected moments, and second an intrinsic tension between the experience of film as continuous, and its reality as a series of frozen moments, made explicit by the representation of the film as a sequence of frames: a true, if uncinematic, state of film.

Expanded projection

In *MFV Maureen* the role of the projector is important as a sculptural presence in the gallery, where its function of reduplicating, through the beam of light, the scope and movements of the camera is made explicit. At the same time, however, its function is subsidiary in the whole structure of the work. In my own four-projector loop

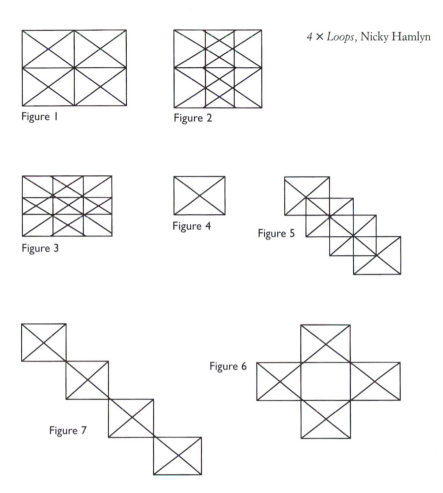

4 × Loops, Nicky Hamlyn

Figure 1

Figure 2

Figure 3

Figure 4

Figure 5

Figure 6

Figure 7

film *4 × LOOPS* (1974), the projectors have a similar status. Each is used to throw a simple image of a black diagonal cross on a white background, which flashes regularly on and off as part of a larger permutatable image composed of four such crosses which flash at different rates. In a conventional two by two configuration (Figure 1), the image appears as a permanently incomplete composition, but when the projectors are moved into different configurations, different aspects of the experience are emphasised. Figures 2 and 3 show increasing degrees of overlap, while Figure 4 represents total superimposition of all four screens. In Figures 2 and 3 the configurations stabilise and the fluctuation of light intensities is foregrounded. In Figure 4 the image reaches maximum stasis, both in terms of light fluctuation and form. This is the closest the piece gets to a conventional single-screen film. In the opposite direction, opening up, the image is increasingly fragmented as the configurations are more dispersed (Figures 6 and 7). Figure 5 offers an ideal balance between light fluctuation and formal stability. The work has an unfixed duration and is performed as a live event in which the projectors are moved into the various configurations (there are a number of other possible ones) every few minutes.

> The role of the projector is radically widened; it is no longer a passive projecting device, but an active tool in the creation of new kinds of films/concepts/spaces. The role of the rectangular screen edges is opened out, by direct use of its shape, and by the employment of images which (conceptually) lead out of its confines into wider spaces. The frame itself is no longer a discrete entity, but an active unit, capable of immeasurably numerous possibilities.[11]

Neil Henderson, a film-maker who works mostly in Super 8, has produced a series of works, each time with an ever-larger number of projectors. His earlier pieces involve more or less straightforward projections of coloured loops or short films, which overlap to create complex colour mixes. In some respects they resemble Paul Sharits' work, except that in Henderson's films colour-mixing effects occur as much on the screen as afterimages do on the retina. Because Super 8 usually runs at eighteen frames per second (18fps), instead of the standard 24fps of 16 and 35mm, the afterimages associated with flicker films are gentler, and the overall experience less frenetic, and more intimate, because of the domestic scale of the medium and the relatively low power of the projector lamps.

As Henderson's work has progressed, paradoxical concepts have entered his thinking and these are evidenced in some of the titles of his films: *Nine for Black and Red* (1996), *Twelve for Black with Splice Marks* (1996) and *Twelve for Black, Green and Red* (1997–8). In each case the number in the title refers to the number of projectors. In *Twelve for Black with Splice Marks* the only image, or rather the only moment when light hits the screen, is when a splice mark passes through the projector gate. But a splice mark, like the dropout from which David Larcher conjured his video work *Videovøid*, is a gap, an absence, which in the case of film is actually substantial, consisting as it does of splicing tape, under which may be trapped dust and air bubbles. In *Thirty Six Working Projectors* (2000), his Slade School of Art MA graduation piece, Henderson developed the sculptural and kinetic implications of the increasing number of projectors. The projectors are placed on Dexion racks, close to the screen/wall in such a way that the spectator cannot easily stand in front of them. One is obliged thereby to view the work through the bank of projectors. This arrangement brings to mind the structure of the eye, in that the nerve ganglia which channel the light from the receptors to the optic nerve lie in front of the retina, so that we see through an invisible mesh of technology. Similarly, we watch Henderson's work through the (visible) machines which generate it. In obstructing our field of vision the projectors also become a central, paradoxical, part of the piece.

Black & Light Movie (2001) is a five-minute work for fifty Super 8 projectors. It is not an installation, however, even though it requires an open space in which to be projected. *Black & Light Movie* has a beginning, middle and end, yet at the same time it overturns those notions, even raising the question of whether it is a film at all. The projectors are again placed quite close to the screen, and are loaded with five-minute (50-foot) rolls of black film (spacing). They are switched on one by one, then each is turned off when its film has run through. Thus it is only at the end of the film that the projectors can begin to fulfil their function of projecting a beam of light onto the screen, but it is at this point that their job is done, and they are turned off. So the film is darkness, and the end of the film light. But whereas with most films the end of the film is the end, this work has a brief but crucial afterlife, between the moment when the film runs out and the projector is turned off: a matter of a few seconds.

This paradoxical work raises numerous questions, some of which may seem banal or obvious, but which take the viewer right back to the fundamentals of the film experience in a novel way, and which raise metaphysical issues about what a thing is and how it can be defined. Can a roll of mute black spacing count as a film? What is a projector when film is running through it and its lamp is switched on, but nothing is projected? On the other hand, can the empty projector beam on the screen be an image? This latter question is similar to one that Clement Greenberg asked: can a stretched, unpainted canvas be a painting? (Greenberg thought it could be a *picture*, though not necessarily a good one.[12]) Yet there is a film, projectors, light: all the necess-

Black & Light Movie, Neil Henderson

ary elements for the event to count as a film screening. There is projector noise too, but can that be a soundtrack?

In addition to these aspects, the work is sculptural and kinetic. Light escapes through the cracks in the projectors' lamp housings. Because of the absence of image on the screen, our attention is drawn to them, and they become the focus of the work, the counters of time passing. As some of the films run out, the projectors are back-silhouetted against the white rectangles on the screen, so that briefly they become the image, rather than its source.

Black & Light Movie divides the viewer's attention between the projectors and the screen on which one is waiting for something to appear. Two states of mind are engaged: the live experience of the projectors, and the state of anticipation regarding the screen. Thus the work focuses around a tension between the actual and the anticipated, a frequent state of mind, since we so often find ourselves in a state of present experience in which what is happening now is coloured by memories, or overcome or alleviated by our looking forward to some future event.

Glass Ground, Nicky Hamlyn

Site-specific film

In my own film installation *Glass Ground* (2001) I aimed to make a piece which was not simply 'installed' in a gallery with no regard for the specificity of the space, but to make a work whose meaning was dependent on being seen in that space.[13] Thus the gallery becomes a necessary part of the work. Although the gallery in which *Glass Ground* was designed to be seen was a thoroughfare, the problems outlined above were dealt with first by the fact that the film was back-projected onto the gallery windows, in order to be seen from outside, and second by the work being the only piece on show at the time.

As a student I made a site-specific piece which consisted of a sequence of photographs taken in a corridor. As I walked along the corridor I took single frames with a Bolex 16mm cine camera, one for each step of the walk. Each frame was enlarged and hung out from the wall at an angle to it, so that the spectator

Corridor Piece, Nicky Hamlyn

would undertake the same walk, viewing the photos as they passed them.

Glass Ground revisited some of the same ideas: a kind of matching of the world with its representations or, rather, a bringing together of the two into critical conjunction. Disjunctions are emphasised as much as coincidences: real space, physically negotiated by a moving body freely controlling its field of view, in contrast with the flat image which fixes the viewer both physically and optically. Real objects and solid surfaces, which exist in determinate relationships to each other, generate phenomena in which normal hierarchies are overturned: shadows can be stronger than the objects which cast them.

Incorporated into the film is a reconstruction of *Grass* (1967), a sculpture by Hans Haacke. The inclusion of this was fortuitous in that it happened to be in the gallery when *Glass Ground* was shot. However, its inclusion serves a number of purposes. I wanted to include other artworks in the film, partly because the subject of the film is an art gallery. The Haacke piece is appropriate because it articulates the otherwise empty middle of the film's subject. Its presence stymies the urge to give inclusive or unambiguous views of the interior space: as a unique object, whose own dimensions are unclear, it cannot easily provide a sense of scale. It is also a conspicuous object in a film mostly of surfaces and ephemeral phenomena. The incorporation of the artwork into the film corresponds to the fact that the gallery incorporates the sculpture. The gallery holds the sculpture, the film holds the gallery, if not in the same kind of way. As an organic object it also provides a link through to the space outside: grass, trees, etc.

Notes

1. The film-maker Guy Sherwin has argued that, on the contrary, Dean's films are gallery works, insofar as most of them have no obvious beginning or end, making them suitable for continuous projection. To this end, like many such contemporary gallery installations, her shorter films are rudimentary in editing terms, being more like a small number of shots joined together than a film constructed and developed through the editing process. (This is not to say, however, that they are lesser works because of this.)

2. The superimposition of a negative image onto its positive derives from Malcolm Le Grice's film *Yes No Maybe Maybe Not* (1967). The device of double-sided projection onto a screen hanging in the middle of the space comes from Michael Snow's *Two Sides to Every Story* (1974) which is discussed in Chapter 11. Sam Taylor-Wood's multi-screen film/video *Third Party* is discussed in Chapter 10.

3. David Hall, who has described himself as 'a sculptor working with film and video', did not participate in the ICA Festival. However, he has also made a number of important video installations which developed his increasingly physically reduced sculpture into the temporal dimension. This work is discussed in Chapter 3 under the heading of 'Expanded Technologies'. For an account of his transition from sculpture into video see David Hall, interviewed by Steve Partridge (which is also the source of the above quotation), in *Transcript* vol. 3 no. 3, pp. 25–40.

4. Deke Dusinberre, Festival of Expanded Cinema, catalogue essay, January (London: Institute of Contemporary Arts, 1976).

5. Ibid.

6. Ibid.

7. Discussions of the work of many of these artists are dispersed throughout the book.

8. Ron Haselden, Festival of Expanded Cinema, catalogue entry.

9. In the film *Untitled,* single frames from the film, printed up as photographs, were handed out to the audience. Audience members could then look out for their frame as it briefly flashed past. This practice dramatises the extreme ephemerality of the photograph as a film frame, concerned with its enduring, physical presence when in the form of a photographic print.

10. For an account of Hall's development, see Steve Partridge, 'David Hall Interview', *Transcript* vol. 3 no. 3, pp. 21–40.

11. Nicky Hamlyn, Festival of Expanded Cinema, catalogue entry.

12. Michael Fried discusses the issues arising from Greenberg's assertion in *Art and Objecthood* (Chicago, IL: Chicago University Press, 1998), pp. 35–7 and p. 168.

13. The work was made and shown at the George Rodger Gallery, Kent Institute of Art and Design, Maidstone, in February 2001.

II

THE APPARATUS

5

The Frame and its Dissolution

[T]hose who acknowledge only the projected 'movie' as a source of their metaphysics tend to impose a value hierarchy which recognises the frame and the strip of film only as potential distractions to the flow of a 'higher' process, that temporal abstraction 'the shot'.[1]

The cinematic apparatus comprises the camera, lenses, tripods and hands, the film strip and the projection event: screen, light, sound, image. It also includes the audience and their interpolation or placement within the projection event (see Chapter 4). But it is the frame, flashed twenty-four times per second onto the screen, that brings the experience to life. The illusion of movement thus generated is at the heart of the viewing experience, and this is why, for a number of film-makers, it has come to represent an obvious starting point. The frame is the fundamental unit of image, duration and rhythm. The concern with the frame also constitutes a rejection of commercial cinema's disinterestedness in the peculiarities of the mechanisms that give rise to the image. Cinema is concerned with sustaining illusory worlds, and so any technology by which this can be achieved is all right. The frame is overlooked in favour of frames, because it is frames, and not the frame, which sustain the illusion. The discussion herein is confined to works which explore the film (as opposed to the video) frame which has notably been passed over by video artists – partly, perhaps, because the video frame is not isolatable in the way the film frame is. It does not exist in the way the film frame does, and thus cannot be treated as a fundamental unit of form like the film frame.

Film-makers as different in approach as Stan Brakhage, a lifelong sole practitioner of film, and Tony Conrad, the musician and occasional film-maker, have identified the frame as a starting point. Although irreducible, however, it is also the nexus of one of the basic dichotomies at the heart of the moving image, for the celluloid moves, but the images do not: image movement is merely an illusion in the eye of the beholder, an effect of the 'persistence of vision'. The very technology of the camera and projector seems to embody this paradox: a feed roller winds the film through the camera at a constant speed, while the claw pulls frames intermittently into and out of the gate, where they are exposed/projected. Indeed, every pulling of a frame into the gate is simultaneously a pushing of a previous frame out of the gate, so there is a push/pull dichotomy within the constant/intermittent one.

The Flicker

One of the most prominent features of films in which the frame is taken as the basic building block of a film is the flicker effect, and Tony Conrad's emblematic film *The Flicker* (1966), although not the earliest example, is a good starting point, because Conrad explicitly stakes his claim on the flicker film as a valid avenue of enquiry. After graduating in mathematics from Harvard University in 1962, Conrad moved to New York, where he worked on the soundtracks of Jack Smith's *Flaming Creatures* (1963) and *Normal Love* (1963) and Ron Rice's *Chumlum* (1964), all classic films of the New York underground period. Although Conrad acknowledged the influence of Smith and Rice on his own work, he was much more influenced by the frenetic slapstick of Louis Malle's *Zazie dans le Metro* (1960) than he was by the loose and laconic works of the former. His ideas about film emerge

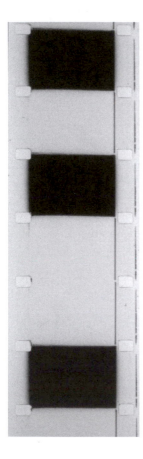

from his intensive period as a musical collaborator with the early minimalist composer/performer Lamonte Young. The concept of 'stasis', embodied in the long pulsating drones produced by the quartet (which included Young's wife Marian Zazeela, and John Cale, who went on to join the Velvet Underground) finds a corollary in Conrad's flicker films:

our music is like Indian music, droningly mono tonal, not even being built on a scale at all, but out of a single chord or cluster of more or less tonically related partials (harmonics). This does not only commute dissonance, but introduces a synchronous pulse beat.[2]

Conrad describes the effects of the music thus: 'pitched pulses, palpitating beyond rhythm and cascading the cochlea with a galaxy of partials, reopen the awareness of the sine tone – the elements of combinatorial hearing'.[3]

The idea of palpitations beyond rhythm describes perfectly the effect of the flicker film. *The Flicker* ought to be rhythmical, composed as it is of sequences of regular numbers of black and white frames. Indeed in its unprojected form it can be seen to be so. But because the eye cannot quite keep up with frames alternating at or

The Flicker, Tony Conrad   close to twenty-four per second, the frames blur into each other, producing 'palpitations'. The idea of 'combinatorial hearing' transfers readily to films like *The Flicker*, in which it is the combination of frames which produces specific effects in the viewer, rather in the way that harmonics combine to produce timbre, the tone 'colour' of musical instruments. This is in contrast to movies, where shot combinations produce semantic 'effects', but rarely perceptual ones: the frame-by-frame combinatorial process is absent.[4] In planning the film, Conrad made simple numerical calculations to work out the sequences of black and white frames, but this is not a constructivist or system film:

> I did not use an overall mathematical composition or systematic device. Math was used only to compute what certain patterns would look like so that I could pick from them which ones seemed to be the most interesting. The whole film is made up of these black and white frames in order to most vividly embody the concept of pulse modulated light ... There are forty-seven different patterns; some of them were repeated a number of times. Each pattern is based on a twenty-four frame per second (24fps) scheme so that I looked at each pattern in terms of both the number of alternations and the duration (or reiterations actually) of black and white frames.[5]

What emerges in these remarks, then, is a tension between flickering/pulsing, and duration. This is something which characterises a range of flicker films, but which is particularly developed in the semi-flicker films of Peter Kubelka, discussed below.

Paul Sharits

In the same year as Conrad produced *The Flicker*, Paul Sharits, a graduate design student in Indiana who then became associated with the Fluxus group of artists in New York, was developing his own flicker films. His earliest pieces, such as *Word Movie/Flux Film 29* (1966), have images, or text as image in this case, but by the end of this very productive year Sharits had moved into abstract colour work. His films exploit the persistence of vision in a very particular way. Film is a presentation of twenty-four discrete frames per second. The persistence of vision bridges the gap between frames, the moment of blackness when the shutter is closed while the next frame is drawn down into the gate. In Sharits' films, persistence of vision creates a collision between one frame and the next: one frame is superimposed on its predecessor on the retina. Thus the eye mixes the frames, creating other levels of visual phenomena; complementary colour afterimages, frame ghostings and pulsations, colour mixes and variable degrees of flicker. To some extent all films are constructed inside the viewer's head, but in Sharits' films one could say that to a large extent what goes on inside the viewer's head is the film, and what appears on the screen are mere frames: if the viewer saw those frames only as discrete coloured rectangles, the experience would be massively diminished. There is a qualitative difference between Tony Conrad's work and Sharits', that is something like the difference between Bridget Riley's black and white paintings and her subsequent colour ones. Although *The Flicker* is a black and white film, it generates colour phenomena in the viewer's brain. Because it is composed of uniformly contrasting black and white frames it has a more pronounced flicker than Sharits' films, where adjacent frames may be of different colours but a similar level of brightness. Sharits varies not only the frame-to-frame colour dissimilarities but also the degree of light/dark contrast between adjacent frames, such that the degree of flicker ranges from pronounced to almost imperceptible.

In some of Sharits' earlier films, such as *Peace Mandala End War* (1966), representational images alternate with colour frames. These films are polemical, setting out an equivalence between image as representation and image as colour field: 'Film ... unlike painting and sculpture, can achieve an autonomous presence without negating iconic references because the phenomenology of the system includes "recording" as a physical fact.'[6] Equally, these films demonstrate the process whereby individual frames are inflected by their neighbours. Later in 1966, with *Ray Gun Virus*, Sharits had abandoned the polemic, settling instead into a more subtle and exploratory dialectic between frames of filmed coloured textured surfaces and frames of pure coloured light which were textureless apart from the grain (see PLATE 10). As well as the colour effects that the film generates there are also textural afterimages which carry over into the non-textured frames and vice versa. This carry-over often appears in negative or in a complementary colour, so that one is aware of two layers in the image, but sometimes a texture seems to transfer itself to the textureless frames, creating a compound image which exists only on the retina.[7]

One can draw an analogy between Sharits' films and Elsworth Kelly's shaped, monochromatic paintings. Individually they generate many of the phenomena described above, and when several are seen in a row, further effects result from the interactions of the different pictures. The distinction that can be drawn between what something is and what it does, is dramatised in both Kelly's and Sharits' work. Apart from the work of people like Kelly and Bridget Riley, most paintings, certainly figurative ones, are more about what they are than what they do. Feature films are only about what they do. Sharits' films both *are* and *do*, and he has dramatised the question of the relationship between what they are and what they do by producing pictorial versions of some of the films, in which the filmstrip is sandwiched between sheets of perspex. One can look at either and see it equally as what it is, at the same time as wanting to see what it does when projected. This wanting focuses one's attention on the material/epistemological duality of the film/experience.

In order to expand the possibilities of the abstract language he was developing, Sharits went on to make a series of films for a projector from which the claw had been removed, so that the film was in constant motion throughout its passage through the

projector (see Chapter 3). Thus he was able to create true movies, in that the images were actually moving on the screen, as well as on the retina. By this treatment, however, the frame surrenders to motion and blurs into a stream of coloured light.

Intermittent flicker

If Sharits' films represent an extreme in terms of abstract optical film, they are also paradigmatic because every frame is different, and therefore every frame is a shot: the frames are the images and this is one way in which his films are unique. In most films, including even Peter Kubelka's, which are intermittently flickery, the images are shots which are several if not hundreds of frames long. Because these shots last longer than a fraction of a second, we can read them as self-contained. In Sharits' films, every frame is a shot but equally every frame is affected – partially obliterated, inflected, coloured, negated – by the adjacent frames, so that every frame both is and is not a self-contained unit.

The same can be said of cinema, but not in the same way. Movie shots are interdependent at the semantic level, but at the optical level each shot contains its own effects: there may be continuity of movement carried over from one shot to the next, and there may be phenomena such as smoke, rain or objects common to adjacent shots, but there is rarely perceptual overspill, whereas in Sharits' films overspill is all. In the cinema, where makers deal with shots, adjacent frames are nearly identical. Because of this they do not appear to interfere with each other although, albeit subtly, they do.

A related point about flicker films is that they are a form of animation, in the sense that they are made frame by frame. And there are film-makers like Robert Breer, whose work straddles the gap between conventional animation and the flicker film. Most of Peter Kubelka's films, although planned in a frame-by-frame sense, are not

TZ (1979), Robert Breer

shot that way, and consequently are not as consistently atomistic in their structure as many of Sharits' are, although they precede the latter's by several years. In fact one finds in Kubelka's oeuvre a complete range of concerns and procedures from the semi-flicker abstraction of a film like *Arnulf Rainer* (1960) to semi-representational works like *Adebar* (1956), in which there is momentary flicker, through to *Unsere Afrikareise* (1970), which, with its highly contentious content – naked African girls dancing seductively for their German big-game hunter clients – dares the viewer to watch it as a purely formal film. None of these films are pure flicker films, but all but the last use small clusters of frames or single frames such that they interact with adjacent shots.

Arnulf Rainer

In *Arnulf Rainer* the frame is treated as a fundamental unit of measurement in a film which fits perfectly P. Adams Sitney's definition of a structural film: 'The structural film insists on its shape, and what content it has is minimal and subsidiary to the outline'.[8] The film is 50 per cent black and 50 per cent white, 50 per cent sound and 50 per cent silence. These four elements constitute a strikingly elemental film experience. They are permutated in various ways, so that there is a gamut of shot length from bursts of single frame flicker, through brief but more enduring moments, to longer 'durational' periods. Bursts, moments, periods: all distinguished simply by length, by degree, yet producing a qualitatively distinct experience in each case.

Because white frames flood the retina, the black frames in the flicker sequences are unable fully to 'darken' the retina, so that the flicker is unequal in its effect, dominated by white.[9] These monochromatic moments invariably produce colour effects in the brain, as well as the sensation of the frame pumping: the screen seeming to expand and contract. The medium-length shots are always inflected in different ways by the sound which is sometimes in sync, sometimes not. The longest periods are experienced variously as respite from the flicker, and as pure artefacts of duration and light, in which time passing is always marked by the movement of clear, but flecked, celluloid through the projector, and of darkness when the frame seems to collapse and disappear briefly. This latter phenomenon is again a product of the fact that the retina takes a little while to recover from white-flooding. During these bedazzled moments the screen becomes indistinguishable from its surrounding masking. In this regard, the film works best when seen in its original 35mm form, which is much brighter, more intense and punchy than the 16mm version, partly because the 35mm projector lamp is so much more powerful.

Rose Lowder

The Anglo-French film-maker Rose Lowder has consistently shot her films frame by frame. In films like *Rue des Teinturiers* (1979) the visual field is split up into focus points along the depth of field axis, and small clusters of frames are shot at each of those points in various juxtapositions. Most of Lowder's films are set in a particular location – in *Les Tournesols* (1982) a field of sunflowers and in *Champ Provençal* (1979) an orchard – but *Parcelle* is an abstract film – her only one – and thus falls within the flicker genre as so far narrowly defined, but which is very different in character to the other works so far discussed. The film has both colour frames and an 'object': a small coloured square in the middle of the frame, which alternates with a circle of the same size (see PLATE 13). The size of this object is crucial. It is just big enough for the viewer to distinguish between the circle and square, but not so big that the alternations between circle and square are gross or dramatic, or threaten to over-whelm the background colour field. The small circle/square and the background are thus in equilibrium, in a manner which recalls Joseph Albers' paintings of coloured rectangles within other rectangles: the figure/ground relationship is not ambiguous, or illusory, as it is in Hans Richter's early films like *Rhythmus 23*. Rather the elements exist in an equilibrium which transcends the figure ground dichotomy.

In Lowder's film, the background colours alternate, the circle/square's colours alternate and there are the alternations between square shape and circle shape. This creates a complex situation in which the background colour-changes affect the viewer's perceptions of the shape changes in various ways. The different conjunc-tions of background colour and object colour render the object more or less visible and, concomitantly, the shape changes more or less visible. As in Sharits' films, the difference of degree of brightness between one colour frame and its differently coloured neighbour also affects the degree of flicker.

Sound and image

Guy Sherwin's film *Cycles 1* (1972/77) is one of a number made by him in which the picture is also used to generate the optical soundtrack.[10] The image could not be more simple: a large dot in the centre of the frame, but Sherwin varies the frequency and contrast of the dot in such a way that retinal afterimages are anticipated, reiter-ated, reinforced or counteracted on the image track. For example, a black dot on a white background may be repeated to a pattern or followed by a white dot on a black or grey ground, sometimes with an intervening empty frame of black or grey, some-times not. The grey may or may not register on the eye, depending on whether it follows a black or white frame or dot. The a-rhythmic pulsing of the dot in this black and white film stimulates the most intense greeny-blue colour effects in the eye, which have the vivid form of the blood vessels in the retina (familiar to anyone who has had an eye test). Furthermore, the dots themselves appear to rotate intermittently, while the background grain drifts through the frame in a gentle arc.

The soundtrack, which is formed from slices – chords – of the dot, has a faltering rhythmic pulse similar to the picture, but above all its on-off character highlights the

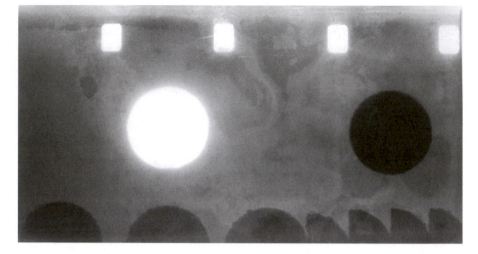

Cycles 1, Guy Sherwin

rapidity of the human auditory system, which is mechanical and hence relatively fast-working, compared to the visual system, whose inherent sluggishness is due to its being a chemical process. Where film frames seen at the rate of twenty-four per second are usually hard to distinguish individually, twenty-four such beats are clearly audible as distinct sounds.

White Light

In my own film *White Light* (1996), I used a frame-by-frame method for some of the sequences. Unlike most flicker films, the images are not abstract, nor are consecutive frames as significantly different from one another as they are in most of the films discussed so far. Some sections of *White Light* are closer to a film like Rose Lowder's *Rue des Teinturiers*, in that the camera doesn't move, but points at a fixed object or scene, while in other sections the camera is moved incrementally for each successive frame. In *White Light* this object is a set of chrome bath taps (see PLATE 11). Every frame is different in terms of focus, aperture, angle and intensity of light, and these variables are permutated in different combinations according to a simple numerical system. As in Sharits' and Lowder's work, there are variable degrees of flicker. Here, though, flicker is a by-product of the making process, not something primarily intended. The aim, rather, was to challenge the threshold between the filmed and the filming, between movement – an effect of the filming procedures – and stasis.[11] In some parts of the film, natural movement impinges on the static scene, as the reflections of the film-maker become visible, reflected in the taps. The viewer sees a record of those fluctuating reflections being made, in a manner which recalls John Hilliard's emblematic work *Camera Recording its own Condition* (1971), in which a camera photographs itself at a sequential variety of aperture settings such that the images vary from fully overexposed (white) through to underexposed (black). In *White Light* there is a mobile, fluctuating triad of stasis: the taps; filmic movements resulting from variations in focus, exposure and lighting placement; and reflected, profilmic, human movement. This latter – human agency – is seen to produce the filmic movement, which produces the static and, in recording itself, the moving parts of the image.

Frameless films

In his book *Visionary Film*, P. Adams Sitney famously elaborates his definition of the structural film as follows:

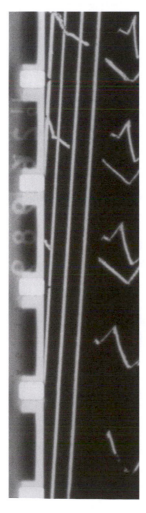

Free Radicals, Len Lye

Four characteristics of the structural film are its fixed camera position (fixed frame from the viewer's perspective), the flicker effect, loop printing, and re-photography off the screen. Very seldom will one find all four characteristics in a single film, and there are structural films which modify these usual elements.[12]

When Sitney says 'frame' here, he really means *framing*, and as such implies the use of a camera: Michael Snow's *Wavelength* (1967) and Ernie Gehr's *Serene Velocity* (1970) are paradigmatic in this respect (see Chapter 6). But in a number of films that share some of Sitney's characteristics, there is no framing, either because there is no image, or because no camera has been used. (For *The Flicker* Conrad used a camera with the lens cap on for the black frames and pointed it at a sheet of paper for the white frames.) What these obvious candidates have in common is that although the way they use the frame challenges the manner in which it is invariably used in 99 per cent of films, they respect the integrity of the frame as an ineliminable unit.

There is, however, a whole class of films in which the integrity of the frame is questioned in various ways. In Sharits' later works for clawless projector, and in projection events like Rob Gawthrop's *Eye of the Projector* (1976), the frame is effaced, or de-defined, through the absence of intermittent movement, which renders the image as a continuous flow of fluctuating colour. In cameraless films by Man Ray, Len Lye, Stan Brakhage,

Ian Kerr, Lis Rhodes, Steve Farrer and others, the film, although conventionally projected, is treated as a continuous strip at the making stage. Man Ray's 1923 film *Return to Reason* and *Emak Bakia* (1926) have been discussed elsewhere, so there is no reason to revisit them except to set out the means by which they were made.[13]

Helspitflexion,
Stan Brakhage

Return to Reason consists partly of Rayograms, where objects, in this case drawing pins, dress pins, a spring, are placed directly onto cine film which is then exposed to light. This procedure ignores the frame line, which in any case does not yet exist on the raw film stock. The film-maker works along the length of the film, knowing that the projector will impose a frame pattern on the work when it is shown. This doesn't mean, of course, that works cannot be planned or effects anticipated.

Brakhage's *Mothlight* (1963) exhibits acute judgment in this respect. It is a film in which a dynamic tension is created between occasional or intermittent events, such as small objects contained within the frame area which flash briefly on the screen, and continuous images, sustained across several frames, which are created by laying long thin objects, such as leaf stems, along the length of the film. Len Lye's late films *Free Radicals* (1958) and *Particles in Space* (1966) similarly combine continuous, longitudinal images with intermittent, in-frame ones by scratching directly into 16mm black spacing. The difference between *Mothlight* and Lye's films is that in the latter the continuous and intermittent images are simultaneously rather than alternately present. This way of working is to a degree experimental, in that the results can never quite be predicted, or at least controlled, at the making stage, in the way they can with conventional filming methods.[14] A film like Brakhage's *Helspitflexion* (1983) grapples with this issue by combining free-flowing hand-painted sections with conventionally filmed frames which arrest and punctuate the former. Within the colour sections there are both transitory and recurring motifs, and these are interspersed with lengths of blue spacing and shots of ambiguous, eclipse-like images. Like much of Brakhage's work, *Helspitflexion* operates on a dividing line between abstraction and representation (a distinction Brakhage hates), a strategy

Brakhage uses to pull representational imagery away from a naturalistic order into a firmly poetic one. Two subtly different strands of meaning are counterposed: abstracted representations on the one hand and anthropomorphic abstractions on the other. It is this dialectic, controlled by the concrete rhythm, that animates *Helspitflexion* and creates its internal drama.[15]

From the mid-1980s through the 1990s Brakhage produced a new series of cameraless films such as *Night Music* (1986) and *Naughts* (1994) in which the unpredictability of the hand-painting process is tempered by reworking the footage in an optical printer so that rhythm and pace can be precisely organised.

Process: *Ten Drawings*

Both *Return to Reason* and *Mothlight* productively exploit the disjunction, the experimental gap between the making process, in which the frame is ignored, and the projection event which (re)imposes the frame-by-frame form. In Steve Farrer's *Ten Drawings* (1976) this disjunctive process is taken a stage further. *Ten Drawings* is:

> a selection of ten short films. For each film, fifty strips (45cms) of clear film were laid side by side to make a rectangle 45cms by 80cms (50 x 16mm). A geometric shape was drawn or sprayed onto each rectangle ... then the strips of acetate were joined together, starting from the top left-hand corner (beginning) and joining the bottom of the first to the top of the following and so on until the bottom right-hand corner (end) to produce the film. The soundtrack is created by the image carried over into the optical soundtrack area ... The surface marks can manifest themselves in three ways:
>   a) a drawing (drawing of a film)
>   b) a film (film of a drawing)
>   c) a soundtrack (sound of a drawing).[16]

Ten Drawings also exists as a Rayogram, made by slipping sheets of photographic paper under the film strips, exposing them to light and developing them, before they are joined up to make the film.

This film, more than any other, dramatises the differences between film as object and film as time-based event. In standard film-making the shooting and projecting procedures are closely analogous; indeed, itinerant film-

Ten Drawings, Steve Farrer

makers in the early 20th century used to use the same machine to shoot, print and project their films. In *Ten Drawings* these stages in the process are as dissimilar as it is possible to imagine: not only is the image not filmed, the filmstrip itself isn't even treated as such, but as conjoined parts of a large 'canvas' on which the images are painted. Consequently, whereas the correlations between the two forms of presentation – object and film – of works like *Ray Gun Virus* or *Arnulf Rainer* are readily graspable, those of *Ten Drawings* are not. In fact the film's efficacy turns partly on the way in which the large-scale image is transformed utterly by projecting it, almost as if the film were created by the projector.

Paradoxical movements

A different approach, with different consequences for the frame and the illusion of movement, is manifest in Ian Kerr's film *Post Office Tower Retowered* (1977–8), which exists in a number of versions. Postcards of the eponymous landmark were cut vertically into 16mm strips, which were printed onto colour film stock. In another version two 35mm colour slides of the tower by day and night were cut into 16mm widths

Post Office Tower Retowered, Ian Kerr

and manipulated by hand at the printing stage. The resulting black and white negative was then reprinted onto positive film with a three-second optical sound loop.

Because of its particular use of photographic imagery, *Post Office Tower Retowered*
raises some interesting paradoxes on the representation of movement and the
relationship between movements and objects. In an ordinary tilt-shot down a tall
building the resulting film would appear, when projected, to recreate the image that
was visible through the viewfinder of the camera (which is not the same thing as
'panning' down the building with the naked eye). The filmstrip itself, however, would
consist of a series of blurred, overlapping views of the building which would not
appear to bear much relationship to the projected experience and, depending on the
speed of the tilt, might well be almost indecipherable. In *Post Office Tower Retowered*
the converse obtains. The filmstrip constitutes a kind of paradigmatic tilt-shot: every
frame is sharp and the contiguity of any one portion of the tower to its neighbouring
portion is exactly preserved in the image on the film, consisting as it does of a complete
but non-overlapping image of the building. When projected, however, this sense of
contiguity is diminished by the fast speed at which the frames move through the

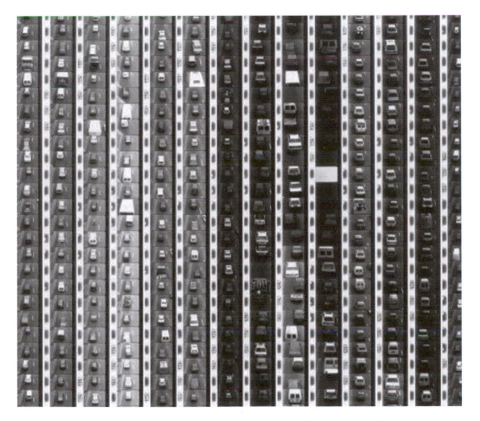

1996 Frames, Dryden Godwin

projector, fragmenting the image into fleeting single-frame moments. But if the projector were slowed down the fragmentation would be replaced by an experience of a series of still images – each, by normal film standards, very different from its neighbour. The film would thus look more and more like a slide show and less and less like a movie.

All this points to an everyday fact about seeing which we tend to overlook. Blur is integral to our perception of moving objects, and even more so of images of moving objects. After all, the shutter speed of a cine camera is slow: at about a fiftieth of a second it corresponds to the approximate borderline shutter speed below which camera shake becomes visible in still photography (somewhere between a thirtieth and a sixtieth of a second). We don't think we are watching blurred images until we see images of moving objects without the blur. This can occur in video footage shot with a high shutter speed, and in computer-generated movies, before blur has been added to make the movement more realistic and less strobe-like.

A more recent example of work in which the dual reality of the frame is explored is Dryden Goodwin's film *1996 Frames* (1996, indefinite) which makes effective use of the contrast between the film image and the technology generating it. Goodwin's film is a loop of 1,996 frames, each one having a different image of a car on it. It was shot from a motorway bridge. As a car passed underneath, a frame was exposed, with an attempt to frame each car as consistently as possible. The work is designed to be presented in a gallery, with the loop fully visible, suspended on guides, so that individual frames can be examined when the piece is not running. The film is 'driven' through the projector; the cars are driven under the bridge from which they were filmed. The filmstrip moves through the projector, but the images of the cars are still images: non-sequential single frames.

Notes

1. Paul Sharits, 'Words per Page', *Afterimage* no. 4, 1972, p. 32.
2. Tony Conrad, 'Inside the Dream Syndicate', *Film Culture* no. 41, Summer 1966, p. 7.
3. Ibid., p. 6.
4. In his brief opening essay in *Film Culture*, Conrad discusses *The Flicker* in terms of colour and harmonics, pp. 1–3.
5. Interview with Toby Mussman, *Film Culture* ibid., p. 4.
6. Sharits, 'Words per Page', p. 29.
7. For a detailed discussion of the experience of this and other Sharits' films, see Regina Cornwell, 'Paul Sharits: Illusion and Object', *Artforum*, September 1971, pp. 46–52.
8. P. Adams Sitney, *Visionary Film*, 2nd edn (Oxford: Oxford University Press, 1979), pp. 369–70.
9. Bright light bleaches the rhodopsin in the retinal cells, which then take time to return to their normal state of receptivity. The brighter the light, the longer the eye takes to recover.

10. In film, the recorded sound is converted into a fluctuating black and white stripe which runs down the edge of the film. When the film is projected, light is passed through the stripe onto a photoelectric cell, which converts the fluctuations into voltages which are passed on to an audio amplifier.

11. William and Birgit Hein's film *Structural Studies* is an exhaustive catalogue of kinds of movement that are produced by filmic procedures, as opposed to movement of the profilmic.

12. Sitney, *Visionary Film*, p. 370.

13. See David Curtis, *Experimental Cinema* (London: Studio Vista, 1971), p. 17 and Malcolm Le Grice, *Abstract Film and Beyond* (London: Studio Vista, 1977), pp. 33–6.

14. 'Video Assist', an innovation in the film industry whereby a video recording is made simultaneously with the filmed take, has removed most of the unforeseeable incidents of a medium in which the results cannot be seen straight away.

15. For an extended discussion of this film, see A. L. Rees, 'Hell Spit Flexion', *Monthly Film Bulletin* vol. 51 no. 609, October 1984, p. 322.

16. Steve Farrer, quoted in Deke Dusinberre, 'See Real Images', *Afterimage* no. 8–9, Spring 1981, p. 99, quoted in Nicky Hamlyn, 'Frameless Film', *Undercut* no. 13, Winter 1984–5, p. 29.

6

Framing

Seven TV Pieces

Flicker film-makers have usually treated the film frame as a temporal and spatial unit, but in the following discussion expanded ideas of the frame overlap with framing. Thus frame/framing may also mean the frame around the TV set, and the idea of frame of reference, with its contextual implications. In the case of David Hall's work it is the TV frame, which frequently coincides with the TV set, which has been the focus point for a number of works, in which he has used film and video to mount a sustained investigation into the ideologies and phenomena of broadcast TV.[1] In a number of Hall's works, the frame as object, image, ideological construct and as the act of framing coincide.

In 1971, Hall made ten *TV Interruptions* for Scottish TV. They were broadcast, unannounced, in August and September of that year. (A selection of seven of the ten was later issued as *Seven TV Pieces*.) These, his first works for broadcast television, are exemplars of what came to be known as *Television Interventions*. Although a number of such interventions have subsequently been made by various artists, the *Seven TV Pieces* have not been surpassed, except perhaps by Hall himself in *This is a Television Receiver* (1975) and *Stooky Bill TV* (1990). In all the pieces the way framing operates – commenting on the poverty of the television image, or changing the way we think about the TV set – is crucial, and in number six, for example, the act of framing is the explicit subject of the work.

In the opening piece we see a time-lapsed scene of a TV cabinet burning in a landscape which contains the empty cabinet, which in turn frames a portion of the same. Periodically, the screen goes black and a voice calls out: 'interruption'. There is an ironic play on the idea of the landscape as pastoral retreat, now sullied by

Seven TV Pieces, David Hall

commercial exploitation, a suggestion that TV is everywhere, omnivorous and insatiable in its quest for subject matter. At the same time there is the implication that a burning TV makes better television than most of the output to which we are subjected. The work also sets out the iconoclastic tone of those that follow.

In the second, a shot of the sky is vertically bisected by the edge of a steel-framed window and its handle. Clouds drift through the frame. This is followed by a high-angle view of open countryside with fast-moving cloud shadows, then a similar view down on a quadrangle with a wind-blown tree and a rectangular shadow on the grass cast by buildings behind the camera. Thus the work sets out a number of framing implications. In the first shot it is as if the real window frame is intrusive, spoiling the view. Yet the TV frame (TV set), which, as a given, we do not really notice, is the real culprit here, since it cuts out what we may not see and forces us to see what it wants us to see. The window frame also stresses the picture plane by appearing to connect the top and bottom of the TV. In the extreme wide shot of open country we enjoy a momentary opening out of space, before the final view of the quadrangle. Now the shots jump through time so that the cast shadow from the buildings behind changes position and finally disappears. The presence of shadow combined with the absence of its cause reminds us again of the fundamentally manipulative nature of most moving-image production, but especially of TV. Why especially TV? Perhaps because the cinema experience trades heavily on off-screen space. There we can project imaginatively into the adjacent darkness in a way that is precluded in the TV experience where the box, which is always visible, functions to contain and inwardly direct the gaze. Designers have tried to make the set less visible by replacing varnished wood with darker, less reflective materials, but in any case TVs are invariably watched in undarkened rooms. The elimination of off-screen space that this occasions is emphasised in most of the *TV Pieces*.[2]

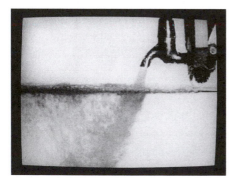

The idea of the TV as a container is neatly explored in *Tap*, the third and probably most well-known of the seven pieces. Unseen hands place a tap inside a glass tank, framed so that the tank's edges coincide with the sides of the TV. The tap is turned on, filling the space with water until it itself is submerged. The tank continues to fill until the meniscus – the surface line of the water – rises out of view. The tap is withdrawn and turned off, leaving that most forbidden of things, a blank screen. After a pause of a few seconds, the plug is pulled and the tank empties, now with the meniscus cutting across the screen at a 45-degree angle. Beyond the reference to the box as glass-fronted

container, the piece serves to demonstrate how framing is crucial in determining how we understand an image, and hence how meaning is created, not just by what framing includes, but also in the sense of the editorial function that it performs. This leads to a wider reading of the work as an implicit critique of the largely invisible editorial practices of programme-makers and indeed the TV institutions.[3]

Dziga Vertov, in the 1920s, held that all stages of film production were editorial,[4] but TV, with its impression of live, unmediated presence, can appear to bypass that truth. By making the framing of an object coincide not just with the shape and size of the TV screen, but also with the physical properties of the set, Hall foregrounds the constructedness of these practices. The concealed reorientation of the camera before the plug is pulled adds to this. The meniscus no longer appears as such, but looks more like a waving line cutting through the void. Its disorientation causes ours: we read it before as a meniscus, not because we could see the water under it, but because of its horizontality and its coincidence with the gushing of the tap. Now, through the act of reframing, and in the absence of these associated cues, we no longer see it in the same way at all. The effect is reminiscent of the end of Bruce Baillie's short film *All My Life* (1966), which ends with a slow tilt up into the sky across a telephone wire. Once the shot clears the ground, it is the wire which appears to move, not the camera.

The fourth piece is a time-lapse of a number of people watching TV – wheat threshing, a Western, folk singers – in a large room. After an abrupt pullout at the beginning, there is a gradual zoom-in to the TV set. The work wryly demonstrates that while watching TV may be engrossing, watching other people watch TV is a lot less so. This leads to the old but nonetheless true conclusion that watching TV is antisocial, unless it is done purposefully and communally.[5] The screen within the screen re-emphasises the paucity of scale and scope that is in the nature of the medium. This is simultaneously conveyed in the fact that the framing reproduces similar conditions to those under which the piece itself would have been seen when broadcast. There is also a play on diegetic/non-diegetic sound, since it is difficult to tell if the increasingly strident movie soundtrack comes from the TV, from another part of the room, or has been dubbed on.

In the fifth, the camera pans from black across a TV-shaped opening through which can be glimpsed an Edinburgh street, shot from a fixed position. This shot structure is repeated ten times, each time with different vehicles and pedestrians in the frame. The soundtrack is in the form of a loop, so that the relationship between sound and picture shifts with each repeat, but all are plausibly synchronous. The work contradicts the normal state of affairs in which a camera pans across a scene, offering a seemingly open and unmediated panorama. Here the refilming camera pans across the scene, but framed within the frame of the TV set. Instead of panoramic plenitude, we get only a frustratingly limited view. Yet this is only the same view we would get if it were shown full frame. The panning highlights how even the most open-seeming view is actually very restricted, partial and centripetal.

In the sixth, three camera operators perform a live filming event at a busy town-centre road junction. The ultimate target of their cameras is a wooden TV cabinet with doors on the front. A woman's voice calls out the shots' durations at five-second intervals while the camera operators race to set up the next shot. The shots are made

in a chain so that each time we see a camera in one shot we see that camera's point of view in the next. Finally the doors of the TV cabinet are opened and in a zoom-in we see Hall himself filming through from the back of the empty cabinet, framed by its screen-shaped opening. Again, the richness of the filmwork and the scale and complexity of the location contrast with the final view seen through the constrictive rectangle of the opening in the cabinet. The presence of Hall's camera pointing directly back at us reminds us that every shot on TV is somebody's point of view, and not some disembodied omniscient perspective.

The last of the seven works presents, in a single, unbroken shot, the constituents of a television programme, but not the programme itself. A man wearing headphones sits, absolutely still and silent at a table, with his back to us – a familiar TV scenario reversed. Behind the table is a plain backdrop. This and the man are lit by two lamps and there is a Bolex cine camera on the desk in front of him. After about one minute of stasis, another man enters the scene, in time-lapse. He replaces the camera with a pile of straw, then reverses these actions, passing between the man and the camera filming him as he does so. Finally the seated man – Hall himself – stands up and removes the headphones, simultaneously revealing that they are not attached to anything. He then picks up the camera and walks out of frame. An electronic beep is heard at five-second intervals throughout the piece. Thus a theme of negation and uncertainty runs through the work: the man never speaks and we don't see his face until the moment he leaves. Until he moves he is so still that we could have been watching a filmed photograph. The backdrop behind the desk is blank, rendering the lighting semi-redundant, and the only movement is the time-lapsed section and the ending. Even here the second man is perceived to be not in motion, but in a series

of static positions. This time-lapsed section retrospectively renders the first part ambiguous, since there is no way of telling if that too was in time-lapse, or in real time. As well as stasis, real time and time-lapse, clock time is also present in the form of the regular beep.

If *Interruption* is literally iconoclastic in its physical destruction of that most familiar emblem of TV, the set itself, this last section adopts an attitude of quiet resistance to the paraphernalia of the TV studio and, by association, its institutions, since it is in such studios that programmes are produced and presented. Instead of designer desks, effusive anchormen, sparkling graphics and 'up' musical stings, we have in Hall's alternative an austere, silent space, a pine table and a mute, inanimate figure who has turned his back on the viewer. His headphones, normally a link to sound, here serve to isolate him from auditory stim-uli. The moving man breaks what was certainly then a TV studio taboo by walking between the camera and its subject, disrupting the spatial unity by which a trans-parent point of view is offered to the viewer. The seated man may be seen as a technician, who probably should be behind the camera, not in front of it. The TV set on which all this would have been seen is the only normal part of the experience, which must have seemed very strange, not to say baffling, in 1971.

Michael Snow: films and photo works

While David Hall's work is strongly formal, it is also politically engaged, driven by an aggressively iconoclastic critique of TV culture. The Canadian artist Michael Snow is more detached. Though equally formal in his foregrounding of the frame and fram-ing, his work is often more abstract in approach. The frame and framing are key preoccupations that unite his diverse output, which is made up of films, photographs, sculptures and hybrid works.

In Snow's most well-known film *Wavelength* (1967) framing is the defining activity in a film which explores the relationship between frame, space, time and memory. Snow claims not to be interested in cinema, but *Wavelength* contains numerous cine-matic points of reference, and not just in the four brief human events which famously intersperse the film, breaking into, but not deterring, the erratic but insistent slow zoom that is the film's overall structure. The opening moments can be understood as a 'master shot', which includes everything of the space we will subsequently see, apart from the human events. Indeed the whole film can be thought of as a master shot, in the sense that there are no cutaways or close-ups, only the forward progression, the zoom, of the film's single point of view. On the other hand the master

The opening of *Wavelength*, Michael Snow

shot ceases to be such the moment it is stated, because it starts to reduce in size, showing us less than in its opening framing. It continues to diminish to the point where, by the end of the film, it has evolved into its opposite – an extreme close-up.

In the opening wide shot, the windows at the end of the loft where the film takes place are framed by the walls, floor and ceiling of the space. The camera is placed well above head height, proposing a self-consciously transcendental viewpoint, but what this high position facilitates is the framing of equal amounts of floor and ceiling, creating a near-even border around the end wall, as well as a symmetrical arena for the human events (all of which upset that symmetry, as they occur to the left of centre). The first two such events, shelves being carried in and two women listening to a radio, occur early on, in quick succession. They serve to give the viewer a sense of the scale of the space, and set up expectations of future human incidents. Once these events have passed, however, attention is drawn increasingly to the grid of windows at the end of the loft. One of these is open and through it can be glimpsed a fragment of New York shop front, across which lorries periodically pass. The passing of these pantechnicons resembles a series of cinematic 'wipes'. The sense of the windows as frames alters constantly with the variation in exposure of the film. When the interior space is correctly exposed, the windows become overexposed and translucent, and the grid of the glazing bars dominates. When the interior space is darkened, however, the windows become transparent, admitting the view beyond, and framing details and activities taking place in the street.

As the film progresses, one becomes increasingly aware that it has a target: the group of pictures on a narrow strip of wall between the windows. One of these is an image called the *Walking Woman*, an ongoing work that occupied Snow for several years during his time in New York. The image appeared in various forms, including a life-size cardboard cut-out which was placed on city streets and photographed with passers-by. In the image of the *Walking Woman*, cropping, paradoxically, also emphasises framing by foregrounding the rectangular limits of the image. The other picture is an unframed photograph of waves. The wall on which the picture is mounted becomes in effect a frame by the way it increasingly encloses the photo as the camera zooms in. The effect of the zoom is to shift the understanding of the photograph as at first barely visible, to being noticeable in the space, to being contained by it, to being framed by it, until it fills the film frame and becomes liberated from its surroundings, at which point it becomes an infinite space. This final image of ocean waves fills the screen, framed only by the camera, and so seemingly unframed in relation both to the enclosed space of the loft and to previous views of the image as framed by the surrounding wall. The non-hierarchical, transient form of waves means that they can be framed in any manner of ways: there seems to be no right way of framing a photograph of a portion of the sea, in the way there can be a right, or at least apposite, way of framing a photo of a building. At the same time the very idea of framing a picture of the ocean exposes the inadequacies and distortions inherent in framing: how can something vast, unbounded and in constant motion be rendered by something which fixes, forms, miniaturises, objectifies? *Wavelength* shows how framing is bound up in a rectilinear pictorial tradition which unites painting, photography and film. Shaped canvasses have never enjoyed a central place in this tradition in the way that rectangular ones have. Shape introduces other issues into painting which seem to dilute the classical dynamic of lines and areas interacting with and bounded by a rectangle. One need only think of Richard Smith's shaped three-dimensional hybrid sculpture/paintings, in which painted-on two-dimensional depth clashes with the work's real three-dimensional depth, or Elsworth Kelly's canvasses, whose curved edges create a quasi-kinetic experience in the way they lead the eye around them, to see how shape challenges the stability of pictorial space.

Wavelength is the ultimate rectilinear film to challenge that stability, by its method of insistent rectilinearity followed by a questioning of that with the image of the waves. The eye is led ever inward by the zoom, with the realisation that it has a target in the middle of the frame. At the same time the film occasionally draws the eye out and back in time, into off-screen space, by superimposing earlier positions of the zoom onto the current one. The human presences, although ignored by the zoom's fixed trajectory, are contrastingly asymmetrical and the image of waves constitutes a final denial of straight lines, as well as reminding us that light and sound travel in wavelengths made up of curved oscillations.

Wavelength, Michael Snow

Sculpture and photo-works

As well as the films, Snow has made numerous photographic and sculptural works which deal explicitly with the issues of framing.

The paradoxical aspect of the frame finds expression in *Portrait* (1967). This is an adjustable aluminium frame that can be fitted into a small gap or opening. The piece explores the kind of paradox or duality – another of Snow's favourite topics – of frames. It is the most un-aesthetic, self-effacing frame imaginable, more like a measuring tool than a frame in the traditional sense. Yet even when they are grand gilt baroque jobs, frames are to some extent self-effacing, their status as objects ambiguous, insofar as their function is to draw attention away from themselves and into the picture. In *Portrait* Snow posits the frame as pure delimiting device, but also as a sculptural object. Where is the 'work' here, for normally it is that which is contained by the frame? Can the view through the frame, then, constitute a kind of work? If so, then perhaps the work becomes as much the creation of the spectator as it is a Michael Snow piece.

8 x 10 (1969), whose punning title refers both to eight by ten inch photographic paper and to the number of pictures in the piece, deals more extensively with framing. It is an exhaustive survey of possible frames and framings in the widest sense: the frame as image, object, concept, process, metaphor. A black frame is photographed in different ways, from fully contained within, and aligned to, the picture

Portrait, Michael Snow

plane and edges, to partially within frame and focus, at oblique angles to the picture plane. These diverse framings manipulate our sense of depth and at other times stress the flatness of the image. Frequently the frame frames nothing, yet we still think of it as a frame. One key image stands out from the others. It is a ghostly shot of the windows of the loft where *Wavelength* was made, but the black frame is absent. Presumably it is off-screen, not visible but present, framed-out (this is the constant activity in *Wavelength* as the camera zooms in). This single picture makes explicit the relationship between framing and contextualisation. We may surmise that the frame, though invisible, is there somewhere, because it is common to all the other images. We are thus invited to consider the idea of an image of something invisible. We are also invited to think of off-screen space as a kind of frame, which is different from the way off-screen space is usually thought of. The unframed image is always framed: there is no escape.

When seen in reproduction, *Of a Ladder* (1971) can appear an overly didactic, narrowly conceptual treatment of ideas about framing, flatness and parallax. Like much so-called conceptual work, it could be characterised as having no afterlife, no other level on which to apprehend it after the idea has been grasped. Seen in the flesh, however, a number of other factors come into play. *Of a Ladder* consists of

Michael Snow in front of *8 x 10*

twelve photographs, taken from the same fixed position, of a ladder leaning against a wall directly in front of the photographer/viewer.

Because the camera must be tilted down and up to frame the extremities of the ladder, progressive parallax distortions are incurred, so that the top and bottom ends of the ladder recede, as towards a vanishing point. This implies that the centre is correctly framed. However, that correctness is relativised in various ways. First the ladder appears to bulge out, and this bulging is a direct result of the centre rungs being closer to the camera than the end rungs. The centre portion is better exposed and slightly sharper than the extremities too. All this begs the question: what is the truth about these images, for arguably the upper and lower rungs are just as truthfully represented as the centre ones, from where they have been photographed? The distortions and loss of focus and illumination at the extremes are truthful reflections of the nature of the process and the apparatus. Thus all the pictures in the sequence, though not all the same, are truthful, but now we can question the status of the middle part: its correctness is not absolute, but simply one kind of result of what happens when something is photographed in a particular way.

The bottom picture of the twelve covers the area where the ladder meets the floor, and here Snow has opted to place the photo flat on the floor, in keeping with the nature of the originary space. But this, of course, introduces a right-angle turn into the work which is not 'in' the original scene. Alternatively, if Snow placed this picture on the wall below the eleven others, as he could have done with equal warrant, the sequence would still have been untrue to the original scene because the bit of floor behind/underneath the ladder would now appear on the wall. This kind of double-bind or paradox is a recurrent theme in Snow; indeed, the behind/underneath duality of the bottom picture alone encapsulates the problematic created by the translation of three into two dimensions.

Of a Ladder, Michael Snow

Behind the distorted rungs lies the relatively undistorted shadow of the ladder on the wall. It plays the role of a reference to how the ladder itself might have looked in the originary scene, but its presence introduces a further puzzlement into the work, for we have both distorted and undistorted parts in an image of the same scene which has been uniformly subjected to the same procedure.

There is no doubt an explanation for this in terms of optics, but that does not diminish the eloquence of the work in highlighting the complexities, uncertainties and inconsistencies incurred in attempts to render the world photographically. All these levels and complications make the work far richer and less didactic than it at first seems.

In addition to all this is the way it situates the viewer. First, perhaps obviously, one is standing in the same place as the photographer, yet one both is and is not experiencing what the photographer experienced: the photographer saw the real ladder, with and without a camera in front of his face, and he has seen the photographs, whereas we only have the photograph. Looking through the camera is not the same as looking at the resulting image. Then Snow, in a manner akin to Eisenstein's use of intellectual montage, uses our knowledge of how ladders are in the real world to construct something that contradicts that knowledge, setting up a dialectic between our assumptions about how the world is and how it comes to be represented. Additionally, and this is what is most obviously missing from the work in reproduction, there is the kinetic effect one experiences as one sweeps the set of images from end to end. This way of looking activates the work, so that it becomes a quasi-movie. It dramatises the bulge, which seems to loom out from the flatness of the images.

Although *Of a Ladder* is a relatively early piece, Snow's concerns have not shifted all that much. Photographic representation and process, self-referentiality, perspective and paradox are all in evidence in *Of a Ladder*. Even the title contains a subtle pun, something of which Snow is inordinately fond: 'Of a Ladder' means both (pictures) of a ladder and a work about a ladder. It encapsulates his approach to photography: a photograph is never simply a picture of something, it is also always about that thing in a substantive way.

Jo Pearson

In Jo Pearson's short film *Extract* (1993), we turn to a more traditional but no less striking form of framing. What is remarkable is the way in which Pearson uses her camera to bring naturally occurring but highly contrasting features into dramatic conjunction. Thus framing is implicitly foregrounded as much as it is taken up explicitly in the work of Hall and Snow.

Extract is based on an epistolary monologue, spoken in a bitter female voice, which charts the breakdown of a relationship. The black and white film is shot mostly in and around an open-air swimming pool, but there are also individual shots of Blackpool beach, and of bingo balls jostling in a current of air. In almost every shot, the idea of a barrier, symbolising the failure of communication between the speaker and her ex-partner, is evoked. The barriers are spoilers, denying the pleasures promised by a swimming pool on a sunny day. Early on we see a wide shot of the pool through a fine steel mesh fence. This is the most explicit of the shots in which a view is barred, negated. They are followed by more subtle variations, such as the railings of a spiral staircase leading to the diving boards. Subtler still are the shots containing rectangular paving slabs, or views of the pool reflected in a casement window. They echo the theme, continuing and reinforcing it by implication, and because there are so many of them, they give the piece its nightmarishly insistent tone: once the barriers are established we see them everywhere – persistent, mute, threatening, like the character described on the soundtrack. The panelled roof of an abandoned factory, a row of street lamps and the torn netting which mars the view from the Blackpool Tower all reinforce the effect, which is a little like that conjured by Alfred Hitchcock in *Spellbound*, where the sight of parallel lines on a white surface induces

Extract, Jo Pearson

psychotic episodes in Gregory Peck. But where Hitchcock's film is (uncharacteristically) laborious, demanding verbal explanations and acted-out seizures, Pearson's is fleet, achieving its effect effortlessly. As the work progresses the barriers become more cruel, for example in the shot of a grand country house, which is seen through a vicious-looking row of heavy iron spikes and, glummer still, a similarly shown cooling tower.

Occasionally there are simple shots which fit the theme of the film, but appear to depart from the framing strategy: a disconnected tannoy horn rocking on its hinges, the winding gear of a coal mine viewed through weeds, fluffy clouds blowing across the top of a lowering facade. By now, however, the viewer is compulsively searching for the rectilinear traces common to the other images in the film: it has induced a mild monomania based on the grid pattern.

The Black Tower

In the classic cinema, the efficacy of the shot/reverse shot system, which establishes two people in the same time and place, talking to each other and maintaining eye contact, nevertheless depends upon a level of suspension of disbelief. Even if we know how films are assembled, we are perfectly willing to enter into that constructed world, in which first one actor, then the other, speaks all of his or her lines to an empty space. We are invited to stretch our credulity in a different way in John Smith's film *The Black Tower* (1987) where we cannot but be aware that what the framing and cutting of the film implies could barely obtain in reality, yet remains plausible, at least within the terms of narrative film construction. If we choose, however, to go along with the film's conceit, we become as vicariously paranoid as the character whose story it tells, partly also through our identification with him. For in the course of the film a man becomes convinced that he has seen a large black tower, which, unfortu-

nately for him, no one else can see. Furthermore, he quickly comes to believe that
the tower is following him around.

A number of diverse filmic forms – documentary, abstraction, psychodrama and
surrealist reverie – are convincingly bound together by the narrator's retelling of his
descent into madness. Indeed, in its ability both to contain these various forms, and
to create a plausible mimetic world, the film is an eloquent statement on the persua-
sive power of narrative, aided by the equal power of the voice-over. The film differs
from most narrative movies, however, in a crucial respect. In movies the shot/reverse
shot system creates an illusory unity of time and of space. (Of course, most
shot/reverse shot sequences are filmed in the same space as that in which the drama
occurs. However, it is perfectly possible to film two people in two different places,
unifying them partly by careful framing but above all by editing.) In *The Black Tower*
the opposite is the case: we are persuaded, at least initially, that what, in reality, is the
same place is, in the film's story, several distinct locations. The film's hero/narrator
becomes convinced that he is being followed by a black tower. At first he sees it
behind some houses, noting only that he had not noticed it before. So far so normal.
Gradually, however, he sees it more often than seems natural. He ventures further
afield, to Brixton prison, where he sees what he assumes to be a similar tower behind

The Black Tower, John Smith

the prison wall. On returning home, however, he is disconcerted by the absence of his 'local' tower, and so starts to believe that there might only be one tower, which, therefore, must be following him around. At one stage the matter seems resolved when the local newsagent confirms that the tower did exist but had been demolished the previous week. (At this stage Smith inserts some footage of the actual demolition of the first of a number of tower blocks at Hackney Wick in East London in 1986.) When the narrator realises that he and the newsagent were talking at cross purposes he is plunged into despair. There follows a semi-abstract sequence in which the character believes he is being followed. Wide shots of the tower taken from alternating angles are cut to the rhythmic sound of his steps on the pavement. The shots become closer and closer until all but a small corner of the frame is filled by blackness. *The Black Tower* is punctuated by such scenes where, without in the least abandoning the narrative mode, Smith offers quasi-kinetic abstract sequences. He thus combines what are normally understood as mutually exclusive categories of film, in this case narrative and abstract forms. It is through the framing of the shots, above all, that these sequences are achieved.

As the narrator slips into a paranoid state, the viewer comes increasingly to realise that the film's meanings have been constructed through carefully selective framing. The utter simplicity and transparency of this strategy forces the viewer to confront his own gullibility, but equally to take pleasure in noticing the details which give the game away, and to understand how easy it is for him/her to be deceived. A funny and telling moment comes late in the film, just before the tower is spotted over the trees in Shropshire. The scene is established with a few shots of tranquil willows and greenery, but there is something about the tightness of the framing of the landscape – one expects a wide shot in these circumstances – and the decrepit state of the foliage – too much moth-eaten bindweed – which hints at the actual location.

Notes

1. Interview with Steve Partridge in *Transcript* vol. 3 no. 3, p. 40.
2. Dolby Stereo, by concretising off-screen space through the placement of speakers which emit off-screen sound, has diminished this pleasure. For an account of the evolving relation of off-screen sound to on-screen action see Michel Chion's discussion of acousmatic sound and his concept of the 'Superfield' in *Audio-Vision* (New York: Columbia University Press, 1994).
3. It is interesting to note, however, how editorial conventions have evolved. Twenty years ago, jump-cuts in interviews were always concealed by a cutaway to the interviewer listening (known in the trade as a 'noddy'), whereas now discreet jump-cuts, softened by a quick dissolve, are commonplace.

4. See Annette Michelson and Kevin O'Brien (eds), *Kino-Eye: The Writings of Dziga Vertov* (London: Pluto Press, 1984), pp. 71–2.

5. In her book of *Cookery and Household Management*, Mrs Beaton gives guidelines for hosting a TV party. As well as catering suggestions, she gives tips on seating and lighting and on the desirability of allowing time to discuss the programmes! *Isabella Beeton, Cookery and Household Management*, 11th edn (London: Ward Lock Ltd, 1971), p. 108.

PLATE 1:
Ich Tank,
David Larcher

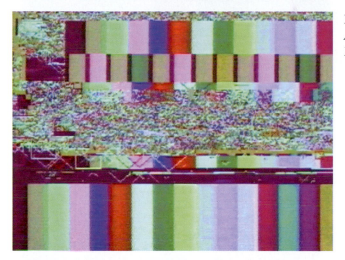

PLATE 2:
Arbitrary Logic,
Malcolm Le Grice

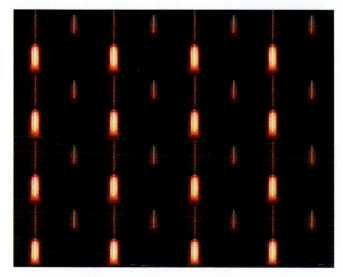

PLATE 3:
Lamp Light,
Gerhard Omsted

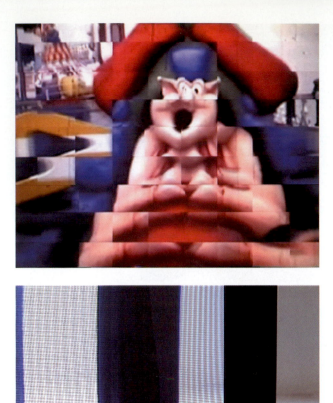

PLATE 4:
Heavens, Joe Read

PLATE 5:
On and Off/Monitor,
Simon Payne

PLATE 6:
*A Situation Envisaged:
The Rite II*, David Hall

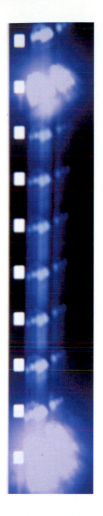

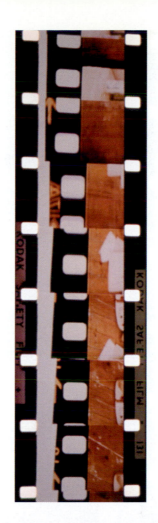

PLATE 7 (FAR LEFT):
Film No. 2,
Jennifer Nightingale

PLATE 8 (LEFT):
Slides,
Annabel Nicolson

PLATE 9 (BELOW):
Fifty Projectors and Colours,
Neil Henderson

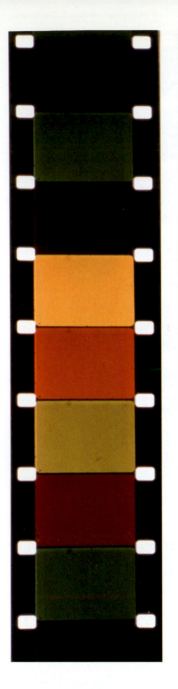

PLATE 10 (FAR LEFT):
Ray Gun Virus,
Paul Sharits

PLATE 11 (LEFT):
White Light,
Nicky Hamlyn

PLATE 12 (BELOW):
Against the Steady Stare,
Steve Farrer

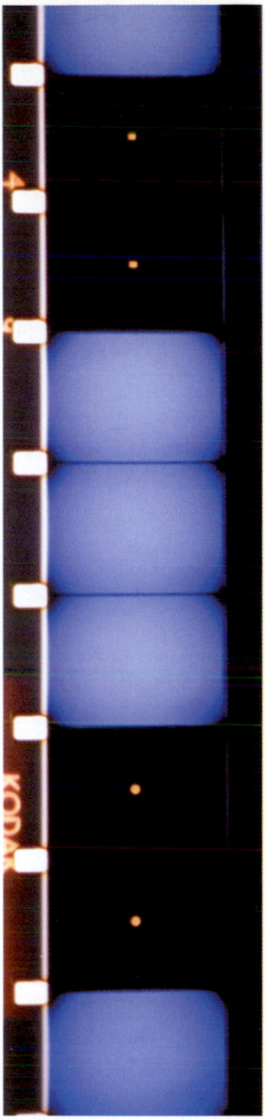

PLATE 13 (FAR LEFT):
Parcelle, Rose Lowder

PLATE 14 (LEFT):
4th Wall, Peter Gidal

PLATE 15:
Text of Light,
Stan Brakhage

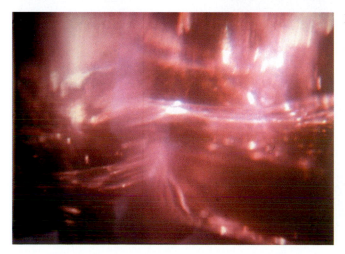

PLATE 16:
Red Shift,
Emily Richardson

PLATE 17:
*Tomorrow and
Tomorrow Let Them
Swing*, Margaret Raspe

PLATE 18:
After Manet,
Malcolm Le Grice

PLATE 19:
A Cold Draft,
Lis Rhodes

PLATE 20:
Angles of Incidence,
William Raban

PLATE 21:
Robinson in Space,
Patrick Keiller

PLATE 22:
Sanday, Nick Collins

PLATE 23:
Slow Glass, John Smith

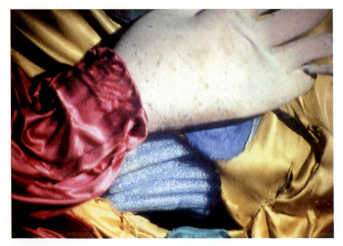

PLATE 24:
Untitled,
William English

7

Holding the Camera

The question of how to support the camera is never a merely technical one, but for a number of film-makers this consideration has gone hand in hand with related questions of modes of vision, and the balancing of the camera's role with other aspects of film-making: principally its subject and the maker's attitude or approach to it. Some superficial similarities of strategy occur in the films of Stan Brakhage and Peter Gidal, which in every other respect are opposed, while in Andy Warhol's film *Horse* (1965), the camera's stasis is crucial to the balance of elements in the work, and central to its meaning.

Stan Brakhage

> The lyrical film postulates the film-maker behind the camera as the first person protagonist of the film. The images of the film are what he sees, filmed in a such a way that we never forget his presence and we know how he is reacting to his vision. In the lyrical form there is no longer a hero; instead the screen is filled with movement, and that movement, both of the camera and the editing, reverberates with the idea of a man looking.[1]

Thus P. Adams Sitney sets out the manner of Stan Brakhage's mature style, after he stopped making psychodramas with actors in the 1950s. The first fully realised film in the new form was *Anticipation of the Night*, completed in 1958.[2] For Sitney, Brakhage's films take us back into their maker's way of seeing, but Brakhage himself puts it more strongly than this: 'I began to feel all history, all life, all that I would have as material with which to work would have to come from the inside of me out rather than as some form imposed from the outside in.'[3] How is Sitney's sense of 'a man looking' realised in Brakhage's oeuvre? More problematically, how does Brakhage reconcile the fact that the camera is an observational tool, whose function is intrinsically concerned with recording the out-there, with a notion of seeing as coming from the inside out?

Brakhage deals with this contradiction by a combination of means. Theoretically, he does it by denying the truth of filmic representation:

here, somewhere, we have an eye (I'll speak for myself) capable of any imagining (the
only reality). And there (right there) we have the camera eye (the limitation of the
original liar) ... its lenses ground to achieve 19th Century Western Compositional
perspective.[4]

Technically, he works constantly to deny '19th Century ... perspective' by destabilis-
ing the field of observation through overexposing, defocusing, turning the camera
upside down, inserting flash frames, negative sections, superimpositions and so on.
But these techniques have been used by other film-makers and do not necessarily
lead us back towards the film-maker's vision (wherever and whatever that might be).
It is the way Brakhage handles the camera, in conjunction with other manipulations
of the image, that constantly refers us back to its operator. Some of these techniques,
such as walking and 'glancing' with the camera to simulate eye/head movement, are
now so ubiquitous that they barely merit attention. More subtly, however, Brakhage's
camera is never quiescent, but always twitching, hovering, circling around its subject.
It is this restlessness that reminds us constantly of the presence behind the eyepiece.
These twitchings, furthermore, when combined with focus pulls and shooting into
light sources, endlessly transform their subject, turning it into an aesthetic object
which becomes more and more divorced from its source. The more the images are
the product of interventionist camera operations, the more they can be understood
as having been generated by their author.

   This tendency can be traced through a strand in Brakhage's work, from the
moment he abandoned the early psychodramas, in which the camera moves relatively
conventionally, to make *Anticipation of the Night* where, within a single film, one
witnesses a move from fairly static shots to dramatically fast and frenetic camera
movement, and where editing, crucial to the film's structure, is used to create conti-
nuities between discontinuous spaces. *Pasht* (1965) is close to being a pure abstract
work, in which the fur of the film's subject – a cat – is manipulated with an anamor-
phic lens and intercut with very short shots, so that it is visible not so much as fur,
but as a slightly different texture to the adjacent shots. One can see in *Pasht* the development of a process of gradual disengagement from the problematics of how to film
the external world – how to balance camera with subject – to an introspective,
hermetic world where every external object is transformed into a synthetic phenomenon which bears at best a vestigial trace of its origins. This trajectory reaches a point
of pure abstraction in *Text of Light* (1974). Where *Pasht* is frenetic, condensed and
organic, *Text of Light* is ethereal, the light crystalline and the colour prismatic (see
PLATE 15). It represents a terminal point in this way of working, before representational details reappear in films like the *Roman Numeral Series* (1979–80).

   Behind *Text of Light* is the well-known anecdote of how the film came to be made.
Brakhage was asked to make a portrait of an old school friend, but he was attracted

Pasht, Stan Brakhage

by a large glass ashtray on the friend's office desk, and this became the subject of the film.[5] The anecdote is important, because it symbolises Brakhage's turning away from the objective world, towards a hermetic realm of optical phenomena where illusory objects are conjured out of light. The ashtray suits perfectly Brakhage's 'outside in' project, because an object like this (in itself a kind of lens) filmed in extreme close-up, with resulting shallow depth of field, is highly susceptible to camera movement. The slightest shake or move in or out can dramatically transform the image, rather in the way that a polished diamond constantly changes as it moves. This scenario allows Brakhage to exert his virtuoso control over a highly volatile light-world, to conjure deep-space, where every twitch or move may be read back as his vision. It is as though he were producing these phenomena like a musician playing a violin. The translucent images are reminiscent of the apocalyptic landscape paintings of the English painter John Martin, or the Turner of *Snowstorm: Steamboat at a Harbour Mouth* (1842), but sometimes these spaces are populated with blurred, floating anthropomorphic forms. At other moments, where the image resembles Christmas tree lights, it is almost perfectly stable, with fluctuating light intensities the only form of movement.

Of course, this strand is not the only one in Brakhage's work and for every *Pasht* and *Text of Light*, there is a *Riddle of Lumen* (1972) or a *Machine of Eden* (1970). Both these films are much more outward looking, although even here there is still a pull, back to the film-maker's controlling presence. In the cryptic *Riddle of Lumen*, it is light, rather than the objects which reflect it, that is the film's subject, and this unites it with *Text of Light*, and with Duns Scotus' aphorism that 'All that is, is light' which has been a crucial principle in Brakhage's work. By declaring the film to be about light, Brakhage is in effect saying this film may have objects in it, but it is not about those objects, it is about the light which is reflected back into the (hand-held) camera. As such the objects are filmed not for what they are, but for their conformity to this idea. Thus the film-maker's vision is the unifying principle of the work.[6] *Machine of Eden* (see Chapter 9), in which a desert

The Riddle of Lumen, Stan Brakhage

landscape and dramatic cloud formations are filmed, is full of strongly assertive zooms into clouds and zooms out/pans which weave a composite image of the landscape. The film draws an analogy between the way a pictorial tapestry is woven and the way the film is built up in horizontal strands.

One might be able to think of *Text of Light* in materialist terms, as the product of an interaction between the camera, its movements, ashtray and light. The resulting phenomena, like a Jackson Pollock painting, could then be seen as being about productive tensions between the film's surface and the illusionistic phenomena which present themselves for consideration for what they are. But the reflexive marks of the work's making have been avoided or cut. There are no reflections of the camera, and even familiar phenomena like the refracted, hexagonal disc which appears when a camera is pointed at a light source are almost entirely absent. If we are to read the work as the wilful production of an individual mind, where are we ultimately led? What and where is the ego, and what would we understand from an acquaintance with it?

Peter Gidal

In Peter Gidal's films an entirely opposite process is at work, in which the film-maker's subjectivity is dispersed into the system of arms/hands, camera, light and subject. In this process, similarly, 'The spectator is produced by the film as subject in process',[7] who must struggle to find a place in relation to the film's unfolding, as opposed to the relatively absorbed spectator of Brakhage's work. Gidal's hand-holding articulates time, tirelessly revivifies the passage of time so that the viewer, instead of having a passive sense of time passing (in which they may become immersed in the image), actively experiences duration as something palpable. In order for that experience to be a pure experience of duration, things have to occur, but these occurrences must not lead back into an experience of image as an expression of the film-maker's subjective vision, as they can do in Brakhage. Neither must the camera move in a pseudo-mechanical way, which would produce an aesthetic effect, or serve to erase the truth that the camera was hand-held. The work creates an experience of duration for the viewer which the viewer negotiates for him/herself, in the production of which aesthetic considerations are relegated. An analogy can be drawn between Gidal's articulation of time and Frank Stella's early monochrome stripe paintings, in which the stripes articulate and thereby secure the flatness of a picture where an unbroken surface could easily appear as an illusionistic void in which the viewer can become immersed.

The hand-holding in Gidal's films is the product as much of avoidance of a number of more or less familiar tropes or patterns onto which the viewer can latch as it is a strategy for the withholding of representation. It is not rhythmic, subjectively embodied (Brakhagian), mechanistic, impressionistic (generative of effects), exploratory or revelatory. Where there is repetition, it is achieved in two ways: first, through printing, whereby the repeats are exact repeats, in order to focus on how seeing exactly the same thing again is different from the first time around, and seeing it three or four times would produce further new experiences and knowledge. Second, where there are manually repeated movements of the camera, these occur several times, over the same object, just to the point where our perception of that object has been exhausted and beyond, into redundancy, but before we can settle down into an abstract rhythm: as soon as a rhythm might become established there is an abrupt shift to a new pattern of movement. Thus we have to confront and go beyond our own boredom or exasperation.

Condition of Illusion

Condition of Illusion (1975) deploys both these strategies. The thrusting moves in on objects obliterate spatial depth, and concomitantly defocus the image (the classic 'mistake' of amateur movie-making). These zooming sequences are alternated with shots where the camera pans slowly over objects. The shots are defocused enough so that recognition of the objects is all but impossible, but not so much as to create abstract illusory spaces in the manner of *Text of Light*. After ten minutes the whole section is repeated, so that the distinction between manual and mechanical repetition is made clear and the inadequacies of memory made explicit.

The repetitions in *Condition of Illusion*, and other Gidal films, are different from repetitions which are the product of a vocabulary of aesthetic gestures, which leads back into familiarity or rhythm or the dead end of the originating mind, as is the case in *Machine of Eden*. Gidal always employs a distinct strategy which evolves out of a balance of forces, to produce a different looking film in each case.

Room Film 1973

In *Room Film 1973* a domestic space is filmed in six four-minute long continuous shots (100-foot rolls at 18fps) that are broken up into ten-second sections. After each section the second five seconds forms a repeat. After five seconds this repeat continues as a new shot for a further five seconds. The film is printed dark through a green filter:

> the only structure was the space that I knew I would try to film in various ways, and then I would film it in various ways, but you wouldn't know what the 'it' was because you would never be able to recognise it half the time anyway. I would go very close to the edge of a shelf having known before hand that at that point I want to be very close so that it doesn't look too much like a bookshelf but it might refer to something that might be a shelf at a certain height, but I want to be sure that you can't tell for sure the height, because if you knew the height you could establish a structure of scale. So to do the second shelf I would have to do it from an angle where the scale is mystified by the way it's shot, otherwise it would be at the scale correctly for the space which would then create a space within narrative illusionism. To undermine that I would have to pre-know that that point wouldn't be, for example, at an eighty degree angle with a medium long shot moving in, because then you could have scale within which a character could exist, and to not have that I would have to start that shot either closer in or darker or less close but out of focus, or more close but in focus. The minute you start pulling out, whatever else happens; flare, beautiful imagery, grain, or optical/ perceptual transformation of foreground/

Condition of Illusion,
Peter Gidal

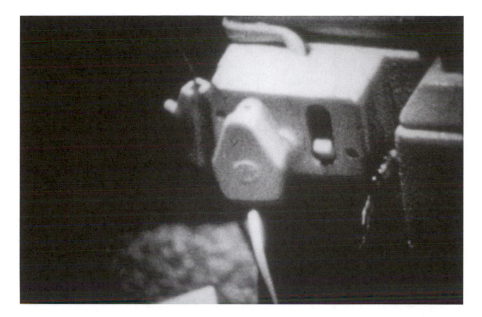

Room Film 1973, Peter Gidal

background, whilst all that is happening, constantly keeping in mind that the clarity of recognition must not go beyond a certain level.[8]

This last sentence pinpoints a difference between Gidal and Brakhage. Gidal accepts that other things are going on in his films apart from what he is attempting to control. That after all is part of the messy complexity of film. There is a recognition that film-making can not only be understood, but also planned, as a system with which one engages. But this doesn't at all mean that various unplanned, autonomous things will not occur in the making process. However, where Brakhage works constantly to produce effects of 'optical transformation', which sooner or later all refer back to 'the film-maker behind the camera', for Gidal these effects are incidental: telling by-products of the engagement with the strategy of withholding clarity. The distinction is not merely conceptual. The by-products in *Room Film 1973* are clearly such, whereas in Brakhage's *Roman Numeral Series*, for example, he creates defocused spaces out of which in-focus artefacts are very deliberately bodied forth for aesthetic consideration.

4th Wall

4th Wall (1978) is similarly a film of a domestic space, but whereas in *Room Film 1973* de/focusing was a crucial technique in combination with others, it is largely absent from *4th Wall*. Instead the camera moves more restlessly, so that the image rarely stabilises for more than a brief moment. Blur and shake do for the image what defocusing does

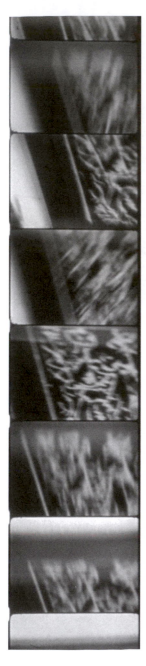

4th Wall, Peter Gidal

in *Room Film 1973*. Nevertheless, there is time to register mundane objects: so the work's concern shifts towards objects; books, lamps, towels etc. In looking at these things as things, and not as narrative props or symbols, one has to grapple with what they mean, if anything (see PLATE 14). To this end, whereas Brakhage sublimates objects, transforming them into optical phenomena, Gidal desublimates, draining his objects of effect. This creates images which are less scintillating but more disconcertingly mysterious. We are confronted with the obduracy of the physical world: what is it, and what does it mean? In *Text of Light* such questions are transcended, because the physicality of the world's stuff is transubstantiated.

Another important distinction between Brakhage's and Gidal's camera strategies is a product of the cameras they use. Brakhage uses a clockwork Bolex, not the most comfortable of cameras to handle, but one of the lightest and most compact of 16mm machines. This, combined with the similarly light and compact lenses and close-up tubes for the Bolex, facilitates a highly sensitive range of movements. Gidal, by contrast, uses an Arriflex ST, an old, silent, news-gathering camera, with an Angenieux 12–120 zoom lens. This front-heavy set-up clearly affects the character of the camera movements. Gidal has stated additionally that the tendency of the eyepiece to mist up has also fed into the often hesitant quality in his work, the sense of moment-to-moment negotiation. Perhaps it was this quality which prompted Michael Snow to remark: 'your film [*Room Film 1973*] had to be worked at. I felt ... as if it were made by a blind man. I felt that searching tentative quality, that quality of trying to see.'[9]

If this sense of discovering, of feeling one's way during the act of filming, seems to contradict the meticulous planning which Gidal describes above, then there are two points to bear in mind. First, film/making is a system, in which, as previously mentioned: 'the film-maker's subjectivity is dispersed into the system'. Part of that system is the uncovering or constructing of new, unforeseen experiences, which by definition cannot be planned. Indeed, too much planning and too little improvisation mitigates against one's opening up to new experience. Second, to approach the filming as a perfunctory process, as Hitchcock did, would contradict the aim of a project which is to defamiliarise, to depose the film-maker as much as the viewer from their assumptions about how the world is, and thrust them into a world where intentional and unintentional acts interact, mitigating against easy understanding. If this seems a trivial point, it is important to remember that for all their mastery and control of the shooting situation, the precise nature of the technology used must affect the outcome. Film, after all, is a technical medium.

Andy Warhol

The foregoing is equally true of Andy Warhol's film work, which, as much as it mirrors the history of the development of cinema, from short, silent black and white films to sync-sound colour, also reflects the use of increasingly sophisticated equipment. The early black and white films *Eat* (1963) and *Henry Geldzahler* (1964) were both shot with a clockwork Bolex, powered by an external electric motor. The films are composed of single takes, 2 minutes 45 seconds long, the length of a 100-foot roll of film (actually four minutes long when they are projected, as intended, at 18fps). The later, longer, sync-sound films were shot with a 16mm Auricon 'single system' camera, which was a ubiquitous news-gathering tool in the US from the early 1950s onwards. Technically, it was like a heavy, bulky version of the video camcorder, in that the sound was recorded straight onto the side of the film in the form of an optical or magnetic soundtrack, giving a much faster turnaround than the conventional route whereby sound and picture are recorded separately. The Auricon could also take a 1,200-foot magazine, which allowed Warhol to make the thirty-three-minute-long takes which are typical of several of the films made in 1965, such as *Beauty No. 2* and *Horse*.

The camera does not move in Warhol's films, not, at least, until Paul Morrisey started to push the work in a more commercial, less interesting direction. For the critic Tony Rayns, the rot set in with *My Hustler* (1965), where, by panning the camera to follow the main character: 'he not only ruptured the formal integrity of Warhol's methods but also, at a stroke, turned Factory films into vehicles for "actors".'[10]

Horse

In *Horse*, the scriptwriter/director, the 'actors', to whom verbal instructions and prompts are issued, passers-by, off-screen voices and the man who reads out the credits, which are interspersed throughout the film's 100 minutes, have equal billing, are equally present. This is even true of the horse, which dominates by virtue of its size, but which, by way of compensation, is quieter and less animated than all the other characters in the scene. In many of Warhol's films the dialogue takes place off-screen, or between characters both on- and off-screen. The equilibrium of the system, in which off-screen sound is so important, depends on the camera not moving. Once the camera

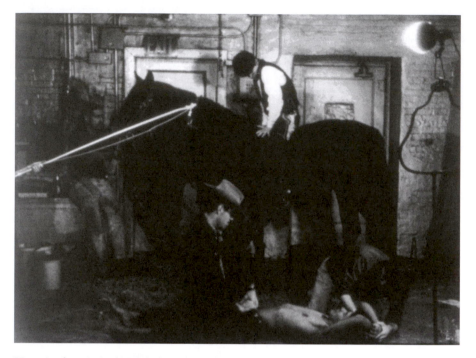

Horse (reel one), Andy Warhol (© 2003 The Andy Warhol Museum, Pittsburgh, PA, a museum of Carnegie Institute)

starts to move, the distinction between on- and off-screen space and sound is eroded.[11]

Horse opens with a mid-shot of a large, dark horse, which stands close to and in front of two doors in the silver Factory. Standing around the horse are a number of characters, dressed semi-cowboy style, i.e. Levis, white shirts, stetsons. Several other people, including Warhol, stand hidden between the horse and the doors, but they are hard to see because it is dark. A voice reads out the opening credits: 'Andy Warhol's *Horse*' and other phrases. It is hard to tell where the voice is coming from. The shot is medium-wide, enough to allow some space around and in front of the horse so that later, when the characters sit down on the floor to play poker, they will still be in shot. The camera does not move for the duration of the film, and the only inter-ruptions are for reel changes, at thirty-three and sixty-six minutes.

Although all the cast and crew are present, and the director is heard issuing instruc-tions, this is not a rehearsal, nor is it a film about a rehearsal, but neither is it 'the film'. It is not even obviously a Brechtian work – there are no speeches addressed to the camera/viewer – nor a Pirandellian filmed play, since many of the roles of the figures are never clearly resolved as either acting or not; yet they could be acting, or performing, since they all have 'roles': that is, they all appear. Taylor Mead's job is director, but it is also a role, since he is in the film. Warhol, too, is in the film, but his role is unclear. (How then is it *his* film?) The characters go through the motions of acting, but don't really 'get into role', and it is clear from the way they interact that they already have a rapport outside the context of the film. Since one gets this sense of an outside rapport, it's fair to assume that they are bringing the campy, role-playing dynamic that they have outside the film into it. At certain points though, this confident interplay falters. When the memorable instruction 'Take off your pants ... real slow' is issued, their finesse breaks down, and they perform this task most clumsily, inadvertently creating a strangely naturalistic moment.

From time to time, people enter the space through one of the two doors behind the horse, or someone in the room enters the set to answer the phone next to the left-hand door. Who are these people, and why does it not matter that they are in front of the camera when it is rolling? Do they become part of the film, even though they don't have a part? Yes, partly because they are an important link between on-screen and off-screen space. This is how that link is made, not by panning the camera, which would privilege them as figures, or incidentally-appearing Factory stars (which some of them are).

The entry of people into the set to answer the phone has the effect of placing the making of the film within the larger space of the Factory, so that it becomes simply one of a number of activities taking place simultaneously. Equally, the off-screen activity itself becomes a kind of invisible 'film', but what kind? Not really a documentary,

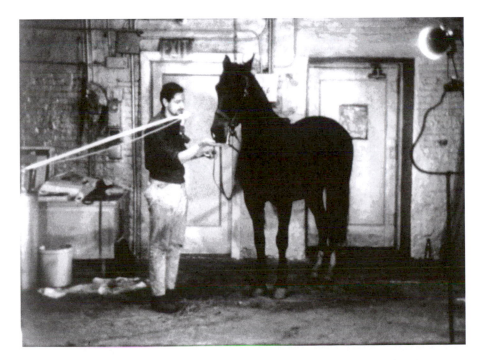

Horse (reel two), Andy Warhol (© 2003 The Andy Warhol Museum, Pittsburgh, PA, a museum of Carnegie Institute)

because we are not told anything about the people in it or what they are doing, but nor a drama, in the sense that the people don't seem to be acting. Nor, since it is neither a documentary nor a drama, is it a prototypical hybrid form, such as docu-soap.

These questions are sharpened in the second reel, where the production has paused, but the camera is rolling, because all the people who were in front of the camera are now off-screen, and the only figures left on screen are the horse and its minder, who remains with the horse for the duration. This is the reel where off-screen space is most intensely felt, where the relative emptiness of the set is contrasted by a corresponding surge of activity off-screen (it sounds like a party). A strong division opens up between what we see: the horse and the minder, off-duty as it were – and the dense chatter coming from behind the camera. What does it mean, that the production has paused, yet the horse and minder are still present, being filmed? Of course, *Horse* is the title of the film, so why should it seem as if activity has ceased, when the film's eponymous hero is present on set?

When Valerie Solanas shot Warhol in 1968, she also accidentally shot some paintings, which Warhol later exhibited as *Shot Marilyns*. In *Poor Little Rich Girl* (1965) Warhol accidentally filmed a reel out of focus, but decided to keep it as the first reel of a two-reel film (the second of which is in focus). Perhaps something like that is going on here, because although reel two of *Horse* has been planned, whereas the *Shot Marilyns* and reel one of *Poor Little Rich Girl* were accidents, they all raise the question: what does it mean for an artist to incorporate into a work something which seems to undermine or contradict the intentionality and the core values of a work, to decide to show a vandalised painting or include a roll of film in which it is not possible (except for the briefest of moments) to see what was in front of the camera? Reel two is a kind of negation of reels one and three, because they contain the 'play' *Horse*, whereas reel two does not. It contains two of the elements of the film, but they are in a kind of limbo or state of inactivity: certainly they are not resting between takes, but nor are they being filmed as part of a documentary about the making of the film.

What, then, is their purpose? By having the horse and minder in reel two Warhol adds another layer to the already complex situation of reel one. It is a layer of quasi-actuality which sits underneath the layers of 'acting', play-acting/role play and documentary incident of reel one. It also gestures towards the question, prompted by TV shows like the *Lone Ranger*, in which the drama is highly compressed, of what cowboys do when they're not riding the range, roping steers or chasing baddies. It also allows us to think about the horse. The horse is an authentic bit of the mythic Western: it's a real horse, just being itself, whereas the cowboys are play-acting phonies. But by isolating the horse and its minder the horse grows slightly in stature, and we also realise that the minder, who looks self-conscious and awkward, is perhaps the one creature in the film, apart from the horse, who really is just being himself: his very discomfiture is a measure of this, since, arguably, discomfiture is the spontaneous state of someone not familiar or comfortable with being filmed. This is a much more natural state than the state of the subjects of social observation documentaries who claim to be behaving naturally because they have 'forgotten' about the presence of the camera. But the horse minder's discomfiture is not the conventional docu-soap type where the camera voyeuristically follows its subject around, hoping for tears and tantrums to occur. The minder's unease is exacerbated by the camera's static stare: he has to obey the camera, to stay in front of it. In the ideal documentary the camera follows its subject; here it's the other way round.

There is a behaviourism in the film which the second reel highlights. With only a horse and one man in the shot, we start to think more about the horse, then make comparisons with the man. We realise that we know as much about the horse as we do about the men in the film. In fact we know more, because there is far more to know about a man than there is about a horse. The horse is just what it is, plus its physical history and its temperament, whereas the men are shrouded in complexity. How can we ever really know them, other than through their behaviour, and what does that tell us, other than their endless appetite for play-acting and posing? Again, the static camera is not only a mechanical counterpart to the behaviourism of the creatures in it, but it allows us to scrutinise the situation in all its misleadingly casual posedness. The joking ineptitude with which the lines are delivered is also exaggerated by the camera's not moving, since there can be no changing angles, close-ups or reaction shots to build the drama and divide the viewer's attention.

Notes

1. P. Adams Sitney, *Visionary Film*, 2nd edn (Oxford: Oxford University Press, 1979), p. 142.
2. The theorising of this new approach can be found in 'Metaphors on Vision', which is reprinted in Stan Brakhage, *Essential Brakhage* (New York: McPherson and Company, 2001). There is a detailed discussion of *Anticipation of the Night* in the chapter 'The Lyrical Film' in Sitney, *Visionary Film*. The film itself is available on VHS through Re-Voir.
3. Stan Brakhage, 'Metaphors on Vision', *Film Culture* no. 30, Autumn 1963, quoted by Sitney *Visionary Film*, p. 147.
4. Ibid., p. 149.
5. For a detailed discussion of *Text of Light* see William C. Wees, *Light Moving in Time* (California: University of California Press, 1992).
6. For an account of the increasingly problematic solipsism of Brakhage's position, see P. Adams Sitney, *Visionary Film*, 3rd edn (Oxford: Oxford University Press, 2003), p. 388.
7. Stephen Heath, 'Repetition Time: Notes around Structural/Materialist Film', in *Questions of Cinema* (Basingstoke: Macmillan, 1981), p. 169.

8. Peter Gidal, conversation with the author, March 2002.

9. Michael Snow, quoted by Peter Gidal, 'Theory and Definition of Structural/Materialist Film', in Peter Gidal (ed.), *Structural Film Anthology*, 2nd edn (London: BFI, 1978), p. 17.

10. Tony Rayns, 'Death at Work. Evolution and Entropy in Factory Films', in Michael O'Pray (ed.), *Andy Warhol Film Factory* (London: BFI, 1989), p. 165.

11. Ibid., p. 167.

8

Point of View

The Expanded Cinema of the 1970s raised questions about point of view that are fundamental to photography and especially moving image work, in which three-dimensional
spaces, seen from diverse positions in space, are presented uniformly in two dimensions in the same place. Recent installations such as Sam Taylor-Wood's *Third Party*
(1999) have avoided this problematic by presenting work on several screens so as to
recreate the spatial disposition of the original (pseudo-narrative) profilmic scenario. At
the same time, TV dramas like the American *24* and the British *Trial and Retribution*
(both 2002) have interspersed double and triple split-screen sequences within conventional narrative structures.[1] In the experimental film and video context, the investigation
into point of view has taken a number of diverse forms, from the aforementioned multi-
screen work in which the spectator's point of view is divided across several images, to
work which uses technological modifications to reconfigure the relationship between
camera and subject, to films which challenge point of view on its own ground by
endlessly redefining the field of view of the camera's singular position.

Multiple simultaneous viewpoints

Malcolm Le Grice's four-screen film *After Manet*, which was shown at the Festival of
Expanded Cinema at the ICA in 1976, is a good example of a work in which the
projection of multiple points of view, which are then presented uniformly on a single
screen, is problematised. There is no creation of narrative (or documentary) space
through montage, because there is no cutting in the film: there are four cameras, and
four points of view. In this way the film focuses around the problematic of the translation of three into two dimensions, by presenting four increasingly disparate points
of view simultaneously on four contiguous screens.

In this playful film the participants/camera operators set out to unsettle the spectator's fixed position, not by fragmenting space or by dispersing the images over two
or more spatially opposed walls, but by structuring the relationships between the four
screens so as to shift the centre of attention around and across the four images.

The film begins with the four cameras 'locked off' on tripods, aligned so as to form
a near-composite image of a single point of view of the picnic. The cameras are started
together and at first do not move. There is a broad shooting system: a set of rules and

After Manet, Malcolm Le Grice

a prearranged sequence of colour, black and white, negative and positive (see
PLATE 18). Each camera had sixteen 100-foot rolls of 16mm film in boxes which were
taped together in a column in the order they were to be used. Each of the four camera
operators – Le Grice, Annabel Nicolson, Gill Eatherley and William Raban – then start
to explore the scene, filming (and at the same time consuming) the picnic, each other
and, later on, the surrounding landscape. Each camera 'belongs' to one of the four people
– thus if there are three people in shot there is one moving and three static cameras.
When all the cameras are moving, i.e. being hand-held, all four operators may be in
each other's field of view. Negative (either B&W or colour) is only used if other cameras
are allowed to appear in shot: they never appear in the 'naturalistic' positive image. Thus
the negative image negates the confirmatory act of definitively locating another camera,
which would imply a full and final point of view. The whole film works to ceaselessly
displace such a point of view as well as the general notion of such: the hermetic self-
sufficiency potentially implied by all four cameras filming each other is blown open at
the end of the film, when they turn away from each other to face outwards around a
360-degree angle of view. This constitutes a maximum contrast to the opening
sequence, where all four cameras share a near-identical angle and point of view.

One twelve-minute section explores a repeated action by Annabel Nicolson, where the repeat is filmed sequentially with one static and three moving cameras, rather than simultaneously. Thus instead of four repeated actions it involved sixteen such actions which are shown as if shot simultaneously. 'As one part of the repeat involved Annabel pouring and drinking a glass of wine, by the 16th take Annabel was having some difficulty getting her sequence right – the inconsistencies were necessary to the "issue" of simultaneity, sequentiality – document – fiction.'[2] The showing of sixteen sequentially shot rolls simultaneously as four groups of four allows the viewer to scrutinise and compare the differences between an action shot from four points of view simultaneously, and one repeated successively for four different cameras. Depending on how four cameras are disposed when a sequence is shot, and how consistent an actor is in repeating an action, it may be very hard to read as simultaneous a sequence shot as such by four cameras. On the other hand, camera positions and framings can mask inconsistencies in the actions and delivery of lines of repeated takes, even when the performer is too drunk to remember and enact them very well. Given the audience assumes from the outset that it is seeing four simultaneously shot sequences, their 'work' consists in recognising occurrences which betray the true manner of shooting. The film, having established a pattern of simultaneity, then plays the audience's expectation of this against the actual state of affairs.

It is instructive to compare *After Manet* with Sam Taylor-Wood's multi-viewpoint work *Third Party* (1999). This film was shot with seven 16mm cameras, which are either static or panning according to a fixed pattern, which in any case repeats every time the work loops round. The overlaps in point of view allow the viewer to reconstruct the space of the party, and to 'reverse-engineer' the execution of the work, a process which has a number of implications. Because it is possible to join up the actions and placements of the figures in the work, the problematics involved in rendering a space by cameras are 'solved'. The invitation to overlook these problematics is strengthened by the fact that the work reconstructs the walls of the profilmic space in the gallery, defusing the issues that arise from rendering a three-dimensional space two-dimensionally. In *After Manet*, by contrast, the space is continually redrawn, reworked, re-examined. The four images are placed on a single flat screen, so that the viewer must constantly struggle with the tensions between the four increasingly disconnected points of view and their contiguity on screen.

Taylor-Wood's piece is dominated by the presence of a number of British icons, notably Ray Winstone and Marianne Faithfull, whose screen is larger than all the others put together. The repeating structure, which soon becomes predictable, throws the focus onto the work's content, and this stress is emphasised by the image of Faithfull, whose iconicity dominates the piece. The set is replete with the conspicuous symbols of wealth: panelled rooms, fine furniture and carpets which are typical of the comfy style of English costume drama. Above all, the work is conventional in

After Manet, Malcolm Le Grice

the formal sense, being simply a scene from a movie which has been divided among several screens. In this respect it is instructive, not least for reasons of historical awareness, to compare it to a work like Tim Bruce's multi-screen film *Corrigan, Having Recovered* (1979). This sophisticated multi-faceted piece explores narrative conventions and point of view through:

> two overt narratives, one a thriller told by a disembodied voice, and the other a dialogue between three actors. Both are open-ended and intermittent. Interwoven with the narrations is a strong formal concern, that of the articulation of space shown by cameras in three positions in each of the locations. The actions of people appearing in front of the cameras have a formal function of linking spaces through editing, and sometimes are invested with significance in the story. Film music codes are utilised to reinforce the suggestion of imminent significant action which is frustrated in the event.[3]

Like *Third Party, Corrigan* is shown on several screens in order to recreate the spatial relationships of the profilmic. Unlike *Third Party*, though, it is a highly reflexive work. For example, the music is seen being rehearsed and played, and then heard as described above, but the musicians are also implicated in the film's narrative.

Reconfiguring the camera–subject relationship

There has always been a strand of film-making in which makers have modified conventional technology or built custom accessories in order to extend the possibilities of the medium. One motive behind this practice is to shift the viewer out of the conventional point of view, in order to destabilise or break the conventional relationship between viewer and what is on the screen:

> the point of view can be – or appear to be – bizarre or paradoxical: the cinema shows extraordinary points of view – at ground level, or from high to low, from low to high etc. But they seem to be subject to a pragmatic rule which is not just valid for the narrative cinema: to avoid falling into an empty aestheticism they must be explained, they must be revealed as normal and regular.[4]

In most films the camera is attached either to the operator – hand-held or Steadicam – or mounted on a tripod. All these methods tend towards an anthropometric or personified camera position. Tripod-mounted cameras are invariably positioned at or around eye-level, giving a human-height perspective on the action. Hand-held cameras suggest, variously, the determining vision of the film-maker (Brakhage), a close-up intimacy in which the camera operator mingles among his subjects as an authentic presence (Jean Rouch, docu-soap) or at the opposite extreme is posited as an invisible protagonist, in which the camera itself is a 'person' as in the 1949 film *The Lady in the Lake*. Steadicam affords us the 'Alien's' point of view as she rampages along the service corridors of a stricken spacecraft.

But there are a number of works which diverge from the above, both in terms of how they were made, and in relation to Deleuze's general principle concerning the rationale by which film-makers give us extraordinary points of view. He gives the example of a ground-level shot of a military parade seen from under the stump of a one-legged soldier. This point of view is subsequently revealed to be that of a completely legless soldier.[5] Narrative cinema demands such explanations, since the viewer must be able to understand how apparently anomalous points of view are relevant, as they always are and must be, to the film's narrative meaning. Film editors speak critically of 'unmotivated' cuts, i.e., cuts which appear not to be driven by narrative demands. Such cuts, and similarly shots, threaten to break the hermetic world of the narrative, and so must be avoided or explained. The 'top shot', like the view down onto the staircase inside the Bates house in *Psycho* (1960) down which Norman's mother will push the detective Arbogast, is the relatively rare exception which proves the rule.

Rather than being explained, and thereby integrated into the narrative flow, the camera positions in the films to be discussed here are explanatory. Where the expression 'point of view' intends an embodied position, the camera positions in these films are notably disembodied, and hence de-psychologised. This frees them to reveal facts about relative motion, gravity, the push and pull of the physical world, and numerous unseen or unnoticed phenomena. The cameras were unconventionally mounted: on bungee ropes, bicycles, planks, trains, specially constructed dollies, even the earth itself. This has been done for different reasons and with very different results.

Cycles

In Tony Hill's films the camera is fixed relative to its moving subject, resulting in a reversal of the usual relationship between fixed and moving elements in a scene. The often extraordinary effects created by this procedure reveal otherwise invisible phenomena, most notably the shadow which rotates around the inside of a car wheel which is itself held static in relation to the camera, in *A Short History of the Wheel* (1992). This film is the most complete and cosmic of relative motion films, because it makes the earth turn around the wheel. Thus the idea of the movements of the spheres is evoked, but the film also champions the beauty of the wheel, here placed in conjunction with the natural object which perhaps inspired it. The film's ecological message is expressed in the fact that the bicycle wheel is the last, and therefore the most sophisticated, of wheels. This argument is grounded in an aesthetic demonstration, since the bicycle wheel is the most elegant and minimal of the structures. It

A Short History of the Wheel, Tony Hill

takes flight at the end, accelerating into an abstract whirl of energy. With a little thought the viewer can work out how this film was made, construct a mental picture of the contraption used, and this process is part of its pleasure.

In Guy Sherwin's *Cycle* (1980) the camera was mounted on a bicycle, overlooking the back wheel and the area of tarmac on which it rolls. A similar procedure to that of Tony Hill is employed except that the bicycle wheel, whose position is fixed in relation to the camera, is also visibly rotating on its own axis in that the tyre tread can be seen to be moving. The bike travels round in a circle, passing through a puddle at each revolution and tracing wet lines on the ground. Transverse movement enters the scene via the bicycle's own shadows, which arc around it from right to left. The shadows are the main movement in the film. Both camera and bicycle are the mutual creators of the image: the bike generates the image, the camera records it. *Cycle* is thus a rare, if not unique, example of a film whose imagery is created by the camera's support: in the three and a half hours of Michael Snow's *La Région centrale*, the camera mount's shadow is glimpsed for only a handful of seconds. Thus *Cycle* can be understood as diametrically opposite to *La Région centrale*. Where the former addresses its technological means, the latter is turned almost entirely away from it, and from gravity, orientation and human presence.

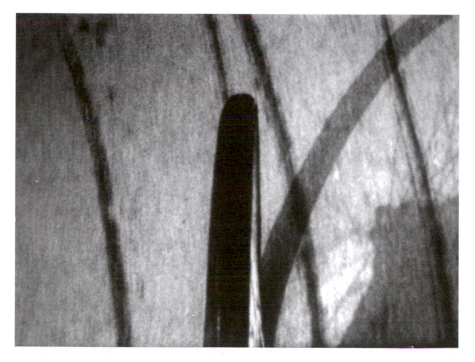

Cycle, Guy Sherwin

In terms of structure *Cycle* is both repetitious, in its retracing the same circular path, and developmental, in the way it builds up a pattern of curved wet lines. These accumulate in a manner reminiscent of the story of Winnie the Pooh and Piglet's encounter with Heffalump footprints. Second, for an audience who grew up in an official culture that was deeply suspicious of avant-garde art, they evoke the philistine public scandals, manufactured in the wake of Jackson Pollock's impact, about (English) action painters who used bicycles to make paintings.

Simon Oxlee built a rotating camera rig from bicycle wheels for his extraordinary videotapes *Revolution 1* and *Revolution 2*, which were both made in 1994 when he was a student at Kent Institute of Art and Design in Maidstone. At every level the works are about wheels within wheels. The big double wheel on which the camera is mounted is constructed from a number of bicycle wheels bolted together in a circle, around which the rim was wrapped. The structure is reminiscent of the space station in *2001*, and the video is similarly gravity defying, except that whereas in *2001* the wheel rotates around the camera in the interior shots, in *Revolution 2* the camera is fixed relative to the wheel. It points at Oxlee, who stands inside the structure, pushing it through the landscape and along corridors. The camera orbits his body, but, because it is travelling, the image of him changes constantly: the piece was shot in bright sunlight, which casts shadows of bicycle spokes onto him as he trundles along. As in Guy Sherwin's *Cycle* the imagery is both repetitive – cyclical – and varied in that the wheel travels through various spaces. With its outdoor-indoor-outdoor form, the overall structure is also cyclical. *Revolution 2* is a kind of performance and has a strong hand-made quality, unlike most of the other works described here, which are more mechanical and cool. Oxlee's videos are part self-portraits, and part exploratory, process driven works, strongly reminiscent of decrepit children's playgrounds in their creaky, erratic progress. His use of a car's steering wheel as a camera mount in *Drive* (1994) links the work with Denise Hawrysio's films.

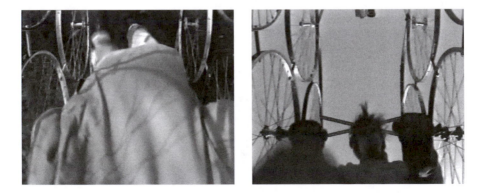

Revolution 2, Simon Oxlee

Men at work

In Hawrysio's Super 8 films the camera assumes the 'impossible' point of view. In cinema terminology this is the position typified by, for example, a view onto a draw-

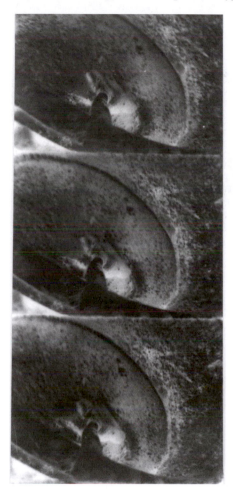

Tar Kettle, Denise Hawrysio

ing room from behind or within the flames of a fire burning in a hearth. Hawrysio has made a series of films in which the camera is attached to various mechanical devices, mostly tools. The films' logic is that by getting really bound in to the activity being depicted, we will get a closer understanding of it, but what we actually get is the opposite: strange semi-abstract images that are almost impossible to interpret. In *Jack Hammer* (1985), *Snow Shovel* and *Tar Kettle* (both 1987) the camera is fixed to the handles of those objects in such a way that the object to which the camera is attached extends into the scene, in the same way as the plank in Tony Hill's *Holding the Viewer* (1993). Because the framing is tight and the subject vibrating we have no reliable clues to guide our reading of the films. Furthermore, snow may fill the frame, steam from the boiling tar obscure the field of vision or lumps of tarmac move and detach themselves from the road as if animated by hand. The difference between camera vision and human vision is pinpointed. The camera gets in between ourselves and our technology. Thus we see how common activities we undertake are transformed through seeing them from the point of view of the tools we employ. But these strategies also generate new kinds of shots which take on a life of their own outside the context in which they were made.

Planks, ropes

Tony Hill's *Holding the Viewer* is a more prosaic work than his *Short History of the Wheel*, but it demonstrates an interesting psychological effect. In the Super 8 films Clare Francis made of her participation in the 1976 solo transatlantic yacht race, the

Holding the Viewer, Tony Hill

camera was bolted to the mast of her boat in such a way that the boat occupied most of the frame area. The boat remains stable relative to the camera while the horizon seesaws alarmingly in the background. In Hill's short film, the plank on which the camera is mounted occupies only a small portion of the picture area, and yet the reverse motion effect nonetheless persists: we the audience are in a stable place while the 'background' moves around.

Confessions, William Raban – preparing the camera

William Raban's brief *Confessions* (2001), in which a video camera makes a bungee jump, offers a momentary experience of pure free fall, the jump without the preceding vertigo or the subsequent pull of gravity. In Kieslowski's film *Three Colours Blue* (1993) an image of bungee jumping appears on a TV set as a metaphor for escape from the world, but the metaphor could also be read as sexual: a laborious, nerve-racking ascent to the top of the crane, followed by a momentary rush during which the world briefly recedes in the adrenalin-filled moment of fall, succeeded by a declining series of bounces as the elastic yields to the pull of gravity and the jumper hangs upside down (echoes of Hitchcock), waiting to be released from the harness. As a film, *Confessions* has moments of near abstraction which dislocate the viewer from the physicality of the fall, so that the sensations that usually accompany simulatory rides/films are absent. This allows the viewer a more detached assessment of the physical fall of the camera and how it records itself. The film opens the question of how picture stability is related to the sense of physical involvement. This is where the continuity between the Diorama, single-screen cinema, 180- and 360-degree projections and simulators becomes apparent.

Fixed mountings

In Guy Sherwin's *Night Train* (1979) where the camera looks out from the inside of a railway carriage window, the mounting – a table – may be only a small step away from a conventional situation, but that small step is crucial in terms of how we understand the resulting film, which is about the way the landscape draws itself across the field of view of the camera. (The film is discussed in detail in Chapter 1.)

In her film *Red Shift* (2001) Emily Richardson goes a step further, taking time-lapsed frames of the stars at night. The camera was mounted on a tripod, and the picture framed so that a portion of the earth and the night sky are both visible (see PLATE 16). The film was shot in Greece and the Canary Islands, and is a mixture of human events – the passing of ferries – and natural ones: the movement of stars and swirling mist and fog. Stars are unusual in that they give out light without seeming to illuminate anything (although night-vision goggles need starlight to work) but in this film they are both the film's light and its subject matter. It could be argued that *Red Shift* does not qualify as having been made with a 'strangely attached' camera, but the point is that it is in effect the earth on which the camera is mounted. Of course this is always the case, but by pointing her camera at the sky and working with time-lapse, Richardson reveals dramatically an invisible truth about all films in which the sky appears: simply, that the earth is turning. The film is animated by the earth's movements, not the camera's, even though the earth appears static. In this way it offers a scintillating, Ptolemaic vision of the cosmos.

Camera helmet

In Margaret Raspe's pioneering *camera helmet* films a simple, silent Super 8 camera is mounted on a helmet worn by the film-maker, permitting her to film herself engaged in activities requiring the use of both hands. From this situation a body of work emerges: the form demands new content, and so a variety of under-the-camera activities are recorded, and a new sub-genre is created. Appropriately for a domestic format, most of the films are of domestic activities – food preparation and washing up – and the intimacy of the medium harmonises with the closeness to the activities that the method of filming brings the viewer.

Tomorrow and Tomorrow Let Them Swing, Margaret Raspe

We are very conscious of looking down on the scene as it is played out, but we do not feel like voyeurs, because we are precisely in the position of the film-maker, sharing her point of view. This sharing is not empathic like our identification with characters in a movie, or even the *Lady in the Lake*, where the protagonist is identical with the camera, because there are no characters and hence no other gazes: we see only Raspe's forearms, dealing with the objects in front of her.

In *The Sadist Beats the Unquestionably Innocent* (1971), there are echoes of the cream separator sequence in Eisenstein's 1930 film *The General Line*, but the cream beating continues past the triumphant stage of thickening until it is reduced to an entropic, coagulated lump. *Tomorrow and Tomorrow Let Them Swing* (1974) is the longest of the films at twenty minutes. It also has the most banal subject matter – washing up – but is the richest and most accomplished in terms of visual complexity and the co-ordination of hand and arm movements with camera movements. The constant to and fro of dirty cups and dishes from the right-hand draining board, into the frothy wash water, to under the rinse, to the left-hand draining board, establishes a rhythmic pattern, a production line, not choreographed, but simply the product of a completely habitual interaction with domestic objects that we can all do with our eyes shut (see PLATE 17). In this sense the piece is partly about 'muscle memory', about how we are a store of familiar routines and patterns of movement from which our daily lives are composed, habitually 'going out, in the old way' like the character in Beckett's novel *The Unnameable*. The camera-moves follow the hands, back and forth. But because the camera and hand movements are co-ordinated, there is a purposive synchronisation that is completely opposite to the exhausting panning back and forth which replaces match cutting in dialogue scenes in TV programmes like *NYPD Blue* and celebrity cook shows, done, apparently, in a spurious and wrong-headed quest for a more 'spontaneous' realism.

La Région centrale

It is tempting to think of Michael Snow's *La Région centrale* (1971) as the big daddy of all the films described here, and it is true that it not only predates all this work, but also dwarfs it in terms of its scale and technological sophistication. However, there are particular differences between Snow's film and and the rest. The work discussed here trades on strangeness: the strangeness of what is shown and how the apparatus defamiliarises what it shows. In *La Région centrale* there is nothing unfamiliar, or even defamiliarised, about the rocky landscape of the location. It is the operations of the apparatus alone which are extraordinary. There is an absolute separation between the subject and its representation: it is the purest possible apparatus film, from which any trace of human presence, either in front of or behind the camera, is conspicuously absent. This is its cool beauty.

By contrast, in the other work described here, the separation between subject and apparatus, if it exists at all, is much less clear cut. Human presence is either strongly implied, as in Hawrysio, Sherwin, Raban and Raspe, or visibly present, as in Hill and Richardson (by implication). In Oxlee, apparatus, operator and subject are all of a piece.

Displacing the cardinal viewpoint

In addressing the question of point of view, some film-makers have sought to attack the efficacy and position of knowledge which the point of view confers on the spectator, by operating from a constrained, and therefore well-defined, point of view.

Michael Maziere's film *Untitled* (1980), produced when he was a student at the Royal College of Art, explores two adjacent spaces: a room and the street outside as seen from the room. Through an exhaustive use of focus-pulls, pans and superimposed zooms, Maziere elaborates a number of ways of seeing these two spaces and their various interpenetrations. Sometimes the room is an interior world illuminated with light from the single window. At other times it is a blackened void and the window a screen. At other moments the window permits a view out and we see the exterior as a view from a window. Then we go outside and the camera teases out a further set of ways in which the space may be experienced. The camera manipulations successively redefine the exterior space, reminding us that seeing is incomplete, and that since each sweep of the camera displaces its predecessor, the notion of a cardinal viewpoint is undermined. The relativism implied by this should not be confused with something apparently similar, namely the subjective expression of an individual's vision. The film sets up a system of objective elements – room, window, view out, exterior, camera, light and darkness – and the film arises from the interplay of these.

The limitations of the recording medium – film – are also inscribed into the work, further complicating the relationship between camera, subject and spectator. Although our eyes can only handle, at any one moment, a small portion of the range of light intensities which exists between near total darkness (one photon) and bright sunlight, they make rapid, constant adjustments as the environment changes, so that most of the time we experience workably consistent levels of illumination. This process only slows down enough to become apparent in extreme situations, such as that of *Untitled*, where strong daylight filters into a unilluminated room through a single window. In most movies the problem this poses for filming is solved by using artificial light to increase the interior lighting to a level so that inside and outside fall within the contrast range, or latitude, of the film stock being used. However, if the true contrast difference between the two is to be preserved, the film must be exposed to prioritise either inside, outside or somewhere in between. These options all involve a compromise, so that if the shot is exposed for the outside, the inside will be under-exposed, or if exposed for the room the outside will be over-exposed and so on. *Untitled* works through a range of possibilities.

Although changes in exposure which lead to different perceptions of a space do not directly affect point of view, to the extent that those changes alter what is perceptible within a shot, they do indirectly affect it, because a point of view could not be such in the absence of any content at all. There has to be something for the camera to look at for there to be a point of view. Point of view, therefore, may be defined by what falls within the shot, as by the apparent position of the camera on a scene. If the former is subtracted from the latter, what is left over? A sense of embodiedness or intentionality, perhaps, whereas in the former there is the sense that the camera is just there, disinterestedly pointing.

Rob Gawthrop was another graduate of the Royal College of Art film school. In *Distancing* (1979) the camera points out, from a fixed position, at a rain-spattered window, a head, a plant, the sea and the horizon. Gawthrop continuously pulls focus and aperture so that the objects dissolve and reform in an ever-changing flux, 'bringing into question the very act and accuracy of cinematic description'.[6]

The field of view is made up of visual phenomena which, in the way they shift into each other or separate out, emphasise the difference between objects and representations. This trenchant distinction is effected without slipping into idealism, a charge sometimes levelled at an experimental film practice which has always stressed the autonomy of the cinematic apparatus. Gawthrop's film can never be accused of ideal-

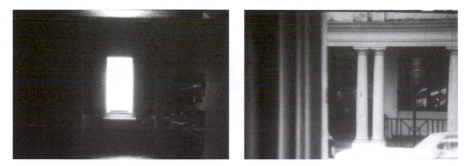

Untitled, Michael Maziere

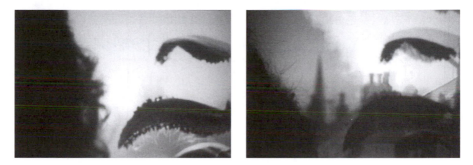

Distancing, Rob Gawthrop

ism: how could images which a camera records from the objects in front of it ever be so described? What occurs is not manipulation, which is something that occurs in post-production, but what Gawthrop is doing is foregrounding as process the moment of constitution of the photographic image.

There is usually a close fit between the profilmic and its representations, which renders invisible these constitutive processes. Instead of appearing ready formed, the images in *Distancing* are brought forth out of a field which is simultaneously seen but unknowable, through a constant pulling back and forth through the various constitutive parameters – focus, depth of field, aperture – so that frequent conjunctions of some of these produce an image momentarily recognisable as an object. The images are latent, or potential, until they briefly appear before dissolving back into a field of infinite possible images. Yet even to describe them in this way is to perpetuate an attitude by which we understand the film as a series of momentarily recognisable objects interspersed with periods of more or less meaningless shadowy shapes. *Distancing* forces us to confront this unconscious hierarchisation of significance.

Both *Distancing* and *Untitled* stress the fact that seeing, as much as film-making, is a constitutive process, an act by which we construct and define ourselves in relation to our surroundings. The distinctions between self and surroundings, observer and observed are blurred. This contrasts with the separation implicit in the cinematic point of view, where there is a clean separation implied in the omniscient invisibility of the spectator in relation to that which they observe. The separation between the profilmic event and its capture, however, can never be a true separation, since the profilmic is constructed through the operations of the camera, but because so much cinema is 'filmed theatre', as Robert Bresson derisively puts it, we tend to make the distinction anyway.

Notes

1. *24* (2002). Consisted of twenty-four, forty-five minute episodes of 'real-time' drama with two- and three-screen sections. In *24* the technique is much more closely confined to its narrative function, taking the place that parallel montage would normally play in tying together two spatially distinct but narratively simultaneous moments. *Trial and Retribution*, by Lynda LaPlante, was broadcast by ITV1, on 19 and 20 June 2002. A typical example of a split-screen scene is where both parties in a phone conversation are seen simultaneously, in itself an old cliché, but here we will get a wide shot and a close-up. In other instances we will see two or three angles on the same object. These examples occasionally mark a partial move from a conventional reorganising of narrative space, as also evidenced in Sam Taylor-Wood's *Third Party*, discussed in this chapter, towards a more autonomous investigation of spatiality and point of view. In *Trial and Retribution* for example, we see, just once, a short interval where an image appears on the left third of the screen, which fades out as a centre screen fades in, which in turn gives way to a right screen. In other words, a brief moment of formal split-screen interplay.
2. Malcolm Le Grice, correspondence with the author.
3. Tim Bruce, London Film-makers' Co-op Catalogue, 1993, p. 21.
4. Gilles Deleuze, *Cinema 1: The Movement Image* (London: Athlone Press, 1992), p. 15.
5. In Ernst Lubitsch's *The Man I Killed*. Ibid., p. 15.
6. Rob Gawthrop, London Film-makers' Co-op Catalogue, 1993, p. 48.

III

AESTHETICS

9

Space

Films that deal with the representation of space also tend to question and reconfigure the relationship between the camera and its subject. Any critical cinema is bound to do this in order to explore how the film apparatus – finite, two-dimensional, enclosing, transient – confronts space – infinite, three-dimensional, continuous, enduring. Thus an examination of films whose subject is principally the depiction of space will be an examination of how those films foreground the contradictory nature of their encounter with their subject.

La Région centrale

In his 1971 film *La Région centrale*, Michael Snow approaches his subject as if it were not just a blank canvas, but a *tabula rasa*. (Blank canvases have the weight of recent art history behind them.) For three and a half hours the camera, mounted on a

La Région centrale, Michael Snow

specially built rig, spins and gyrates in a desolate mountain landscape. Snow's choice of location must have been guided by the fact that his subject suggests no one approach or structure over another. There is no obvious fit between the mountain – formless, chaotic, unfathomable – and the synthetic purity of the cycling arcs and loops of the camera. On the contrary, the two are heroically counterposed: chaos versus form, nature versus culture, raw matter versus technology. Snow spent a long time looking for a location devoid of human traces (but accessible by car). He also made a thirty-minute section of the film which documented the assembling of the camera apparatus and equipment, but this was discarded at the editing stage.[1]

Measured against a 'primitive' film like the Lumière brothers' *Sortie de l'usine* (1895), where, classically, a static camera is placed square-on to the scene which is then animated by human activity, *La Région centrale* can be construed as exactly opposite, with its inanimate subject and ever-mobile camera. It is the most pure kind of apparatus film, in that the animation is entirely with the camera. Snow develops ideas about movement as a function of the apparatus that are increasingly present from *Wavelength* (1967) through *Back and Forth* (1969) to the work in question.

There is a distinction to be made between a tracking shot and a shot made from a camera which, for all its mobility, is rooted to a spot. The tracking shot slices through, both spatially and temporally. Space is passed by and left behind. It isn't even off-screen space because our mind is always with the leading edge of the film. The trailing

La Région centrale, Michael Snow

edge is past and largely forgotten. In *La Région centrale* there is always the under-standing that the camera is not going away, that it will return to parts already visited. This creates a sense of the camera perpetually redrawing the space, as opposed to cutting it up. The limitless variations in these redrawings serve to remind us that there can never be a definitive description of a space or set of phenomena, even when there is a commanding viewpoint from which to survey the scene, with a camera mount-ing that permits any imaginable movement or angle of view. Yet as much as it is about the apparatus, this spirographic film is also about the spectator's sense of gravity and orientation. Our experience of the world as embodied spectators is engaged, but not at all in the way of the simulated ride, where the physiological mechanisms by which we anticipate and manage shifts of weight and balance are tricked into responding as if we were really there. Precisely because Snow's framing and camera movements are so patterned and measured, they assert themselves as images, and not as a simu-lation. We are spectators, as opposed to participants.

Seeing as

William Raban's *Angles of Incidence* (1973) was shot in a basement room in East London. The camera faces a window, and is tilted up so as to take in the neigh-bouring tower blocks. Over a twenty-four-hour period, the tripod-mounted camera moves in a semicircle around the window, in such a way that the position of the window within the film-frame is consistent (see PLATE 20). To facilitate this consis-tency of framing, the camera is attached to the centre of the window by a cord which occasionally is visible.

Slowly, methodically, the camera moves from one position to the next, sometimes in jumps, sometimes incrementally. At this stage the film is a sequence of static views of an invariably static scene: a study in framing, parallax and light changes. Gradually the pace increases and the film becomes more animated: now it is becoming a 'camera piece', in that the camera dances around its subject, its movements animated by the rapid shift from one position to the next.

As the motion accelerates, and the camera starts to jump from one acute angle to the opposite in larger and larger steps, our perception of the image as the camera moving around the window shifts over to a perception of the window as flipping in space, as if the camera is static and the world moving. As the film slows down again, however, one's 'seeing as' does not revert to its initial aspect, but stays in window-flipping mode almost until the end, which is marked by a brief sequence of blurred time exposures which destroys the spatial depth and reinforces the sense of the space dancing before the camera.

First, then, there is a shift from stasis to movement. This can also be expressed as a shift of subject from window to camera. Then there is a shift from camera move-ment to window movement. Finally, there is a return to stasis, but this is not

Angles of Incidence, William Raban

accompanied by a corresponding shift back from window movement to camera movement.

In Raban's film this illusion is a psychological effect, occurring in the mind of the beholder, like the Duck-Rabbit or the Necker Cube, but whereas in these famous examples the flip from one perceptual aspect to the other is instantaneous, in the film it occurs gradually as the motion gathers pace.

In one of Guy Sherwin's ongoing *Short Film Series* films *Canon* (2001), a tall chimney was filmed from a train window as it passed through the industrial landscape of the English West Midlands. Each time a vertical feature crosses the sightline of the chimney, the film jumps back a few seconds, proceeding forwards past the same vertical feature for the second time until a new one prompts another backward jump. The image of the chimney gradually changes, becoming a grainy silhouette as the camera swings round to face the sun. Because the chimney is always framed centrally, the straight line of the train's trajectory becomes an apparently circular one: we seem to be on a giant carousel, which is rotating around the chimney. This effect is reinforced by the similar motion of objects beyond the chimney.

Angles of Incidence also operates in this way, but in a completely different kind of space. In Raban's film the window is both a (transparent) threshold and the fulcrum around which the camera and the buildings outside rotate. Both these films thus show how the way the camera moves through a space creates different kinds of spatial experience.

Relative motion

In several of Tony Hill's films, but most dramatically in *A Short History of the Wheel* (1992), different processes are in play. The camera films one of the wheels of a succes-

Canon, Guy Sherwin

sion of moving vehicles in such a way that the ground, and everything else, rotates about the wheel. Here the work depends not on psychological illusion for its effect but on a reversal of the relations of stasis and motion which we take for granted: cars move, roads do not. Hill deploys coolly objective camerawork to revelatory ends. The extraordinary results of his camera motion machines trade as much on the indexical veracity of his images as on his not revealing the technology that produces them. This encourages the spectator to ponder on how it was done, and this process of analysis is an important effect of much of Hill's work.[2] It invites us to ponder our understanding of the external world: space, time and motion and our apprehension of it. Technology enters into the work as a semantic agent, in that the deductions the viewer has to make in order to work out how the films were made lead to insights beyond the narrowly technological.

A Short History of the Wheel also constitutes a humorous critique of the position of the spectator. In each shot the hub of the wheel is in the centre of the frame, thereby placing the spectator in the classical transcendental, Archimedean (sic) point of view. Simultaneously though, the stable world that this position usually guarantees the viewer now spins out of his/her control. An aside: Hill stresses the importance of giving special thought to the shooting of his work. Without in any way impugning video as a technology, he is critical of the 'sort it out in the edit suite' mentality, whereby poorly shot footage can be lashed together and digitally spiced up in post-production in ways that would be impossible with film. It is telling, in this regard, that video-makers often talk about the camera as a 'gathering' device, whereas filmmakers rarely do.

Spatial ambiguities

In Bruce Baillie's short film *All My Life* (1966) the camera appears to pan round a rose-covered fence surrounding a road. At the end of the pan it unexpectedly tilts up

All My Life, Bruce Baillie

across a telephone wire, into the sky. The film lasts about three minutes, the same length as it takes Ella Fitzgerald to sing the title song.

A seemingly simple film, easily described, but an extremely difficult film to decipher. Because the fence is overgrown with roses, it is almost impossible to judge its geometry: is it rectangular or circular? Does the camera track and pan, or just pan? One has to study the way the fence appears to approach and recede to try to work these things out, but the kinds of clues which might confirm the assumption of a rectangular configuration, such as a corner, where two straight runs of fencing would meet and which would therefore recede visually, are crucially obscured by rose bushes.

Finally, when the camera tilts up at the end, another conundrum of a different kind makes its entry. Once the camera has cleared the ground, it is the telegraph wire which appears to move through the frame, rather than the camera moving across it. Then, finally, the camera hits clear sky, so that its movement is no longer discernible. Given, however, that the camera has moved for the entire film, we are entitled to assume that it is still moving, or are we, given that we can't confirm this visually? Thus the film takes us to a place of epistemological doubt, where habitual patterns of assumption are brought into question.

In *Sculptures for a Windless Space* (1995) the Dutch film-maker Barbara Meter uses the documentation of a roomful of sculptures by fellow artist Anneke Walvoort as the starting point for an exploration of figure/ground relationships within a confined space. In this film the camera interacts choreographically with the objects, rather than simply recording them, so that the work animates the interrelationships between the various sculptures, creating a quasi-dance film.

The dance analogy is strengthened by the fact that the sculptures resemble a group of figures. Each work consists of an object atop a tall, slender pedestal whose breadth and depth is approximately that of the sculpture itself. In some cases the sculpture grows out of the pedestal and in many of the works the distinction between object and pedestal is eroded in various ways.

The sculptures are almost all white, as is the space. They appear small, but since there are no familiar objects in the room with which to compare them, there is actually no way of judging their size. The scene is similar to a desert where, in the absence of references, one soon loses all sense of scale and distance. This can make deserts seem limitless, but although Meter's room is obviously not so, there are often moments when the texture of the walls blends with the film's grain movement, so that the walls cease to function as enclosures, or even discernible, locatable surfaces, because they appear to move into the same plane as the grain. (This plane is defined not so much by the grainy surface, although grain is highly visible, as by the orientation of forms in relation to the vertical and horizontal edges of the frame.)

In a desert everything can become reduced to light and shade – that is, texture – and here there are further similarities to *Sculptures*, with its coarse-grained surface and absence of colour. Yet in automatically assigning 'whiteness' to the objects and

Sculptures for a Windless Space, Barbara Meter

surfaces of the space, we temporarily blind ourselves to the colour-cast of the image. To remind us of the bluish colour-cast and to reinvigorate it for the spectator subjectively, Meter inserts a vivid flash of complementary orange into the film after a minute or so. This is followed by further inserts of varying hues.

The similarity of tone between sculptures and wall creates a number of perceptual puzzles which reinforce the film's reflexivity over its documentary function. The objects are lit from one side so that the shaded faces of the pedestals blend into the darker wall areas in the background. Thus the dichotomy between object and space, on which the very existence of sculpture depends, partly breaks down. In two-dimensional terms this dichotomy is one of figure and ground, and in *Sculptures* the breakdown manifests itself as a blurring into modulated surface. The alcoves and chimney breasts of the room, and the shadows they cast, create additional vertical features which interact with the pedestals. This interaction, which compounds the confusion of figure and ground, is again facilitated by the very grainy texture of the film.

Camera and sound strategies also stress the primacy of the medium. Meter frequently animates the scene by moving across a foreground object to reveal a more distant one. Thus static objects come to life, effectively dancing in relation to one another through the agency of the camera. Focus-pulls are also employed, but here, strikingly, they change the disposition of lights and shadows, more than merely bringing parts of a scene into focus. Camera movement and grain movement interact, and also form one of a number of complementary relations within the film; the sculptures retain a notional solidity, even as they pulsate and threaten to merge with their surroundings.

The one black-pedestalled sculpture in the room signals the difference between two kinds of absence of light. It plays on the assumptions of the viewer who has assumed that in a roomful of white things this black thing must be a cast shadow. It is soon revealed, however, as a non-reflecting object – the only such to be defined, negatively, by its surroundings and not by its reflectivity, as is the case with all the other objects in the space.

Tracking shots

Linear tracking shots, where the camera is fixed relative to the dolly, especially if at 90 degrees, straighten out space. This is evident in examples like the car pile-up scene in Godard's *Week End* (1967) or the supermarket tracking shot in *British Sounds* (1969). This is Godard at his most spectacular and uninteresting, since the relationship between camera and subject is not problematised in any way: the camera tracks smoothly, and at a comfortable rate, allowing it to disappear, so that the viewer is focused entirely on the profilmic events, which in themselves are not disrupted as representations. Although *Week End* and *British Sounds* as a whole offer a critique of

Week End, Jean-Luc Godard

narrative in that they are episodic and heterogeneous, they are less radical than Godard's earlier non-explicit political films like *Une Femme est une femme* (1961) or *Pierrot le fou* (1965), where highly disjunctive sounds disrupt naturalistic scenes, exposing their constructedness through a focusing on the manner by which mimetic audiovisual worlds are artificially sustained.

In spatial terms the farmyard sequence, also in *Week End*,[3] is far more interesting, because it successively redraws a space in such a way that the viewer must struggle with the representations to come to an understanding both of what the real space might be like, and how the camera's movements through it redefine it very much in its own terms. Here there is a dialectic between the real space and its representations which functions through the varying degrees of autonomy of the camera movements from what is being represented. The piano, which pulls the viewer to itself through its sounds being audible almost unbroken throughout the entire scene, would seem to be the camera's proper destination, but the camera moves on, and the piano has eventually occupied only a small amount of the total time of the seven-minute shot.

Politics of space

In Peter Gidal's *Room Film 1973*, the camera moves around and through a confined space, sometimes revisiting the same parts of the room.[4] Because the film is printed very dark, only small areas of the room are visible at a time, and these are subject

Room Film 1973, Peter Gidal

to a constant, moment-to-moment refocusing and repositioning of the camera, so that it is impossible to build up a mental picture of the room, even though one would suppose that, from the set of visual co-ordinates which the viewer receives during the fifty-minute film, that should be easy. But Gidal's project is precisely to confound and frustrate the temptation so to do. The shooting of the film is planned around a thorough knowledge of the space, so that at each point in the room, the interaction between camera – angle, focus, depth of field, framing – objects in the room and the level of illumination, something is withheld which will prevent straightforward identification of those objects. Since one's sense of space is co-ordinated by the placement, size and shape of objects, the rendering indistinct of the latter also renders ambiguous and highly problematic the former: what is space, where is it, how deep is it? How do we know that a darker area is a space and not an underlit surface?

The struggle in naturalistic figure painting is to make a figure sit convincingly on a ground, whose space must make perspectival sense. In movies this task is made to appear to be an effortless product of the apparatus. Gidal's films refuse this facility, and in considering the numerous factors involved in the apparatus and its complex interaction with its subject, and the room for 'error' in those interactions, one can see how the aim for clarity enforces a particular configuration of those factors, which are always designated as technical, not ideological, and hence natural and inevitable.

Gidal's work thus partly serves to confront the viewer with their own gestalt-forming tendencies, a mental process which seems to be hard-wired in the brain, but which is also endlessly reinforced by our lens-based culture. The process, whereby the brain interpolates missing information from a combination of partial information provided and previous experience, facilitates the production of a filled-in, struggle-free world of consistent features. In many respects this facility is necessary for a person to function efficiently in the world, hence the (evolutionary) hard-wiredness, but it is also a process which can be accompanied by a quotidian blindness to anomalous or contradictory phenomena and experience. The resulting acceptance of the way things seem to be may be extrapolated to the wider cultural and social sphere. The film's political project, then, is to destroy this tendency (indeed it is the force behind much of the work discussed herein). But Gidal's project is equally a critique of film's supposed efficacy in representing three-dimensional space convincingly or exhaustively. Film is turned against itself, becomes its own worst enemy in its demonstrable inability here to represent anything adequately (that it appears to be able to do so is an illusion). But if it could, it would render itself redundant, for what would be the point of a perfect simulacrum of reality, other than to delude or divert? This kind of work, then, must be opposed to the escapist utopianism of virtual reality, which offers to replace the real world in all its messy, compelling complexity with an inane, simplified simulation, lorded over by an infantile master encased in video goggles and a data glove.

Gidal's films are not political allegories intended to supply an alternative ideology with which to mount a critique of the dominant culture, although they may stimulate such a critique. The viewer's act of attempted apprehension, revision and struggle that the films engender is itself a political process in that it is an ongoing act of questioning and doubting.

Lis Rhodes

In Lis Rhodes' films the representation of space is also questioned, even as it may be the arena for a self-questioning, even self-negating account of concrete, historical events, as in more recent works like *Running Light* (1996) and *ORIFSO* (1998). Forms are posited, implied, superimposed on each other, partially obliterated, never resolved. Through rapid cutting, repetition, freezing of movement, mixing of painting with photographed images, in images in which light effects burn through a scene, or in spaces which are glimpsed, only to be denied when a silhouetted figure passes through, Rhodes constantly deploys cinematic representation in order immediately to arrest or deny it. Her spaces are flattened out, cluttered, partially obscured: provisional, even as they engage with naturalism. They are also strongly claustrophobic: the viewer feels trapped on or near the surface, compelled to endlessly repeat the process of trying to enter, and hence enlarge, the space. In Gidal's films the dialec-

ORIFSO (top) and *Running Light* (above), Lis Rhodes

tic is between the viewer and the never fully represented spaces with which he/she grapples. In Rhodes' intensely restless films there is a double dialectic, between the viewer and the surface, and within the image itself, which is invariably contradictory, self-negating.

Every statement on the soundtrack is countermanded or fractured by abrupt switches into violent metaphor. When the monologue becomes momentarily descriptive, it is full of images of disintegration and disorientation:

> the picture hung askew/the room reeled over/splashing into the yellow liquid/days slipping through the drawn curtains/withdrew in the late afternoon/as condensation gathered and dripped/swollen plaster split open/the geometry of creeping lines/bloated and stained.

The repetitions within the image are paralled by recurring phrases on the soundtrack which have a comparably claustrophobic effect. These formal parallels invite the viewer to search for semantic correspondences which rarely exist.

Space is neither an arena for action, nor a historically concrete setting, nor is it virtual or abstract. Rhodes' spaces constantly seem as if they might become some of these things, however, and this striving to become that which is then denied is what energises the works.

In *A Cold Draft* (1988) there is a recurring image of a sunset – glorious, golden – framed by a barbed wire fence – silhouetted, jagged (see PLATE 19). This shot dissolves into drawn images which infiltrate and tinge the sunset, whence there is another transition to an image of illegible text. Thus beauty is encroached upon by its opposite, representation infected, then supplanted, by abstraction, and the readable rendered illegible, except as image. As well as the abstract and semi-abstract painted images, Rhodes frequently employs projected slides, which similarly declare themselves as flat, as image, especially when a figure appears in front of them. The forms we see are barely that: something like the substrate of form, or the provisional arrangement of materials that look like forms but which do not function as anything – they are there, but what are they for? They seem to raise the question of what something has to be to count as a form. On the other hand, can there be such a thing as formlessness? This problematic is not to be confused with the *informe* because Rhodes is always operating a tension between form and its dissolution, meaning and meaninglessness, not seeking a retreat into entropy by taking refuge in formlessness.[5]

In *Deadline* (1991) live action imagery is superimposed on paintings, hands move in front of slide projections and we see blurred black and white images which may be photographs, and which, like the slides, declare their flatness. There are brief moments when a figure passes in front of a space, offering the possibility of a momentary figure/ground gestalt. But these figures invariably pass too close to the camera, obliterating the background, and repelling the viewer back to the picture plane. Their actions defy the viewer to read the space three-dimensionally, insisting rather on the image's flatness, its impenetrability. It is this which creates the unbearable sense of claustrophobia.[6]

Stan Brakhage's Wild West

A completely contrasting work to Rhodes' in spatial terms is Stan Brakhage's film *Machine of Eden* (1970) which, for all its romanticism, can nevertheless be construed as a work about the contradictions of enclosing space within the film frame. It opens with a sequence of shots of a loom, whose operations inform the way the rest of the film is made: on a loom a pictorial surface is built up by the movement of the shuttle to and fro as it weaves the thread between the vertical fibres. There is a seamless transition from this sequence to shots of the Colorado landscape, in which the camera tirelessly pans and zooms, often simultaneously, and often from a moving car.

Brakhage animates the landscape, opening it up with the rapid and dramatic zooms out. But for every zoom out there are zooms in onto clouds. The transitory nature of the clouds contrasts with the physical mass of mountains in the background of the horizontal shots, yet at the same time they have a dark three-dimensionality and solidity stronger than the mountains, which are paled by the thickness of atmosphere between them and the camera. Whereas the scale of the ground shots can be judged by reference to trees in the landscape, the clouds are of indeterminate size. The zooms in even make them appear larger, once they are isolated from the mountains and trees. Strangely too, zooming in, which usually flattens spatial depth, does not seem to flatten the clouds in the way it flattens space in determinate, enclosed locations, as in the loft in *Wavelength*. The sense of depth comes about from the way (flattened) wisps, curlicues and tonal variations in the clouds imply depth.

Machine of Eden, Stan Brakhage

These zooms into the clouds are repeated in groups of two or three, emphasising the agency of the camera and reminding the viewer of the constructedness of the film: any shot, however apparently inclusive and right-seeming, is a construction (and a constriction). The very idea of construction already stands against the reality of space, which can only be enclosed at the cost of fragmenting and distorting it, and certainly not opened infinitely. Given this impossibility, Brakhage opts to weave an image of the space through a rhythmic building-up of part-shots, where the horizontal to and fro moves are crossed by the vertical zooms into the sky. Thus the film counterposes the horizontality of most landscape films by insisting on the importance of up-down looking. The spectator is offered a sense of what that space would be like if they were to stand in it. In the wide open landscape our eyes are immediately drawn upwards to the sky, of which there is a lot, yet this almost never happens in the cinema, and only occasionally in experimental work.

Sculptural correspondences

Richard Serra's recent very large sculptures provide an even rarer example of artworks in which the spectator is invited to look upwards. *Snake*, a permanent exhibit which was made for the opening exhibition at the Bilbao Guggenheim Museum in 1997, is such an example. The work consists of three wave-shaped steel plates, 104 feet long by 13 feet high, which stand close together, forming two narrow passageways along which the viewer can pass. The experience is intensely physical: the spectator is already aware of the mass of the metal and as he passes into and through the passageways he is abruptly enveloped by the cool, rusty, unyielding walls. Field of vision, too, is severely restricted, even forward vision, because the curves in the steel plates mean that the path ahead is only revealed bit by bit as one curve opens onto another. However, in looking up while walking through the work, the tops of the metal walls form a mobile, wavy frame beyond which the ceiling passes like a film. A similar kind of swapping of motion between fixed and moving parts to that in Tony Hill's film *A Short History of the Wheel* may be experienced. The distance of the ceiling is hard to judge because comparative references are blocked by the high walls of the sculpture. Although the ceiling is flattish, the effect of seeing it in this way is to flatten it still further, enhancing the film-like effect.

Although limited, this interaction between the sculpture and its space allows the work to hold its own in the Guggenheim's vast, complex space in which other works – by Robert Ryman, Robert Morris, Lawrence Weiner and Claus Oldenberg – are dwarfed or overpowered. The nature of the experience, which is purely phenomenal, generated and hence controllable by the spectator's own movements, contrasts strikingly with the more constrained, very bodily interaction which he has with the sculpture as he walks along the passageway.

Between space and location

In *Blowup* (1966), the first of Michelangelo Antonioni's three English language films, Thomas, played by David Hemmings, photographs an apparently amorous couple in an innocuous-looking municipal park in South London. Later, in his darkroom, Thomas discovers that he has recorded the opposite of what he thought: the woman had lured the man to the park so that he could be murdered by a third party. Antonioni says of the Hemmings character: 'It is precisely through the photographs he made that he discovers what he never saw.' In other words, the act of photographing or filming is not simply an act of recording, but an act of discovery, in which unanticipated results beckon the artist in an unforeseen direction. The artist can either allow himself to be pulled in that direction, which, in the case of Thomas, a bully and control freak,

Blowup, Michelangelo Antonioni

precipitates an existential crisis, or he can ignore or repress this direction in the interests of other priorities, which, in the case of movies, are narrative coherence and momentum. One could say that Thomas is Antonioni himself, a successful film director who is frightened of stepping out of that world into the realm of experimental film. Although the film is unfaithful to the geography of London in the way it jumps from one area to another while implying contiguity through the editing, the scenes in the park are as much an analysis of a space and how the placement of figures invites certain kinds of readings of that space which may or may not be right, as it is about the activities of the couple whom Thomas encounters, whose repercussions generate the film's themes. It is significant that the park is not identified in the film. It is unimportant for the film's vestigial narrative, and if it were identified the film would become too documentarised, too parochial, detracting from its real themes.

How do we get a sense of the layout of a given space? In most narrative films spaces are passed through and seen from the limited points of view of the salient characters. A similar thing happens in *Blowup*, except Antonioni extends the scene, in order partly to explore psychological tensions in the encounter between the three people, but equally to use the figures as a way of exploring depth, distance, proportion and placement, of both figure and camera. Similar things happen in Thomas' studio, where the space is fragmented and redescribed, and which becomes a frame for the photographs taken in the park, which add another layer both to the elaboration of the studio space and, retrospectively, to the space of the park. *Blowup* has always been wrongly identified as a film about Swinging London. It is actually a film about space, among other things, one of a few such narrative films.

Notes

1.   Regina Cornwell, 'De-romanticising Art and Artist: *La Région centrale*, *Snow Seen* (Toronto: Peter Martin Associates, 1980), p. 110.

2.   Hill built a camera dolly like the outrigger of a canoe, which is pulled by the vehicle being filmed. The camera is mounted centrally on the hub of the dolly's wheel, facing the hub of the wheel of the vehicle being filmed. The camera rotates about its own axis at the same speed as the speed of rotation of the wheel it is filming, thus holding that wheel static relative to itself, so that everything else moves around it.

3.   This scene is discussed in detail in Chapter 12.

4.   See also Chapter 7.

5.   For a discussion of formlessness in twentieth-century art see Rosalind Krauss and Yve-Alain Bois, *Formless: A Users Guide* (New York: Zone Books, 1997).

6.   For critical analyses of Rhodes' work see Susan Stein, 'On *Pictures on Pink Paper* by Lis Rhodes', *Undercut* no. 14–15, London Film-makers' Co-operative, 1985, pp. 62–8 and Peter Gidal, 'Lis Rhodes' *Light Reading*', *Materialist Film* (London: Routledge, 1989), pp. 65–75.

10

Location

One of the ways of making a rough distinction between narrative and experimental film is to look at how locations figure in the work. The more a film becomes preoccupied with space in itself, or with a location as an end in itself, the more likely it is to be an experimental film. Documentaries are set in but are not often about actual, named places. Even wildlife films set in specific locations are always at least as much about flora and fauna as they are about landscape. Narrative films are set either in real locations or fictional ones, but, if the former, they will very likely have been shot in a studio or a substitute location.

Experimental films tend to explore a location, whereas in movies they are invariably treated as a backdrop for drama. Of course there are exceptions to this. *Mean Streets* (1973), *Dear Diary* (1993), *Nil by Mouth* (1998), even *Alphaville* (1965), which is a special case, being filmed in a deliberately recognisable yet set-elsewhere Paris. These examples, all non-Hollywood films, may be thought of as home movies, in that they were made in the places their directors have lived in or know intimately. As such they are untypical of the commercial cinema as a whole. Even so, although closely observed, it is more accurate to talk about milieu than location in these cases.

The instrumentalism of locations is reflected in the job of the 'location scout', crucial in a film industry which operates year-round on planned-out shooting schedules. In order to film snow scenes in summer, or a war movie somewhere other than the real battle zone, one has either to work in a studio or use a location. Thus much of *Lord of the Rings* was shot in New Zealand for its July snow and the Philippines substitute for Vietnam in *Apocalypse Now* (1979). Even very precisely located dramas may be filmed elsewhere, for example Zeffirelli's Romeo and Juliet (1968) which is set in Verona, but was filmed in the Umbrian town of Gubbio.

Despite the importance of locations, however, their function is normally confined to contributing to the look of a film, or at best help to create a particular ambience or state of mind, as in *The Searchers* (1956) or *Apocalypse Now*. The location provides an appropriate background against which the story can unfold. Rarely are we invited to contemplate the location in itself: however striking it appears, we always leave a place when the story moves on to somewhere else. The fact that a story set in an identified place can be shot elsewhere without changing the meaning of the film shows how locations can be interchangeable and thus non-specific. This generic quality harmonises with the generic nature of much cinema.

One could assemble a list of examples of TV programmes and films in which location can be seen to be increasingly important. Soap operas rely on a complete familiarity with the characters so that we can easily follow the multiple situations that constantly unfold and develop. The soap opera's setting, too, becomes as familiar, and thus as unremarkable, to viewers as the layout and contents of their own home.

Los Angeles

At the opposite end of the scale are films like Antonioni's *Zabriskie Point* (1969) which weaves the extraordinary billboards, signs and streets of Los Angeles into the film's putative narrative. Antonioni strays as far from narrative conventions as it is possible to go, highlighting, perhaps inadvertently, the fundamental tension, indeed incompatibility, between the exploration of a location as an end in itself and the demands of narrative form. The more he strives adequately to render the hyper-real landscape, the more these passages threaten to derail the narrative.

Zabriskie Point begins with a group of students debating radical politics in a crowded room. This initial scene establishes the film's milieu and its main character, such as he is, Mark. In the next scene we are introduced to the contrastingly slick office block of the property developers where the film's female lead, Daria, works.

Following these establishing scenes, there is a cut from the office block to a painting of a cow in a Western landscape which fills the screen. This image starts to move: it is painted on the side of a truck which drives off to the left, revealing another painting of a desert behind. This image also starts to move, but this time it's the camera, zooming, then panning, to include the street beyond this image, which is on a gigantic billboard. Telegraph poles which appear to be part of the painting are thus revealed to be in the street itself. The theme of layers of image continues as Mark drives down the street in his pickup truck. The camera zooms out beyond the windscreen to take in distant agglomerations of billboards, petrol stations, industrial installations and shop fronts. In one extended shot the out-of-focus rear-view mirror fills the centre of the screen. By filming Mark with a telephoto lens, at an oblique angle so that objects in the space partially obscure him, cluttering the image, Antonioni works to imply the narrative layer as another layer of image among the layers of billboard and landscape. Through the way the shots are framed, emphasising the dominance of the billboard images, he attempts to create an equivalence between these layers. He also uses montage to this end, notably in an early scene which intercuts a group of property developers with figures in a scale model of a desert housing development, filming the model as if it were a real film set with real people on it.

On a visual level this strategy succeeds, but simultaneously creates tension in the structure, because these visual passages take on their own momentum, and threaten

Zabriskie Point, Michelangelo Antonioni   *L'eclisse*, Michelangelo Antonioni

to pull the film apart. In order to stop them taking over completely, Antonioni withdraws back into a relatively conventional narrative mode. At the end of the sequence of Mark in his truck, for example, there is an abrupt cut to a clichéd shot of him jumping a red light. This shifting between registers results in a film which is uneven, but which, more interestingly, delimits the gulf between narrative cinema and experimental work.

Antonioni, for all that he remains within a narrative mode, has often created remarkable, autonomous images in overlooked, unvisited, unlovely places, consciously turning his back on the picturesque landscapes of Italy. He chooses not the Byzantine town centre, but the industrial hinterland of Ravenna for *Il deserto rosso* (1964), suburban Milan and Rome for *La notte* (1960) and *L'eclisse* (1962) respectively. (This approach is light-heartedly reprised in Nanni Moretti's film *Dear Diary* (1993), in which Moretti travels around Rome's modern suburbs on a suburban form of transport, the scooter.) But it has been artists and film-makers who have made ugly, bleak or mundane locations the primary subject of their work. In 1977, Joseph Beuys cast a large abstract sculpture, *Unschlitt/Tallow*, whose mould was the space under a pedestrian ramp in Munster. The piece transforms negative into positive, and polemically elevates the absent and abject into something imposing and monumental. The size of the work, once installed in a gallery, is also a reminder of how big even contained urban dead spaces are compared to objects. Even when the object is the same size as the space from which it derived, it seems bigger.

Great Britain

In Patrick Keiller's film *Robinson in Space* (1997), Robinson and his unseen companion, who delivers the film's narrative monologue, also visit unlovely and often unvisited places, travelling around modern Britain, observing the mix of old and new landmarks in the Thames Valley, Avon, Liverpool, the North East and elsewhere. They visit a plasterboard factory on the Isle of Sheppey (see PLATE 21), Immingham Docks and Europe's largest shopping complex, Merry Hill, near Dudley in the West

Midlands. The sequence of locations is based on the routes taken by Daniel Defoe in his *Tour Through the Whole Island of Great Britain*, completed in 1727. The film's understated drama stems from the enormous differences between the way the land-scape must have looked in the 18th century, when most of the population still worked on the land, and what it has now become: increasingly developed and managed, yet massively depopulated in terms of the people who make their living from it.

The images in the film are striking for the way they reveal that within a geographi-cally small, densely populated country, massive economic activity quietly proceeds, largely unseen, right under people's noses. The plasterboard factory for example, a nondescript shed on an industrial estate, produces 120 square metres per minute: 'the fastest running production line in Europe'. Immingham Docks, the second largest in the UK after Teesside, imports 3 million tons of coal per annum, as well as iron ore and cars, yet employs only a handful of workers. Menwith Hill, the US National Security Agency's Signals Intelligence Base, near Harrogate, is the largest in the world.

The beauty of the shots of the numerous industrial sites visited in the film is disturbing because of the massive environmental threat they also represent, not simply because of what they produce, but also for what they import, such as hundreds of thousands of new cars. The knowledge that many are privatised industries, owned by foreign or transnational corporations, adds to the sense of disquiet. Behind the often placid exteriors of these installations lie massive investments of foreign capital and political-economic ambition. They are part of a global strategy whose planners are powerful enough to override local conditions: most employ non-union staff in a deregulated labour market where worker 'flexibility' is compulsory. Against this hard, predominantly industrial view, the Oxford colleges and the homes of famous English authors appear in the film as anachronistic and quaint, condemned, by comparison,

Robinson in Space,
Patrick Keiller

to occupy a place in a puny heritage Britain. In a way *Robinson in Space* seems to be a corrective exercise to the limitations of photography criticised by Bertolt Brecht and quoted by Walter Benjamin in his essay 'A Small History of Photography',[1] in that Keiller's near-static images are counterposed to statistics, delivered in a cool voice, tinged with irony, which create a shocking supplement to those images, thereby showing them as the outward signs of a specific nexus of politics and culture, capital and labour at a particular moment in time. However, the film moves decisively beyond this old photo/text dichotomy, when we are shown the image of a roundabout with a direction sign to a Toyota plant. This one image alone indicates how the idea of a national topography – made up of towns, places and natural features – has been supplanted, or at least overlaid, by a far more significant network of corporations. The film offers a detailed presentation of the micro-level changes to the country which at the macro level are evidenced by the way the nation state has been superseded by global structures. Toyota has become a place, a part of England. It is ironic indeed that while the government obsesses over what to do with small numbers of 'illegal' immigrants, the country has already been taken over wholesale by foreign interests with real power and influence. The England of *Robinson in Space* is a lurid palimpsest, in which the geographical and cultural forms of old have been overwritten by invisible forces, of which the Toyota sign is the visible tip of an iceberg. The film's political project is to make more of those forces visible.

East London

The political realities of specific locations are taken up by the film-maker John Smith, who has lived and worked for the past twenty years in Leytonstone, a still unfashionable suburb of East London. His film *Slow Glass* (1988–91) stands in opposition to cinema in terms of its approach to its locations. As Smith's oeuvre has developed, the peculiarities of the locations have become increasingly important, particularly in more recent films like *Blight* (1994–6) and *Home Suite* (1993–4), where topical issues affecting the local community feature in the subject matter.

The locations in *Slow Glass* had to be observed and researched over a period of several months in order for Smith to record the changes to the urban landscape that are a feature of the film (see PLATE 23). Smith would take note of 'For Sale' signboards on properties, then make before and after shots of the buildings with the signboards framed-out. He rang breweries to find out which pubs in the area were due for a makeover and so on. In this sense the film is like an enormously extended time-lapse study which speeds up imperceptibly slow changes to the landscape. Londoners are accustomed to parts of the city like the Isle of Dogs being in a state of constant redevelopment, but do not expect this of semi-dormitory suburbs, composed of large tracts of late Victorian terraced housing. In fact, as the film dramatically reveals, the landscape of East London is undergoing constant and sometimes dramatic change. In *The Black Tower* (1985–7, see Chapter 6) this is seen in the spectacular, botched demolition by explosion of the first of an estate of tower blocks on the edge of Hackney Marsh. In *Slow Glass*, even bigger developments are touched on. The bricking-up of windows towards the end of the film, in preparation for the demolition of houses to make way for the M11 Link Road, is poignantly recorded. The shutting out of the light, the replacement of glass by its antithesis, symbolises the benighting of whole communities for the sake of the convenience of car drivers for whom the area is a mere inconvenience.

In *Blight* and *Home Suite* Smith's exploration of familiar locales is explicitly conjoined with personal circumstances. *Blight* combines a painstakingly formal approach to image creation with characteristic word-play, but the documentary element gains urgency from the environmental issue at the heart of the film: the building of the contentious M11 motorway link road through East London, which required the demolition of large areas of housing, including Smith's own, and provoked a prolonged tree-top protest.

In visual terms the film records the demolition of a number of Victorian terraced houses in Leytonstone. Like *Slow Glass*, it was shot over an eighteen-month period using a ratio of fifteen to one. The care and deliberation with which one of the houses

Blight, John Smith

is demolished is due to the fact that it was attached to the house in which Smith was living at the time! This gave Smith the time to make a rigorously composed, poignant record of that process. Although sombre in mood, *Blight* is leavened by an intermittent play on a spider theme. There is the neighbour's story on the soundtrack about her fear of spiders, the classic tattoo of the spider's web on the elbow of a labourer, and finally the web-like map of the (incomplete) London motorway system, in which radiating lines cross the concentric threads of the North Circular Road and the M25 London orbital motorway. Like most of Smith's work, *Blight* is a hybrid film, in which politics are combined with documentary, quasi-autobiography and formal abstraction. The latter comes in a sequence where passing vehicles function as vertical 'wipes' which effect shot changes between a series of close-ups of graffitied corrugated iron.

Home Suite is the most explicitly autobiographical of all Smith's works. Overall, it tells the story of his enforced move from his old house to his new flat nearby, via the streets in which the M11 protest occupations were held in 1993–4. It was shot on Hi-8 tape, in three continuous half-hour sections. The first part, which was made some time before the second two, is shot in the toilet of the old house and describes, in extensive detail, the history of the cracked pan, the motorised toilet-roll holder, the shoddy paintwork and other minute details of the smallest room. The space gradu-

Home Suite, John Smith

ally fills with its history – complex, eccentric, funny – until it has become a kind of monumental environment, about which epic stories could be told for ever more. The work serves to remind us about the complexities of the history of even simple spaces and objects, a complexity to which most films do not even begin to do justice. In part two, Smith continues with a similar survey of his bathroom, which features a hilarious study of the gloopy, freeform Artex applied to the walls to hide an accumulation of cooking grease left by the house's previous occupants. In the contrasting third part, Smith walks the camcorder through the streets to his new flat, greeting neighbours and stopping at the M11 street protests on the way. Much of the history recounted in the first hour of the work now gains both a retrospective poignancy and an outer, political context, to do with the impact the road development will have on individuals' lives and circumstances. This is the closest Smith comes to straight documentary, but unlike most TV documentaries, the camera operator, director and narrator are all the same person, making a work about very immediate local issues. Thus the camera is not disinterested, but personalised. This is emphasised by Smith's voice being literally close by, his face close to the microphone, commenting on events as they unfold visually.

Orkney

Nick Collins' films are often concerned with the experience of place in terms of historical resonance. This resonance sometimes comes through an encounter with physical evidence of the previous inhabitants of a location, but also simply through a knowledge of a place's history. The concern to evoke the layerings of times is realised through an acute engagement with a particular place, invariably, as in John Smith's work, over an extended period of time. The locations in his films, and the manner of their treatment, evoke an emotional response to places rather than being about them in a dispassionately observed way. He seeks to create the sense of a physical encounter with a place and its history, and this is achieved through a range of means, from factual intertitles, to the replication of subjectivity by various devices: swinging or snatching camera movements, jittery shifts of focus and an interpolative manner of construction.

Sanday (1988) was shot on an island in the Orkneys. Superficially it recalls the photographic work of Hamish Fulton in the choice of a remote and empty landscape, with the stillness that that implies. Like a number of Collins' films *Sanday* is composed of titled sections, and it is also the most heavily worked, all the original footage having been reshaped in an optical printer. In 'Burial Mound' a low-angle camera looks up at a flower-covered hillock from various angles (see PLATE 22). The frame-by-frame (optical printing) reworking serves to create hesitant rhythms in the scudding clouds, but also emphasises the extremes in the frequently changing light levels as the sun

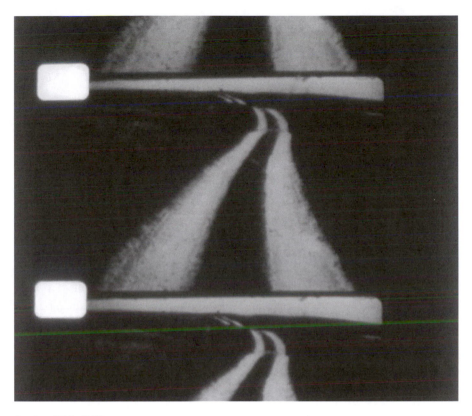

Sanday, Nick Collins

goes in and out, bouncing off granite slabs, which glow in the palpable, deep blue light, while at the other extreme the entire land mass is momentarily reduced to a dark shadow out of which the flowers radiate pastel light. In 'Quoy Aire – Funerary Road', the camera, having established a curving shore line and promontory, swings loosely back and forth in a close-up across the two white stripes of a dirt road cut into purplish-black turf. The hand-held rhythms create a gently kinetic abstract sequence like a slowed-down flicker film. This gives way to a similarly treated section of what looks like seaweed poking through white sand, which is echoed in the follow-ing shot of grey sea birds against a flat white sky. In 'Odinsgarth' the footage is even more heavily reworked, and the contrast increased, so that the shadows scudding down the dirt road towards the camera merge with the road's surface, so that it appears to shift and disintegrate. In the final section, 'Two Houses', the image is divided into horizontal bands; clouds, sky, promontory, breakers, houses and bay. From another high-angle view it later seems that what appeared to be clouds are really breakers, lying at the top of the frame but in reality situated beyond the houses. In another low-angle shot the cloud movements in the sky at the top are balanced by the light fluctuations in the beach at the bottom.

Time in *Sanday* is concomitantly manipulated: frozen, reversed, repeated. This repetition seems to simulate the mental remembering of experience that we do even as we stand in the place of that experience: the way our steps create various kinds of physical and visual rhythms as we walk through a landscape composed of regular features, like the road, and irregular or undifferentiated areas, like the masses of dark turf. Throughout the film the regular repetitive cries of sea birds are heard, adding a layer of aural rhythm to the physical/visual ones. These too are sometimes reworked, with added echoes and repetitions. Thus even as the piece is very much about a particular location, Collins pushes both the intrinsic abstract qualities of the land-scape and the abstracting, plastic possibilities of the camera, optical printer and audio sequencer.

From the intertitles we learn that Sanday has been inhabited since 3500 BC. It is this knowledge, combined with the evident inhospitability of the place, that produces a strong sense of melancholy, infusing one's perception of the empty landscape with thoughts about how people could possibly have lived here. This process whereby a single thought irrevocably inflects the way a place is perceived is at the heart of the film. It is in turn underpinned by the realisation that even in an empty landscape the very act of filming is a form of inhabitation that is as irreversible for the viewer as the building of a settlement is.

Non Places

Non Places (1999), by Karen Mirza and Brad Butler, offers a completely different way of thinking about location. The film consists of black and white sequences of perhaps four or five locations: a group of glass office blocks, a pedestrian underpass, a pair of doors and a lamp post in a street, possibly the underneath of a railway arch, another passage in a different (?) underpass. Each sequence is composed of a group of similar looking shots, distinguished only by a slight shift of camera position or degree of closeness. The images are accompanied by four anonymous stories, related in the form of subtitles which appear a few words at a time. These stories do not fit neatly within the image sequences but sometimes span the cut to an apparently new location, implying that those locations are in fact one and the same. Hence the reason for qualifying the description of the film in various ways is that there is really no way of telling if the locations are all one place, or a group of adjacent spaces, or entirely distinct locations.

In the first sequence a connection between the story and the location, a modern glass office building, is implied. The story unfolds in short sections, so that the mean-ing continuously evolves, and we become aware of the precise construction of the account, of its rhythms and its character as narration: 'Next to these high ... mirrored

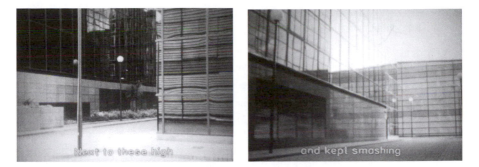

Non Places, Karen Mirza and Brad Butler

buildings ... some white guy ... came after a black guy ... and smashed him.' We don't know if by 'these' the narrator means these very buildings, or is merely saying 'these' instead of 'some'. There follows a dissolve to a very similar shot, so that we assume that we are in the same place. The tale continues: ' ... and then picked ... this black guy up and kept smashing this guy's head ... into the car ... windscreen wiper ... we had blood on us and the other two people who had actually ... been in the fight ...'.

We don't know the narrator's relation to the people involved in the fight, and we have to keep adjusting our mental picture of the disposition of people in the scene, as well as introducing precise details into the existing picture, as in, 'into the car', then, 'windscreen wiper'. The film gives us the time and space to combine photographic representations with mental pictures. How do we do this? Where are the mental pictures in relation to the ones on the screen? How do we fit the mental images into the represented spaces? When we add new bits to the mental picture, like the head to the windscreen wiper, already hitting the car, do we move the head from its previous position, or form a close-up, or a separate new image to incorporate the new information? Such questions are raised by the film.

The second, quite different, story commences over the same shot in which the first one ambiguously ends. After a pause we see the words: '1961 ... platform 16.' This is at first baffling, but then a train passes through the shot along what, it now becomes clear, is a viaduct. The appearance of the train elegantly shifts the scene, changes the meaning of that self-same shot. The next shot change takes us to a different location: distinct in the sense that we move from a sequence of office buildings to a pedestrian underpass. Yet this underpass could be connected to the railway viaduct in the previous shot. One cannot tell.

The underpass is framed so that the top half of the shot is filled with out-of-focus ceiling. The effect is claustrophobic, and the anonymous figures who descend into and pass through the space are further distanced by their being flattened and silhouetted by the use of a telephoto lens pointing towards the light. They appear as apparitions floating from one unknown place to another. They move, but do not seem

to get closer to the camera. The sense of alienation this induces fits with the nature
of the story, which continues:

> making my decision my big decision ... what to do ... pregnant ... whether to get married
> or abortion ... how in 1961? ... or go for adoption ... or jump in front of the train ... at
> platform 16 ... sad, desperate, surreal ... one of the worst moments of my life ... everyone
> else had ... somewhere ... they were going to ...

We seem to be getting closer to films like *Taxi Driver* or *Apocalypse Now*, where the
landscape forms an objective correlative of the protagonists' state of mind, but the
sense of despair here is pinpointed and concretised in what is surely an authentic
story. The location is not a metaphor for, or a reflection of, a woman's fictionalised
state of mind, but the kind of real place where the familiar urban experience of feeling isolated in a crowd would be compounded by her circumstances.

We do not need to know whether this experience occurred in this actual location,
and it is not important for the impact or veracity of the event that it occurred here
and not there. The scene examines the nature of a *type* of location – the public thoroughfare – and people's experience of it, and thus the question of interchangeability
does not arise as an ethical question about the veracity of a film in the way it might
in a film which fictionally reconstructs one historical location in another.

If the first story deals with a small-group close encounter – 'we had blood on us'
– and the second with isolation in populous places, the third is about being lost in
the crowd:

> I lost my mum in the crowd ... and was sheltering from the rain which was ... pouring ...
> I listened ... I have a memory of a doorway on a central London high street ... I was
> very young and ended up there because I lost my mum in the crowd ... on a central
> London high street ... I was very young and ended up there because I lost my mum ...
> in the crowd ... I listened ... for her voice ... but I could only hear the sound of the rain
> cars and people ... passed oblivious to me ... the constant ... sound of rain ...

surrounded me ... I found this comforting and no longer felt lost unseen unnoticed in
the rain ... rain is now ... my favourite sound ...

As before, the new story begins in the old location, then cuts to an image of a stretch of pavement with a double door and a lamp post, the framing of which shifts from time to time. In this instance, the shot change from the underpass to the street is followed by the line: 'I have a memory of a doorway on a central London high street.' Thus the image of a real but unidentified doorway stands in for a remembered part of an actual but forgotten location. It could, of course, be that location, but it doesn't matter if it is not. On the other hand, the shifting from one camera position to another suggests a kind of searching for the position which would retrieve the precise memory of the space.

It is a truism that we are invariably disappointed by the film of the book because it falls short of our mental pictures. Here, the reverse might be the case, in that the image appears before the memory it realises without seeming to offend it (yet it may do this at the cost of permanently displacing the memory if the memory is vague). Why is it that we feel disappointed when the the mental images of books are not satisfactorily realised in the film, yet we do not feel correspondingly let down by verbal descriptions which follow the image?

(A further question about memory arises here, albeit tangentially: what might it mean to remember a doorway without having a mental picture of it? Is such a thing possible, and what is the nature of the memory of a space that only exists in the form of words?)

The surface meaning of *Non Places* is to do with the idea of the dead spaces that proliferate as part of the process of urban renewal and construction: the land beneath motorway arches, the anomalous gaps between old and new buildings, the dead corners in intersections where leaves and rubbish accumulate. Even though these accumulations are often of human detritus, they say more about the wind movements funnelled by buildings than they do about people: people leave traces, rubbish just gathers. But the non-places are not only the dead corners of thoroughfares. They are also the parts through which people walk *en masse*. These streams of people are in effect not people, but movements or processes. The idea of place suggests definable space, space with a boundary, but a thoroughfare is the antithesis of this.

These issues echo throughout the film, but are dealt with most explicitly in a section filmed beneath what appears to be a railway arch. A strip of sunlight high on the massive wall is occasionally interrupted by unseen vehicles or trains passing overhead. At the beginning of the sequence, a car enters the frame but is immediately edited out by a camera-stop/flash frame. (There are three such momentary, 'accidental' human appearances in the film.) Like the previous section, this one is also about crowds, and it is also the only section in which a specific location – Millwall football ground – is named:

> walking through ... the underpass ... under Cold Blow Lane ... near Millwall ... football ground ... surrounded by mad fans ... fighting ... [At this point there is a cut to another underpass] ... and police ... while carrying two bags ... of food and drink ... I just walked ... through it all ... like walking through a film ... [and here a man steps briefly into the shot].

The threatening tone of the story is counterbalanced by the framing of the first few shots, which gets progressively wider, so that a strong strip of sunlit ground comes into the bottom of the frame, lightening the scene both literally and in terms of mood.

A theme running through the whole of *Non Places* is of the non-specificity of locations. At a certain level, objects, buildings, even whole areas can be substituted in a film, in the manner mentioned in the feature film examples above. Even in a John Smith work, a corner shop in Manchester could be made to stand in for one in Leytonstone. Thus in any kind of film this sleight of hand is usually possible, if unethical. In *Apocalypse Now* we believe ourselves to be in Vietnam for the purposes of entering the story, even though we know we are really seeing the Philippines.

The problematic of *Non Places*, however, is precisely to address this question of interchangeability. This is perhaps another meaning of the title: that since the places are not identified, and could be anywhere, they are not anywhere, they are non-places. In all but the Millwall sequence the places in the film remain, like the authors of the stories, unidentified and unidentifiable. This may be contrasted with the locations in *Blowup*, for example, where specific locations – the Economist Plaza, Stockwell Road – are easily recognisable.

Non Places is also about the fit between a story and its location. *Apocalypse Now* could be made anywhere with a swampy jungle, partly because the fecund, chaotic, scary otherness of the location functions principally as an objective correlative of Martin Sheen's state of mind. The two are in harmony, as they are in *Blade Runner*, *Taxi Driver* and countless other movies. In *Non Places* this kind of fit is questioned.

The base violence of the first story, which conjures up graphic mental pictures, jars with what the buildings seem to symbolise: rationality, industry, efficiency, wealth and so on. In the second we see the kind of environment whose relationship to the story is contingent, but where the sense of isolation the protagonist feels might be compounded. In the third we see a type of location – the 'street' – which raises questions about the specificity of locations and the relationship between visual and verbal memory and what happens when they are brought into conjunction with photographic representation. In the final section, the desolate place and the frightening encounter are gradually prised apart by the introduction of sunlight into the scene.

Because its stories are written, *Non Places* has more the character of a book, but not an illustrated one, because the images do not illustrate, or even complement, the stories, but nor do they have an arbitrary relationship to them. Rather, the film gives us the components of a narrative in their original form: a visual location, a written story, narrating characters. We are invited to fit the stories to the locations, and the film makes us conscious of this process, makes us self-conscious constructors of the film's meanings. It also makes us think about how locations function in a general sense, as the ground in a kind of figure/ground relationship, or as an arena for action, as an objective correlative for the protagonist's state of mind: we have to think about how locations become settings, or not. To this end, there are only three moments when people appear accidentally. On two occasions they are immediately edited out, while the third is an act of self-removal by a man who steps into shot, sees the camera and immediately withdraws. These cuts serve to stress the fact that the other scenes in which people are present are intentionally so, but that, since the film was shot on location and not staged, some human appearances were unintended and hence had to be cut. Thus the intended appearances become pseudo-stagings, or rather they raise the question of what the nature of intentionality is in relation to the desired appearance in a scene of people who are only fortuitously present?

Note

1. Walter Benjamin, 'A Small History of Photography', *One Way Street* (London: New Left Books, 1979).

||

Interactivity

The disorientating in art is the as yet unperceived new structure.[1]

Seeing is the decisive act, and ultimately it places the maker and the viewer on the same level.[2]

The encounter with an artwork of fixed form involves the confrontation between one structure, the artwork – with another – different kind of structure – the mental forms and habits of the spectator. The extent to which the former differs from and makes demands on the latter is the extent to which the artwork may be experienced as challenging or 'difficult'. The effort required, by both maker and viewer, in realising and understanding an image is equally demanding and equally rewarding. This is also a democratising process, in that both parties are equally, and actively, engaged.

One of the arguments in favour of interactive cultural products – artworks, games, strategy novels, certain radio plays and films – is that their environments are more participatory and thereby more democratic, less passive, since the participant must 'do' things and that this makes a more creative experience for the consumer/spectator. (Interactive encyclopaedias, e-commerce websites and other informational or commercially driven examples are here excluded, because their principal claim is simply to do more easily, in electronic environments, what can be done in physical ones.)

The assumption behind these arguments is that by modifying or affecting an existing structure or environment, rather than just contemplating it, the spectator becomes a creative participant, actively involved in shaping the outcome of the work, and so becomes a kind of artist in his/her own right. The process of feedback, wherein the participant learns how to play within the environment, supposedly leads to a more intimate and reciprocal level of engagement with the work. A typical, and typically crude, early example was an interactive installation by the Australian art duo Severed Heads, which was installed at the first Video Positive Festival in Liverpool in 1989. In this work a room contained slide and video projectors. By stepping on pressure pads the participant could activate different projectors. Because the pads were concealed, a rudimentary learning process had to take place before the participant could control the elements of the work.

The conception of interactivity trades heavily on the opposed terms 'spectator' and 'participant'. These terms are value-laden: spectators are passive, participants active. The implication is that artworks which presuppose a contemplative attitude on the part of the spectator necessarily position that spectator as passive. The spectator's lack of agency is construed as a form of powerlessness and therefore inferior compared to the maker's relationship with the work. Interactive work remedies this by empowering the spectator through active participation. However, this interactivity is achieved at the cost of the insight and understanding achieved through contemplation. The dialectic set up between the structure of the non-interactive work and the viewer's mental formations is deliberately collapsed, leading to a static homogeneity of work and mind.

In the case of computer games, interactivity replaces emotional and intellectual challenges with banal demands on the participant's hand–eye motor skills. Interactivity holds out the promise of a fluid and creative exchange with the product. Yet in being able to rearrange elements within a work in any way that one wants, one is effectively talking to oneself, and meaning drains away. It is an onanistic kind of activity, actually a non-engagement, since one does not have to move one's own mind in any direction to apprehend the work. If anything, the activity of interaction renders contemplative consideration of what one has done impossible.

When we interact with a painting or a sculpture, we are constrained in various ways. But these constraints do not prevent us from returning to a work repeatedly, each time to find something new, or rather to experience a different kind of interaction. It is the fact that the work exists in a certain form, with which we then engage, that makes the experience meaningful. Furthermore, the constraints we experience come increasingly to be seen as contributory, as we come to a better understanding of a given work. For example, the rectangular form of a painting can seem limiting and arbitrary, all the more so for its ubiquity and conventionality, until we realise that most good paintings use those rectilinear boundaries as compositional devices to energise and focus the picture. They become, in effect, (inter)active elements in the composition.

If, in the case of interactive works, we are encouraged to manipulate forms then it becomes possible for us to accommodate them within our existing mental furniture, and the possibility of new kinds of experience and knowledge is avoided.

There are, nevertheless, examples of time-based art – film, video, sound and performance, which require modes of participation which are not inimical to simultaneous critical consciousness. In these works it is partly the scope and nature of the spectator's participation itself that is the focus of the participatory act. In other words, the spectator is not wholly absorbed, to the point of self-forgetting, in a hand/eye co-ordination activity, as is the case in computer games, for example, but becomes a tentative self-conscious intervener in processes which in themselves are either fixed or too complex to be predictably manipulated.

Two Sides to Every Story

Michael Snow's film *Two Sides to Every Story* (1974) comprises two films of the same event, which are projected simultaneously onto a double-sided screen hanging in the middle of the projection space. Because both films cannot be viewed simultaneously, the viewer is obliged to make choices about how and when to view them. Each film is conventionally linear, a record of a sequence of actions performed in a large studio space. These are filmed by two cameras placed opposite each other and facing onto the scene of the action. The cameras are in each other's field of view, as are the technicians and the participants, including Michael Snow, who sits in a chair with a script, issuing instructions to the performers and the camera operators. The thirty-minute work takes place in real time. Every aspect of the process is thereby not only rendered transparent, but is part of the work's reflexive strategy.

Against this transparency the form of presentation dramatises the often radical disparity between front and back views, and offers the spectator a double dilemma. One option is blindly to construct the back view from the front (an old exercise from the life drawing room) or move constantly from one side of the screen to the other. The first option requires an effort of imaginative intellection, in order to reconstruct hypothetically one half of a human form from a view of the other half by a process of extrapolation, filling in the details in a mental picture which must be constructed while its opposite is in front of one's eyes. In the process of doing this the conventional opposition of dry intellect and lively imagination is transformed into a dynamic process; imaginative or speculative mental picturing is guided by intellection and empirical hypotheses, or the intellectual act of extrapolation is driven by that imaginative picturing. The demands of this process are compounded by the fact that the film is running on in the meantime. It thereby induces, under special conditions, the common experience of doing one thing: walking (and seeing), say – while thinking of something else, or of looking at one thing while mentally picturing something different.

The second option for the spectator in viewing the work is to move between the two screens in order to compare the front and back views. The problem here is that one is bound always to be behind the action, because in the time it takes to walk round the screen the action has moved on. Thus one can never really know the whole story, and one is always behind, a truth which is here actualised as a spatio-temporal dilemma. The title therefore is ironic, since even though we know that there may be at least two sides to every story we can, in principal, never know them all. In this work this is especially true, because no matter how many times we were to revisit the piece

Two Sides to Every Story, Michael Snow

we could never, in principle, experience all of it. The most we could ever experience would be less than half of a version of the whole thing.

In this way *Two Sides to Every Story* focuses on the passing of time and on the unevenness of the experience of time passing and of levels of attention. In attending to one thing, one inevitably overlooks, misrecognises or under-appreciates something else. In the first option the spectators are confronted with this fact in a literal way, because the film asks them to introspect in front of the ongoing film, a process which must draw their attention away, while the second option, of running between the two screens, allegorises that same fact.

In interactive terms, the work in itself is unalterable, but the spectator has maximum flexibility in terms of what to look at when and for how long. In this respect there is an absolute division between the work and its reception, which has the effect of putting the onus on the spectator to consider how and why they want to order their experience in the way they do, since no one way will be more inclusive than any other: there are no mistakes to be made as there are in playing computer games. The interpretative process is foregrounded, since it rests on the spectator deciding when to swap sides. The spectators must physically construct their own sequence of events, based on consciously made decisions. Thus constructive and interpretative actions are fused, so that in a sense the viewer is, if not the maker of the work, the assembler of his/her own version of it. Not withstanding the clear separation between the work and its organisation and reception by the spectator, insofar as the experience of the work is here a form of construction, then the spectator becomes an author, if not the author, of it.

Arbitrary Logic

In Malcolm Le Grice's computer piece *Arbitrary Logic* (1988) the artist interacts live with imagery generated from a software program written by him. Interactivity is fundamental to the existence and manifestation of the work, to its forms. This distinguishes it from interactive games, in which the user enters, but at the end of which the core environment remains unchanged. *Arbitrary Logic* exists as semi-formed raw material which does not have a stable base condition. This material consists of an array of shifting, rectilinear coloured shapes which are manipulated in a live event to create evolving patterns which also do not have a final form (see PLATE 2):

> both the visual and the sound elements are entirely synthesised. There is no initally-recorded data and the programme is constructed entirely from formulae which generate the initial (rectangular) forms, the colour sequences by values of red, green and blue, and the selection of instrumental timbres. The programme controls a basic, and consistent system of changes in value which is modified and interrupted by the movements of the mouse. Different movements and conditions of the buttons change the instrument voices, pitches, volumes and speeds as well as controlling an incursion of random values. These mouse movements also control a system by which the visual vertical stripes are copied to other sections of the screen and combined (superimposed) according to the system of computer logical operators (and, or, nand, nor etc.).[3]

As the mouse is moved towards each of the four corners of the screen, so each of the parameters exerts a changing degree of influence on the progression of the shapes.

On one level the work falls within a tradition of colour organs and the abstract films of the Fischingers, Mary Ellen Bute and others, in which colour takes on a force and autonomy, driving the work as much as, if not more so than, line and shadow, rhythm and montage. As in Le Grice's earlier, most well-known film *Berlin Horse* (1970) colour exists to a large extent for itself, and is not subordinate in the balance of ingredients.[4] This is *Arbitrary Logic*'s formal provenance and rationale. However, the work also demonstrates Le Grice's point that digital media can be output in any form.[5] It is perfectly conceivable that this work could exist as sounds or a printed image, but it is also designed to explore specific issues in relation to digital art, objects and processes, as well as the wider issues of what interactivity is and can be. *Arbitrary*

Logic, as well as the other examples discussed here, offers an implicit critique of the pervasive assumption that interactive productions offer a royal road to a more creative and democratic participation, especially in mass culture.

There is a similarity between Le Grice's improvised abstract electronic pieces and Peter Gidal's films. In both cases it is the viewer's engagement with the work which is core. This engagement is of a similar order to that demanded by, for example, Richard Serra's large sculptures, which require the active physical participation of the viewer to complete the work. One has to walk into and through these pieces, and they exist as much as facilitators/catalysts as they do as objects. The meaning of the work is the experience produced by the spectator's moving in and around them. They do not necessarily have an autonomous aesthetic existence independent of this. Similarly, in *Arbitrary Logic* the meaning is in the interactive process between the raw material and Le Grice. The apprehension of this process demands the viewer follow the logic of the unfolding piece. This requires a particular kind of concentration, specifically an attention to moment-to-moment developments. This is different from watching most films, where the following of moment-to-moment events is over-shadowed by the film's dramatic arc, its push towards narrative resolution and the release of tension.

The experience of a work like *Arbitrary Logic* is closer to the experience of listening to freely improvised as opposed to composed music, where the knowledge that what one is listening to is pre-structured affects the experience. In these films and film/video performances, the viewer must consciously reflect on the mental processes involved in engaging with the work itself as he/she is watching the work. The work is thus a kind of meta-discourse on that process, but not, as Gidal would insist, in the sense of presenting the viewer with a documentation of that process that can be watched outside of the reflexive process that his films demand. *Arbitrary Logic*, uniquely, raises the question of the status of improvised video. We are used to the idea of improvised music, i.e. something that only exists in the form and at the time of its performance, whereas time-based media are designed to record and hence preserve an event for repeated playings. *Arbitrary Logic* is a rare example of the former, a video work which only exists at the time of its performance (although versions of it have been reworked for videotape). It therefore demands a particular kind of attention that is distinct from our state of mind when we watch a video or listen to a CD in the knowledge that they can be replayed. This state of attention to moment-to-moment shifts in Le Grice's interaction with the program is important if the work is to be seen as more than simply a display of animated coloured rectangles.

The motive which drives the computer games player is mastery and completion – 'closure' to use a currently fashionable term. Games designers (who are also players) understand this too, which is why computer games are arranged in levels of increasing difficulty. *Arbitrary Logic* challenges this drive. First, the viewer must understand the interactive process as an observer, and thereby gain an objective understanding of how one form of interaction unfolds. In a version of *Arbitrary Logic* which Le Grice presented at the London Film-makers' Co-op in 1988, he collaborated with Keith Rowe, a musician with the free improvising group AMM. Thereby the video work was inflected by outside forces – Rowe's guitar improvisation – to which Le Grice would respond, taking control of the piece to some extent out of his hands. (The ethic of group improvisation is that one cannot simply ignore others' input, but must respond to it and modify one's own output accordingly.)

Second, because *Arbitrary Logic* has no fixed final form – left to themselves, the rectangles cycle through a pattern of movements until the the mouse is moved – there can be no closure on that level. Both performer and audience, therefore, must come to terms with incompletion, with process as something definitively incomplete. *Arbitrary Logic* is so designed that a final form would in any case be a banal negation of the richness of the work as process. This corresponds to the anticlimax experienced by gamers when they complete the final level and, obviously, is a common enough experience in all sorts of situations.

Feedback

The mental feedback process with which *Arbitrary Logic* works has a familiar corollary in electronic feedback. It is an originally unwanted by-product of electrical systems that has, characteristically, been turned to advantage both by guitarists and videomakers. As an intrinsic, spontaneous and only partly controllable phenomenon, however, the challenge has always been how to put it to meaningful use.

Many artists have been suspicious at the ease with which feedback can be generated, and have therefore tended to avoid it. (The *mise en abîme* that occurs when a camera is pointed at the monitor to which it is connected induces a strong sensation of empty self-referentiality.) At the other extreme, it has been used gratuitously to generate moving wallpaper in clubs. Elliott Ashton's *Interactive Feedback No.1* (1995), however, unusually steers a path between these opposed attitudes.

By creating a large, convoluted loop in which each camera is connected not to the monitor opposite, but to the next one downstream, he has expanded and elaborated the crude feedback loop that is created when a video camera is pointed at its own monitor. In Ashton's arrangement feedback does not actually generate itself alone, but requires the intervention of the viewer who, by passing between the rows of camcorders and monitors, generates an image which instantly passes from one screen to the next, then back to the top of the line. As an image travels down the chain it evolves and disintegrates as the signal is endlessly reprocessed. (One is reminded of the way in which the blues guitarist Albert King's notes mutate into pure feedback before slowly dying away.) Besides 'illustrating' the effect of electronic circuitry on a given signal then, *Interactive Feedback No. 1* may be seen as the product of an interaction – or interference – between the spectator and the live camera–monitor array. The physical presence of the spectators and the visual relationship between them and the images they generate, also becomes part of the work.

As well as the camera–monitor feedback loop, a feedback situation between the technology and the viewer/participant is established, whereby the viewer, through a process of trial and error, comes to understand and partially control the production of images. In this sense the viewer becomes the originator of imagery in a way that he/she never is in other interactive environments, be they video installations or multi-media computer programs. Such systems are cumbersome and unresponsive compared to Ashton's installation, yet are technologically far more complex to produce. Like much good art, the strength of *Interactive Feedback No. 1* lies in its conceptual simplicity, harnessed to an unconventional employment of video technology.

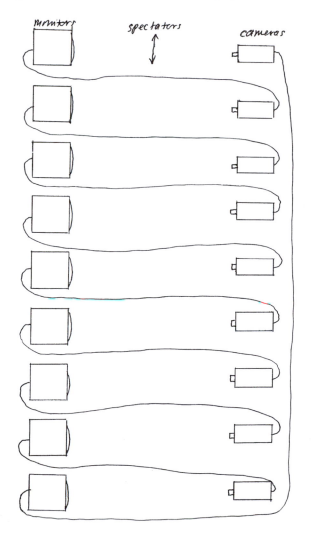

Interactive Feedback No. 1,
Elliot Ashton

The indeterminacy in work like *Arbitrary Logic* or *Interactive Feedback No. 1* and the sensitivity of the system to human input has often best been realised in sound works, because sound is much more intractable than coloured shapes on a screen. In John Cage's *Inlets* (1977), which was performed at the Almeida Festival in London in 1982, the performers hold conch shells of different sizes, each of which contains a small quantity of water.[6] The shells are slowly rotated so that as they move, the water moves around, making a noise. The progress of the work consists in the performers' efforts to gain control of this gurgling, which of course they can never fully do, partly because they cannot see the water and partly because the interior of the shell is too complicated, and water too unmanageable, for them to get a feeling for where it is. This situation dramatises Cage's desire to wrest the control of sound production from the musician, to let forces outside his/her control shape the organisation of sounds. Human agency is reduced to that of precipitating an initial event which triggers a series of further events at a distance. By using water, an emphatically uncontrollable substance, Cage forces us to appreciate the liberatory possibilities of allowing events to create their own momentum in order to take us into new areas of experience beyond those defined by habit and familiarity. Thus the work's ethos is the antithesis of that which dominates most interactive environments, where it is the bringing under control of, or the getting to grips with, events which is supposed to be its own reward.

In terms of interactivity, however, *Inlets* is rich for both performer and spectator. The latter can focus on the relationship between shell movements and water noises, and is in a similar position of not knowing to the former. Thus the work 'places the maker and the viewer on the same level', as Gerhard Richter puts it. On that level playing field, *Inlets* focuses our attention on the differences between observing/reflecting and performing/reflecting. In this case the difference can be seen to be very small. All of this obviously requires that the performance be seen and not only heard. (At least until the time of the Greenaway documentary, Cage was averse to recordings, and in the film he tells two very funny anecdotes which illuminate the detrimental effects of recordings on the mind of the listener.)

Acoustic environments

Another sound artist who is averse to recordings of any kind is Espen Jensen:

> I feel I ought to mention that I never document my work, hence me not being able to supply you with any photographic or sound images ... I believe that all art should be site and time specific, even extending so far as work never being re-shown or re-presented after its initial showing, and part of that would inevitably be documentation. The negation of the object, including objects of documentation bar writing – or other personal recollections – is crucial to my ... idea of 'present' art.[7]

In 2001 Jensen presented a sound installation *Interactive Room 12* which was:

a site/time-specific sound installation. Very simply put, essentially built to create an indefinite audio-loop, using the sound from the outside, fed into the space, and then re-amplified through the means of an internal microphone and powered speaker. The set-up (see illustration) generated a loop/interaction between the internal/external sound-sources, designed to gradually, and very slowly, go from nearly inaudible to, over a period of two weeks, a physically painful delayed soundscape.

As with all of my installations, and on a certain level my performances, this was fully interactive. This particular one on two main levels; physically interacting with the equipment used, i.e. tweaking levels on the mixer, amp and delay/pre-amp units. It has to be added here that as part of my artistic/aesthetical approach, I never hide or cover up any equipment used in my work, as I feel that this approach both demystifies the work on display and leaves the audience free to deal with the concepts/ideas behind the work, as opposed to how it was made.

So for this particular piece, the audience interfered with, and temporarily broke the loop, through changing the changeable levels, thus creating new oscillating frequencies, adding to the initial loop. This made for very interesting discourse amongst the members of the audience as some would want the high-pitched squealing of the feedback generated by the internal mic, and others would want the droning, low-frequency quiet hum of the external mic.

The other interactive aspect of the piece was intentionally more subtle, and, in fact, only very few members of the audience even knew they were interacting at all. Basically, by the way the installation was set up; it was designed to generate a direct line of sound between the internal microphone and the secondary sound-source (the powered amp). This set up led to the feedback loop being cut or disturbed by people walking in the line of fire. Essentially, the complex physics of sound waves, and how they behave, being shown to you by an unsuspecting/unknowing audience.

To me the latter interactive option is the more interesting for a couple of reasons; the subtle simplicity, and the fact that it is a non-interactive interaction, if that makes any sense …? What I'm getting at is that the audience, unless so informed, would not know that they were affecting the sound through their movements, effectively turning them into (unwitting) performers, as well as viewers/listeners, blurring the age-old line between art/artist/audience, which is something I try to achieve in my work.[8]

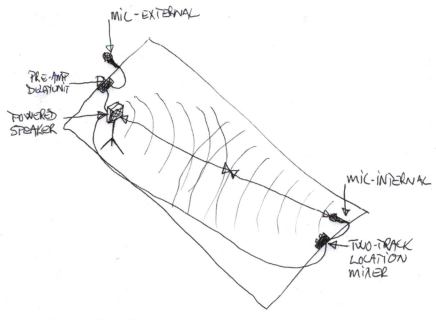

Interactive Room 12, Espen Jensen

Jensen's installation was created in a medium-sized, first-floor room in a Victorian studio block in Anlaby Road, Hull, as part of his finals show for the degree in Fine Art and Phonic Art at the Hull School of Art. The work demonstrated the extreme sensitivity of soundscapes to interference. As his account of the work indicates, any small movement, even silent, on the part of the spectator could trigger an event that is unpredictable in its effects and potentially infinite in its duration. In terms of interactivity, then, the piece is highly responsive to outside interference, but almost wholly uncontrollable in the effects thereby generated. Interaction becomes a voyage of creation and discovery, an opening up to new experiences, as opposed to the computer game paradigm, where the aim is the avoidance or frustration of uncontrollable elements in the pursuit of an increasingly sure and narrow goal, namely winning.

John Cage said: 'It is better to make a piece of music than to perform one, better to perform one than to listen to one, better to listen to one than to misuse it as a means of distraction, entertainment, or acquisition of culture.'[9] In the Cageian performance, the player is essential to bring the work into existence, in that it must be re-created as opposed to reproduced, following the guidelines laid down by the composer. In the case of *Interactive Room 12* the guidelines are the technical set-up, and the player may be a bird or passing car picked up by the outside microphone, or the unwitting or aware spectator moving within the space. The spectator is both performer and listener, and given that the act of performing within the space alters the developing structure, performing becomes an intrinsically compositional act, if composition is not the wrong word in this context. Furthermore, because of the delay between performance and resulting sound, the performer can listen to the results of his/her act of production with full concentration.

The computer game – its architecture, structural parameters, characters, objects, spaces and ambiences, will in most respects continue to exist regardless of what, if anything, the player does. The game requires the complete involvement of the player, but their performance is futile in that it produces nothing. Interactive artworks, where one can choose how to navigate through a virtual space, or a network of texts, or rearrange a story, or trigger an audiovisual recording, similarly remain untransformed, all of which raises the question: what has the participant really gained? How, at the end of the process, has his/her relationship to the work moved beyond the traditional role of spectator?

Notes

1. Robert Morris, 'Some Notes on the Phenomenology of Making', *Artforum* vol. 8 no. 8, April 1970, p. 62, quoted in Michael Compton and David Sylvester, *Robert Morris* (London: Tate Gallery, 1971), p. 115.
2. Gerhard Richter, *The Daily Practice of Painting* (London: Thames and Hudson, 1995), p. 217.
3. Malcolm Le Grice, 'Art in the Land of Hydra Media', *Experimental Cinema in the Digital Age* (London: BFI, 2001), p. 306.
4. For a discussion of the cultural history of the subordination of colour to form, see David Bachelor, *Chromophobia* (London: Reaktion Books, 2000).
5. See Malcolm Le Grice, 'Mapping in Multi-Space: Expanded Cinema to Virtuality', *Experimental Cinema in the Digital Age* (London: BFI, 2001).
6. This and other Cage works, including documentary footage of performances at the 1982 Almeida Festival, were the subject of an excellent documentary made by Peter Greenaway for Channel 4 Television called *Four American Composers* (1983).
7. Espen Jensen, letter to the author, July 2002.
8. Ibid.
9. John Cage, 'Forerunners of Modern Music', *Silence*, (Hanover, NH: Wesleyan University Press, 1973), p. 64.

12

Sound, Sync, Performance

Don't believe much of what you see on the box – even the news uses dubbed bangs on war footage. Real bangs are delayed by five seconds per mile, like thunder.[1]

Experimental film-makers have been extremely wary of sound, and not without reason. In talking pictures the spectator's attention is inevitably divided, and the resulting loss of attention serves the illusionism of cinema as much as do the master shots and eye-line matches of narrative grammar.

Cinema's mimetic power rests in large part on the binding together of sound and image. Music controls the emotional response to a scene. Synchronous speech serves to sustain a self-contained, self-sufficient world. The deployment of sound effects to punctuate and dramatise the audiovisual field has been extended in recent years with the practice of enforcing key visual moments with unnaturally loud cracks and bangs on the soundtrack as in, for example, an early scene in *The Lord of the Rings: The Fellowship of the Ring*, where the ring falls down some steps to an accompanying set of booming thuds. The practice of smoothing shifts in level and ambience between different sounds within a scene performs the same function as eye-line matching in the picture editing process: to erase the marks of production and sustain an illusory world that is consistent and homogeneous.

In the light of this, it is not surprising that experimental film-makers have approached sound with caution. Some have opted to avoid the use of sound as far as possible, while others have produced works in which the fit between sound and image – and, in a more technical sense, synchronisation – is examined, and in which these concerns become a key structuring element.

All but one of the examples discussed here involve performance – that is, the production of sound within the work. Perhaps this is because the live production of sound allows the maker to reveal and foreground processes that in pre-recorded sounds are concealed. Once sound is divorced from the source of its production – so called acousmatic sound – important clues about its nature and origin are lost. This is not to argue that performed sync sound is more genuine or unproblematic, as is argued by advocates of 'direct' sound, such as Straub/Huillet and some documentary-makers. On the contrary, all the work discussed here problematises precisely the question of the origins of sound synchronicity.

In film conventions, sounds are divided into sync – speech and effects – and non-sync 'wild tracks' – atmospheres such as birdsong, traffic noise, wind etc. Yet, insofar as all sounds ultimately have a source, they are all 'sync', so the sync/wild distinction is not a natural one but is, rather, a product of the medium, which, in bringing together pictures and sound within a small rectangle, creates and trades on this distinction. (Musical scores, which are both acousmatic and non-diegetic, form their own category.)

One of Jean-Luc Godard's most enduring contributions to critical cinema has been his disruptive use of sound. Whereas he has often accepted the givenness of photographic reproduction, he has not been afraid to question the role of sound in sound/image relationships. It is in this area that he has come closest to a materialist cinema, one which questions its own construction at the level of sound and image production, leading to a disassembling of the mimetic world of the film and the supposed veracity of representation on which that depends.

In much experimental film and video there is a bottom-up questioning of the very project of photographic reproduction, which there is not in Godard. Godard often

Pierrot le fou, Jean-Luc Godard

puts things in quotation marks, notably in *Pierrot le Fou* (1965), as a way of foregrounding the constructedness and referentiality of his images, while remaining indulgent and uncritical in the way he accepts visual representation *per se*, most obviously of women. (When he has attempted to question the way he represents women – most contentiously, for example, in *British Sounds* (1969) – he has seemingly been unable to resist the opportunity yet again to objectify and fetishise the female form, while purporting to wrestle with the issue of how to represent it.[2]) On the other hand, Godard's disjunctive use of sound does justice to the complex, unfixed nature of the experience of sound and image in cinema. This is particularly true of his earlier films. Besides his established practice of abruptly cutting-in scraps of music in films such as *Pierrot le fou*, he uses direct sound not as an index of authenticity, but in order to foreground the way sync sound is subject to all sorts of modifying factors, both natural and artificial, as the product of recording technology. In an early scene, Anna Karina sings a love song in the Parisian flat which she and Jean-Paul Belmondo are about to leave. As she moves from room to room the sound's ambience changes, sometimes gradually as she moves off-mike or into another room, sometimes abruptly, when there is a picture cut. Periodically the song breaks off, then restarts, so it is not heard in its unbroken entirety (anticipating perhaps the fraught pair of films on the Rolling Stones songs: *One plus One/Sympathy for the Devil*, 1968).

Week End

In the long tracking-cum-circular pan around a farm in *Week End* (1967) it is the sound/image relationship and the spectator's shifting understanding of it that is most remarkable. As the shot begins with a long track along some outbuildings, we hear non-diegetic music. After a while the music stops and a man's voice starts to talk about Mozart, whose last piano sonata we have been hearing, indicating that this may be diegetic sound, even though we have yet to see its source. The track seamlessly becomes a pan around the farmyard, slows down and eventually comes to rest on a medium-wide shot of the piano that is the source of the sound. The pianist stops, starts to talk. We never see his hands, but if we could, what would we be able to discern? Piano playing often looks out of sync (where do we get our idea of something looking 'in sync' from?): even professional pianists find it hard to 'read' music by observing a pianist's hands. The question then begins to arise: what and where is the ultimate source of the sound? The pianist's hands must make a slight noise as they hit the keys, and this starts a mechanical chain reaction of near-silent functions which result in the hammers hitting the strings. The sounds that the mechanism makes are masked by the resulting sound of the strings vibrating. This is a reminder that for any given sound event there will be other, quieter sounds which are masked by that event. (Some forms of audio compression work on this principle, and the sounds of his blood circulation and nervous system firing that John Cage heard in his epiphanic experience in the anechoic chamber at Harvard University were unmasked sounds.[3]) The causal chain of fingers, mechanism, hammer blow and string vibration are all, in a sense, equal candidates for the cause of the sound, even though obviously a key link in the chain is the vibrating strings. Yet it is not the vibrating strings that we hear, nor even the disturbances of air movement, the fluctuations in atmospheric pressure that result in an experience of sound. Therefore one could argue that the seemingly pivotal event, the hammer hitting the string, should not necessarily be prioritised. There is a further complication in the fact that different forms of attack by the pianist on the keys will produce different tone colours, yet there is no visible, synchronous

Week End, Jean-Luc Godard

correlation between the character of the finger pressings and the resulting sounds. All this boils down to the fact that we cannot 'see' sync. Sync is simply the coincidence of two distinct phenomena, the origin of whose causal connection may not be pinpointable. Most of the coincidences between even apparently tight synchronous events are complex, and in the case of films, where framing can render ambiguities in the audiovisual field, the semantic relationship between sound and image is also indeterminate – a fact which allows, for example, the sound of frying eggs to stand for falling rain in John Smith's film *Shepherd's Delight* (1980–84), or which similarly enables Foley artists to create fitting effects for movies from materials unrelated to either the visual events of the film or their accompanying sounds.

Once the piano sound in *Week End* has been established as diegetic, the camera tracks on past it, the sound continuing for the entire eight-minute take. After some time we start to re-experience the music as non-diegetic, even though we know it is not. Thus the sound, without changing, runs through the entire gamut of functions available to film sound. At the opening of the scene it is non-diegetic and non-sync: the standard musical score. Then it becomes diegetic sync, then, at the point where the camera moves off the piano, diegetic non-sync/off screen sound. Finally it returns, in effect, to being non-diegetic non-sync music. At the mid-point where the pianist stops, starts and stops again, it becomes a sync effect. As a diegetic non-sync sound it is also part of the atmosphere at certain points. Thus, in a single unbroken eight-minute shot, Godard breaks down the (instrumental) distinctions between sync and wild sound, diegetic and non-diegetic. The only possible permutation omitted is non-diegetic sync sound, a special category occurring almost exclusively in cartoons like *Tom and Jerry*, where music synchronises with specific actions.

Lip-sync

In *Synch Sound* (1974) Mike Dunford takes the processes explored by Godard in *Week End* a stage or two further. The image is an extreme close-up of a woman's mouth. An off-screen male voice asks her questions about the early history of sync sound in the movies, and she gives prepared answers.

After several seconds the mouth becomes abstract, divorced as it is from its surrounding features. One starts to concentrate on small areas of the image. The dark gap between the woman's upper incisors expands and contracts slightly, depending on the amount of light falling on her teeth, the level of illumination of which is regulated by the opening and closing of the lips.

The premise of the film is that by isolating the mouth from surrounding distractions, the source of synchronisation can be isolated and identified but, as indicated in the discussion of piano sound in *Week End*, the opposite occurs, and the close-up disconnects the image from the sound. The former is fleshy and palpable. The elastic movement of the lips works sometimes with, sometimes against, the more

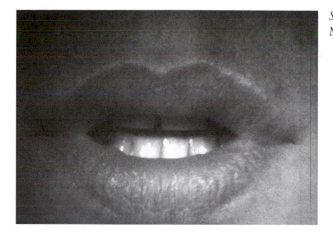

Synch Sound,
Mike Dunford

mechanical movement of the teeth, setting up complex visual counter-rhythms. The sound, by contrast, is ghostly, ephemeral and above all dislocated. This is because, in trying to trace the sound to its ultimate source, we encounter the same difficulties as in *Week End*, except here there is a more acute sense of bafflement because the concept of lip-sync has its origins and justification in the representation of speaking, yet to where can one trace the fundamental source of the sound? The vibrations of the vocal chords, which are both activated by the air passing across them and influential on the subsequent movement of that air? The shaping of the vibrations by the mouth, lips and tongue? Although not explicitly didactic, *Synch Sound* forcefully demonstrates the distinct character of sounds and images, and shows how there is very little perceptible, moment-by-moment correspondence between a sound and the mechanisms that generate it.

Breath

In William Raban's *Breath* (1974) the duration of individual sounds is the method by which shot length is determined, and the film's climax arises partly out of a gradual coming into sync of sound and picture. Three camera operators, Raban, Malcolm Le Grice and Gill Eatherley, positioned by a Nagra tape recorder with an omnidirectional microphone, at the top of a hill on Dartmoor, walk downhill, away from the recorder and each other, for eight minutes.[4] At this point, Le Grice blows a whistle, a signal for them all to turn round and walk back towards the Nagra, taking it in turns to film as they do so. Each camera points in the direction of its successor, which establishes a triangular, inwardly spiralling chain of looks. Because they cannot see each other at this stage, each blows a whistle as they film, one high, one low in turn, to inform the other two that they are filming. The third, Raban, films silently. While a whistle blower is filming, the other two refrain. While Raban is filming, the whistle blower whose turn is next has to estimate the duration of Raban's shot. The filming

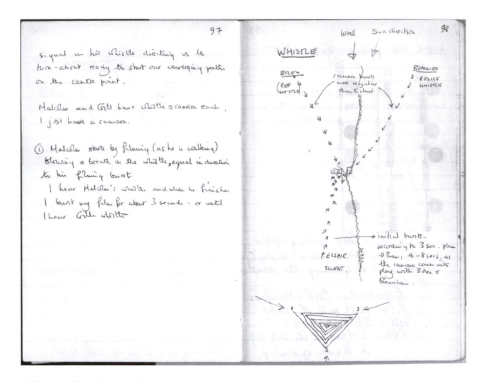

William Raban: breath-plan and shooting scheme

sequence is thus: low whistle, high whistle, silence. Each shot lasts the length of one breath/whistle blow.

The film's increasing pace, its rhythm, crescendo and climax all arise out of the conditions of filming and recording. In this sense it is a classic record of its own making, except that whereas most typical such-process works in the tradition of minimal painting and sculpture are ongoing and non-hierarchical, *Breath* has some of the characteristics of a narrative movie: situation, development and climax, if not resolution.[5] At first each shot is fairly quiet, and the whistles all but lost in the background atmosphere. There are long periods of black between one shot and the next. This is because when one camera has stopped, its accompanying sound is still travelling to the next camera operator, who is waiting for it to stop before starting to film. However, at points where Eatherley, the camera operator following Raban, starts filming before the latter has finished, their shots tend to overlap, and are superimposed in the edited film. This is because although Eatherley has to guess the duration of Raban's shots, Raban himself waits until he hears Eatherley's whistle before stopping. Thus Raban's shots will tend to overlap Eatherley's because by the time the sound has reached him she has already started to film, but these overlaps do not begin to occur until a good way into the film because at the beginning the sound and picture is so out of sync

Breath, William Raban

that one person's whistle coincides with another's shot.

As the cameras move closer to each other the black spacings get shorter and then cease, quickening the pace. At the same time as the sound comes into sync the whistling gets louder, drowning out the background sounds. Eventually, as they breast the hill, the cameras come into each other's view, as does the Nagra. The shot sequence has progressed from a series of disparate, disconnected views of the landscape to the climactic moments in which the cameras mutually locate each other.

This neatly resolving structure is accidentally modified when one of the cameras runs out of film before arriving at the Nagra. We see the end-roll flare, after which the film continues as a two-person performance. Rather than spoiling the film, the absence of the third camera's shots enhances the innate drama of the rhythm, turning it from an erratic slow waltz into an emphatic march. In the absence of the third camera, the meeting of the two cameras feels more confrontational: with three cameras the passing movement is rotational, via a third party, whereas with two it is directly back and forth.

At the beginning, the whistling does not cut when the picture does, because of the difference between the speeds of sound and light. One comes to experience this discrepancy as a feeling that the sound is out of sync, which of course it is not, at any point in the film. There is here a confrontation between what we know about the synchronicity of distant, observable events, such as batsmen hitting cricket balls, and the tendency that we nevertheless expect sound events to coincide with their observable causes in films, a false expectation which prompted David Brinicombe's remarks in the opening quotation. This process, where one kind of empirically derived understanding is confronted with another whose filmic truth is in a dialectical relationship to the former, is akin to intellectual montage, except that whereas in, for example, the crane scene in Eisenstein's *Strike* (1924) this dialectic is constructed, in *Breath* it arises automatically from the natural processes which shape it.[6]

The film as a whole is one in which natural processes and artificial procedures form the plan, but do not predetermine the precise outcome, of the work. The built-in imponderables guarantee this. First, the duration of the shots produced by the silent camera operator must be guessed at by his successor, while he waits for her signal to stop himself. Thus her signal passes back to him, reversing the movement of signals and shots, at the same time as it signals forward to her successor. This ensures that the business of passing from one camera to the next will not be a neat one. Second, not only is the accidental running out of film by one camera allowed to stand, but the resulting change to the structure is embraced. Thus an accident is allowed to alter the course of what is, on paper, a systemic film. Raban could, after all, have inserted spacing to preserve the three-party rhythm. Doing this, however, would have offended the principle that the film is the authentic, material record of an event performed according to a set of rules. To retrospectively insert 'missing footage' – footage not produced as part of the event at the time of its enactment – would be to break the film's ethical principles.[7]

Sound/image disjunction

Colin Crockatt has made a sequence of sound videos in a variety of distinctive locations in London. He appears in all of them as a mobile sound recordist. His *Video Tape with Bicycle Sound* (2001) demonstrates not only how the distinction between sync and wild sound is a function of framing, but also how the perception of synchronisation depends on the viewer's position relative to the camera and microphone: what is sync for the sound recordist may not be sync for the camera/spectator, depending on how far apart they are from each other.

Video Tape was shot in Queens Park, in North West London, on a rectangular circuit. A static camera frames a short stretch of road, behind which lies the park. A cyclist (Crockatt) mounts his bicycle, switches on a minidisc recorder in the front basket and pedals away out of frame. We will not see him again until the end of the tape, six minutes later, when he reappears from the left, having completed one lap of the circuit. Like *Breath*, the work turns upon the speed difference between sound and light, but reaches a maximum point of disjunction at the halfway point, when the bicycle is furthest from the camera.

After it has pulled away, there is little activity within the frame, apart from the odd jogger in the middle distance who, it is safe to assume, generates nothing audible to the viewer. We set to thinking about the birdsong that pervades the image. It is perfectly plausible, yet we know it is being recorded from a moving point substantially distant from ours, so is it true? The bark of an off-screen dog, intrusive and with a relatively close perspective, does not yet disturb the naturalistic continuum. It is not until a car passes silently through the frame that the unity of the scene is disturbed. Soon after this we hear a car quite loud on the soundtrack. Is it the same one, passing by the bicycle? Possibly. This prompts us to construct a mental picture of the off-screen scenario.

The work is animated, its structure activated and worked through, by human movement. In *Synch Sound* this is done by mouth movements, in *Breath* by walking and filming, in *Video Tape* by the action of the cyclist/sound recordist moving through the landscape. Our relationship to Crockatt's scene is completely opposite to his. Our only sync point is at the introduction/scene set and the conclusion and coda, both mostly dead moments. At the beginning we wait for the cyclist to mount his machine

Video Tape with Bicycle Sound, Colin Crockatt

and switch on the recorder, while the end point is an exact reversal of this procedure. The sound common to both moments is that of the bicycle's stand being flipped up and down. While Crockatt enjoys a continuous sync-sound experience we are stuck with our limited point of view and fed bewilderingly disconnected visual and aural events. Crockatt's experience of motion is more complex, because he is moving in relation both to the ground and to other vehicles and people, while we are in a fixed relationship to most of what we see.

In films the camera's point of view is always our point of view (which is sometimes also a character's point of view and sometimes not). In *Video Tape with Bicycle Sound* there is no point of view because it is not a video work. The true point of 'view' is the sound recordist's, which is ours too, in which case it is really a point of audition. Crockatt is the director/cameraman/sound recordist, only he has left the camera behind on its tripod, much as one might leave a tape recorder and microphone in one place, while filming nearby. This is how the piece is really a sound work with video track, and not vice versa. The static camera enforces this, since we know that Crockatt's point of view conforms with the sound he is recording: he experiences an integrated (sync) visual and aural experience. The camera's function is merely to artic-ulate the sound/image disjunctions that comprise the work. The work is not about how we see a space. By being elsewhere in relation to the work's actual place of happening, the camera declares not only its inadequacy as a recording device, but its redundancy as a focal point.

False unity of sound and image

In *The Sound Recordist Walks Away, Alone; The End* (2001) the camera points down a long avenue of widely spaced trees in Kew Gardens. Crockatt stands in the foreground with a Nagra tape recorder and microphone. He switches on the recorder and walks towards and past the camera. At this point the music from *The Third Man* (1949), on whose final scene the work is based, is switched on. Then Crockatt reappears, walking away from the camera with the microphone pointing towards it. The music fades as he walks down the avenue of trees. The ambient sound continues for a further two and a half minutes after he has disappeared, yet we continue to hear 'his' sound until the same burst of tone that commenced the work announces its end.

The title establishes a contract with the viewer: what you are about to see was recorded as you see it, no tricks were used. Crockatt then uses this contract to stretch our acceptance of conventional sound/image relationships, to confront the complex discrepancies between sound and vision as directly experienced and as experienced in the form of recording and image.

We watch Crockatt disappearing, but the sound he records does not change or evolve concomitantly as we might expect. On the contrary it remains, steady and constant, almost entirely atmospheric, with a preponderance of aeroplanes passing overhead. The fit between the location and the sound seems appropriate in terms of content, level and ambience, yet it is this easy fit which the work sets out to question.

The maximally directional microphone that Crockatt uses here (a hyper cardioid Sennheiser 816) would typically be used to conduct interviews in a noisy location. It is designed to admit sound from a narrow angle of source. Yet the sound does not seem to have been highly selected. This is partly a result of the way microphones work. The closer a directional microphone is to its sound source the more directional in effect it will be, as in the interview situation, for example. If, on the other hand, it is pointed into a landscape it will pick up a relatively broad swathe of sound. Nevertheless, had Crockatt used an omnidirectional microphone the results would certainly have been different: busier, more varied and perhaps less dominated by aeroplanes. In the event, the soundscape is convincing, despite the fact that it cannot possibly include all the sounds occurring simultaneously in that environment.

This is because sound/image relationships can be very indeterminate, especially in outdoor situations like this, where there are no sync-sound generating features. If there were birdsong, or distant traffic or even nearby road drills, instead of aeroplanes, we would still not necessarily question the veracity of the scene. Only if we heard reverb, for example, imparting to the open parkland a cave-like resonance,

The Sound Recordist Walks Away, Alone: The End, Colin Crockatt

would it immediately strike us as wrong. Therefore it is perfectly possible that the entire soundtrack could have been recorded elsewhere. It is this indeterminacy between a location and its sound that makes possible the creation of convincing soundtracks that were not recorded where they were filmed.

It is useful to compare this piece with *Video Tape with Bicycle Sound*, which used the same procedures to very different ends. There the combination of stationary camera and mobile sound recordist produced dramatic mismatches between sound and image, whereas here a similar procedure produces a strikingly conventional synthesis. The difference hinges partly on the fact that in the latter work we can see the recordist. The evident unity of recorder and the sounds he is recording seems to neutralise the kinds of discrepancies that, when they occur in *Video Tape*, are so disturbing, and confirm the integrity of the recording. On the other hand the sound is remarkably unvarying, given that the recordist walks a considerable distance in the seven and a half minutes of the piece. That the sound continues largely unchanged well after he has disappeared from view introduces a note of doubt that the sound might, after all, have been recorded elsewhere, even though it seems realistic. It is the very plausibility of the scenario, reinforced by the title, that confronts us with our over-willing acceptance of what are so often concocted combinations of sound and image in film.

In *Video Tape with Bicycle Sound* the difference of position between the recordist and the viewer produced dramatic disruptions of synchronisation and timing. Here, by contrast, we seem to share the same sound world as the recordist. Yet how can we be sure that this is so? How can we know that the plane he hears is the same one that we are hearing, or that he is hearing it in the same way as we would were it recorded from our point of view?

Ambience

The question of the ambience in which a sound is recorded is neatly explored in James Allen's *Whistle Blower* (1994). Each shot consists of Allen blowing a whistle in a different location each time. The whistle generates the sound, but the ambience inflects it, so that in each shot the whistle sounds different. Arguably, therefore, the whistle has no sound of its own in practice, but only the sound it makes in a particular space. Even in an anechoic chamber, where no reflections can colour or add to the whistle's own sound, it will have a particular quality unlike anywhere else: a dead space is still an acoustic space of sorts. Once we understand this, we must accept that the distinction between sound and ambience is artificial, for the listener, if not for the audio engineer, being nothing more than the product of filming/recording procedures, just like the distinction between sync and wild sound. The sound and the ambience in which it is recorded is one particular sound.

Sound/image permutations

William English's ongoing two-screen film *Untitled* (1990–present) can be presented with variable sound and image conjunctions, since it uses a mixture of silent film, sync and wild (non-sync) sound that can be combined in different ways. The work is presented as a semi-live event in which English plays a selection of audiocassettes on each occasion that the work is presented. Like the aforementioned example of *Shepherd's Delight*, in which the frying eggs stands for falling rain (or vice versa), *Untitled* similarly plays on the way an image can cue misidentifications of a sound.

Untitled is composed of several three-minute sections – 100-foot rolls of 16mm Kodachrome film – which were originally intended to be self-contained shorts. The sequence of rolls is staggered so that the left roll changes before the right, multiplying the actual and possible juxtapositions of image with image and images with sound. This method also preserves flow by having an image on one screen carry across the cut on the other.

In every section the abstract aspect of representational images is stressed, and the sound is ambiguous. In the first pairing two illuminated cranes form an composite image which creates a continuity across the two screens. The cranes are defined solely by the strings of lights hanging on them, and they appear as twinkling images in a dark space, the antithesis of what they are in reality. They evoke Christmas lights, but

the effect is incongruous, given the objects they outline. Because it is dark it is difficult to read the cranes three-dimensionally and this is compounded by the way the
image forms a projecting angle whose apex lies on the join between the two screens.
This composite three-dimensional form is at odds with the true disposition of the
cranes on the building site they occupy. The image is akin to stellar constellations,
which appear to be on the same plane but are formed from stars that are actually far
apart in all dimensions. The sound seems to be a tube train, but turns out to be a
rollercoaster, whose image appears later on.

The next image on the right screen is a close up of a foghorn, and on the left a
funnel. The foghorn sound is a variable element, sometimes occurring over its image,
and sometimes afterwards, over the succeeding roll of a bouncy castle. This vibrates
spasmodically in front of a municipal building which is in the process of being demolished by a crane whose presence continues the theme from part one. On the left
screen, meanwhile, is an extreme close-up of a mechanical, coin-operated laughing
clown, whose colourful but forlorn costume has torn to reveal a layer of blue foam
(see PLATE 24).[8] The clown has its own manic laugh, but the foghorn sound which
sometimes follows the clown's laugh becomes a mournful echo of that laughter.
Themes of creation and construction, decay and demolition emerge. This is
compounded by the image of the rusty red ramp up which rollercoaster cars are pulled
to the beginning of their descent. This, too, may be seen as a metaphor for the entropy
that follows the big bang. The climb to the top of the ride, often the most frightening part of the roller coaster experience, is followed by the gradual and inevitable
downhill path to stasis. The sounds which were misinterpreted as tube trains here
find their proper image. In the final section two identical shots, of water cascading
down a dam overflow in Wales, are played with their own sync soundtracks. Here
though, sync is at its most redundant. The sound, like the image, is an undifferentiated, continuous rush. The playing of both tracks doubles the sound without adding
anything to it qualitatively. The roaring is sufficiently close to traffic noise that it could
fit convincingly into the urban setting of the opening sequence.

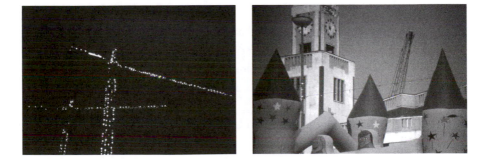

Untitled, William English

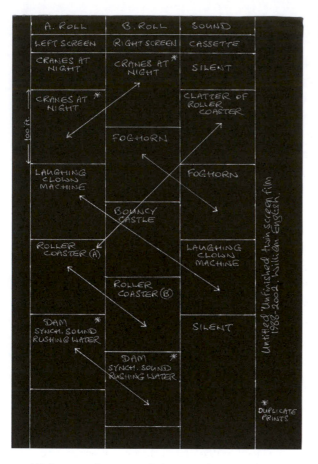

Untitled – Projection Scheme,
William English

All the sounds in *Untitled* are mechanical, but in different ways. The rollercoaster cars produce a typically unintended and indirect machine noise. The foghorn and its intended sound is direct and of a piece, like a football rattle or a klaxon. When the work is performed, English plays it through a large wooden horn which reinforces the timbre of the foghorn.

To the extent that its sound is the product of a process of human intervention, the water noise, too, could be said to be mechanical. Water itself is a naturally occurring substance, but the manner in which it is channelled is artificial, and hence the sounds it makes are, like those of the rollercoaster, the indirect product of human intervention. The clown's cackling is a caricature of laughter, whose manic, repetitious approximation turns it into its opposite: sinister and discomfiting, like an obviously forced or insincere laugh.

Notes

1. David Brinicombe, sound recordist, in a letter to the *Guardian* newspaper, 14 May 1998.

2. See Laura Mulvey and Colin McCabe, 'Images of Woman, Images of Sexuality', *Godard: Images, Sounds, Politics* (London: BFI, 1980), pp. 79–105.

3. John Cage, 'Experimental Music', *Silence* (Hanover, NH: Wesleyan University Press, 1973), p. 8.

4. *Breath* was made on the way back to London from filming Malcolm Le Grice's four-screen film *After Manet* (see Chapter 8). Raban used an Eclair, Le Grice a Bolex, Eatherley a Beaulieu. Each had a single roll of Kodachrome film.

5. The classic work of this kind is Robert Morris's sculpture *Box with the Sound of its Own Making* (1961), which consists of a simple wooden box containing a tape recorder which plays the sounds of the box being made. The idea that the process by which something was made could be the subject of a work has inspired a number of experimental films, including *C/CU/CUT OFF/FF/F* (1976) by Lis Rhodes and Ian Kerr. This was a performance/installation consisting of two 100-foot 16mm film loops, one clear, the other black. The loops were projected in the main gallery at the ICA, London, during the Festival of Expanded Cinema, in January 1976. They were projected in such a way that they dragged on the floor and became scratched. The black loop thus became progressively clearer, while the clear one became darker, through the refractive agency of the scratches, and through its acquiring dirt and dust. Each was periodically photocopied and the copies displayed chronologically. At the same event Steve Farrer made a photo-performance called *Exposed* (1975). In a darkened room Farrer stapled sheets of 10 by 8 photographic paper to a board with a staple gun to which was attached a small pen torch. The sheets were then processed using spray guns and the lights turned on at the end. The lines of movement made by the staple gun were recorded, like the mark of Zorro, on the sheets of paper. The image here is built up through a series of repetitive functional actions. To this extent the work's aesthetic qualities are a by-product of that process. A similar attitude informs Farrer's film *Ten Drawings*, discussed in Chapter 1, except there a composite drawing is broken down into 16mm frame-sized fragments.

6. The example of the crane is used by Noel Burch to explain the theory of intellectual montage in 'Eisenstein', in Richard Roud (ed.), *Cinema: A Critical Dictionary*, vol. 1 (London: Secker and Warburg, 1980), p. 315.

7. The artist David Cunningham made a set of sound works called *Error System* in which mistakes in the performance are deliberately incorporated into the work: 'The players play a repeating phrase. As soon as one player makes a mistake that mistake is made the basis of his repetition unless it is modified by a further mistake. Thus each player proceeds at his own rate to change the sound in an uncontrollable manner. On no account should "mistakes" be made deliberately to introduce a change in performance.

In short . . . sustain your errors.' David Cunningham, sleeve notes to the album *Grey Scale* (London: Piano 001, 1977). Coincidentally, Cunningham has worked on the soundtracks of some of Raban's recent films.

8.   The clown section, called *Ha,* was originally made as a one-minute work for the BBC2 programme *The Late Show,* and was screened in 1990. It has a palindromic structure, with the clown's hand rotating one way until it stops and recommences in the opposite direction. When the piece was broadcast, the BBC cut ten seconds from the end, upsetting the symmetry.

Film, Art, Ideology

If modern painting failed to encompass a reflection on its own limitations, ignored its own crises, it would be dismissed as naive, yet film and video have often been so used without attracting similar criticism, especially in the work of a younger generation of so-called 'gallery' artists. For most of these contemporary practitioners, questions about the specificities and effects, both ideological and aesthetic, of the media have never been urgent. They are perceived as forming part of a moribund debate, by now irrelevant or superseded, which took place in the 1970s. Besides, in a lot of work which emulates or borrows from narrative cinema (overwhelmingly Hitchcock) or deploys some of its conventions, such questions simply do not fall within the scope of the work. In Mark Lewis' films, for example, the production values of cinema are enthusiastically emulated, and in Douglas Gordon's *Feature Film* (1999) they are embraced aspirationally. Alternatively, in the installations of Jane and Louise Wilson, one sees images composed of long, shapeless takes made with hand-held DV cameras, whereby the medium is treated in the same instrumental manner as it is in TV docu-soap.

Recently there have been attempts to distinguish two strands of artists' film and video: on the one hand, 'gallery' artists who use the media, and on the other those makers – the subject of this book – who come out of the experimental, Film-makers' Co-op tradition. A more useful distinction might be made, however, between those who use the media unreflexively and those whose work necessarily includes an investigation of their manner of operation. Leger/Murphy's *Ballet mécanique* (1924) is paradigmatic.[1] Gallery artists like Robert Morris and Richard Serra, primarily sculptors, made single-screen films in the 1960s and 1970s which exhibit a sophisticated engagement with the workings and forms of the medium. Equally, 'Co-op' film-makers such as Steve Farrer and Anthony McCall have made gallery work which addresses the spatiality of its situation and the spectator's place within it. Such examples blur the 'gallery artists' versus 'Co-op film-makers' distinction. What all the above works share is an engagement with the problematics of making and presenting moving image work. In their concern with the peculiarities of film projection they may be defined as site-specific. Such work stands in contrast to that of numerous gallery artists, such as Douglas Gordon. His *24 Hour Psycho* (1993), originally a single-screen work, was shown again as a double projection on a hanging screen in his retro-spective show *What I Have Done*, at the Hayward Gallery in 2002. This latter decision was evidently justified by a desire that the work conform to a theme of the double which ran through the show, but in relation to its original form was meaningless, in that it added nothing to the original version of the work. By comparison, Michael Snow's *Two Sides to Every Story* (1974) exhaustively addresses the specificities of its form of presentation.[2]

In recent years many film and video works have been projected within specially constructed but generic rooms, designed so that a large image exactly fills one wall. The format (whose precedents lie in the Camera Obscura and the Diorama) has become a popular mode of presentation, in recognition of the fact that time-based media need dedicated, sheltered spaces if they are to be shown in galleries. However, the uniformity of this enclosed wall form means that it often bears little relation to the particular form of the film itself. Installations like Steve McQueen's 1999 Turner Prize film *Deadpan*, and Catherine Yass's 2002 Turner Prize exhibits *Flight* and *Descent*, are all very different pieces, but were shown in an identical manner in near-identical rooms. This resulted in *Flight*, which was shot from a model helicopter flying around the BBC's Broadcasting House building in central London, acquiring a spuri-ous, inappropriate monumentality. *Descent*, an undeniably beautiful film, works much better, with the projection wall forming a kind of window onto the gradually chang-ing scene: an upside-down descent past a half-built office block, shot on a foggy day on a building site at Canary Wharf in London. (However, just as works like Stan Douglas' *Der Sandmann* (1994) and Gordon's *24 Hour Psycho* inevitably invite comparisons with *Two Sides to Every Story*, so *Descent*, a baldly descriptive work, may be compared to Ernie Gehr's *Side/Walk/Shuttle* (1991), a virtuoso forty-minute film in which the complexities of vision in a large urban space are elaborated in a set of twenty-four variations on the view from an external glass elevator on a skyscraper in San Francisco.)

I have tried to touch on the ideological ramifications of the work under discussion, and to examine the relations between this and the aesthetic aspects of the work. In Gerhard Richter's Baader Meinhof paintings *October 18th 1977* (1988), the political lies not in whether the paintings are intended, or able, to raise consciousness, or induce pity or anger in the viewer. Rather, the pictures raise a question about how or whether art can engage with politics without compromising the specificity of its own discourse. An image of a political event is not necessarily a political image, but it can contribute to a meditation on the limits of painting's possible engagement with politics.

The same goes for experimental film. In the work of Peter Gidal, representation, explicitly theorised as a political process, is withheld, on the grounds that it is necess-arily conservative, since it reproduces what is already there and hence is complicit in the maintenance of an ideological status quo. The political effect in these films comes through the stimulation in the viewer of self-conscious sensations of boredom, frustration, engagement. This subject may be surprised by him/herself, and put into a position of not-knowing. This is in contrast to, for example, suspense films, where 'surprises' are expected and anticipated – unsurprising. That the effects of this work may be political, as distinct from being 'about' ideological questions, comes about through the viewers having to rethink themselves as persons through the process of confronting incipient boredom: the desire to see a work through to the end, in tension with an immediate impatience. Then: why the urge to leave? Why not stay for an experience which is already becoming more than an experience of consumption, one of self-evaluation? What is the 'end' in this context?

In a different way, political implications are also present in work like that discussed in Chapter 3. There, the use of modified technology to develop new aesthetic possibilities for film and video also constitutes a resistance to the norms maintained in the uniformly un-self-questioning products of the TV and film industries. These norms are entrenched in a well-developed ideology of 'professionalism': media transparency, notions of 'broadcast standards' and so on. If resistance to this seems a romantic notion, it needs to be set against the mind set of, for example, students embarking on media production courses. Most have experienced nothing in their lives other than a diet of Hollywood films, TV and video games, or MTV, where experimental tropes are reduced to meaningless graphical conceits. These students' understanding of media is so wholly instrumental that most of them are unaware that film and video are even distinct media.

In David Hall's work, the engagement with broadcast TV and the politics of representation is always also an engagement with aesthetic issues, because it is at this level that much of the work that is subject to attack, either implicitly or explicitly, functions. I have tried to show this, for example, in my discussion of the role of framing in *Seven TV Pieces*, where Hall explores a number of aesthetic ideas which also address the ideological implications for how TV presents the world to its viewers. Many of the works discussed herein exhibit a strong sensitivity to the play of light and the way in which objects and surfaces mutate under its influence. But this beguiling quality in the work is deepened by the fact that it points towards a profound indeterminacy in the relation between the apparatus and the profilmic, whose effects are effaced in the products of the dominant media. The 'place of epistemological doubt' that many of the works thereby take the viewer to is one area where aesthetic effects constitute both a philosophical comment on the problems of knowledge, as mediated by cinema and TV, and a refusal to collude with their ideology of truthfulness, impartiality and transparency. Regardless of how problematic their relationship may be, if ideological issues are divorced from the aesthetic there is a risk that the latter may be reduced to a merely decorative function. The aesthetic experience is surely deepened when it is allied to the various challenges it makes on the viewer: this is the point of the argument made at the beginning of Chapter 11.

All the work discussed in this book manifests the practice of putting the indexical moment of the photo-recording process (mediated differently in film and video) into tension with the peculiarities of the apparatus. In this way, new medium-specific forms develop. Such developments render obsolete the wranglings over essentialism that dogged previous debates about medium-specificity, for film and video can be seen to be distinct in the same way that watercolour painting is distinct from oil painting, without having to appeal to notions of unique properties in the two media. (By the same token, the assertion that video supersedes film is as unwarranted as the idea that acrylic paint might supersede oil: both have their own look and effect. In the end, the continuing use of film will ensure its survival, unless or until it becomes uneconomical to manufacture and process.)

In work where the nature of the originating medium is not the focal issue, and in which the camera, for example, is used in a relatively straightforward manner, as in Bruce Baillie's *All My Life*, the tension between indexical moment and apparatus might seem to be evaded. This is not the case, however. The work's problematic is simply pushed outwards from the apparatus *per se* and into the profilmic arena. The profilmic, in being defined as the object of the camera's gaze, is drawn into the apparatus by that gaze (although it stands at the opposite end of the system from film grain/video tape). The realisation that everything that falls within the purview of the apparatus becomes part of it leads to the understanding that the index/apparatus problematic cannot be avoided. This understanding underpins the works' aesthetic and defines their ethical position in relation to other kinds of unquestioning, manipulative or mendacious uses of the apparatus.

By discussing both old and new work, I hope to have demonstrated that there is a continuing and vital tradition of film- and video-making in which the issues and approaches, described above, that have exercised film-makers since the 1920s, continue through new generations today, and that their work stands against both the dominant media and the trivialising convergence of MTV, fashion, art and media that is evidenced in the work of artists like Mariko Mori, Wolfgang Tillmans and others, and whose ideology is disseminated in magazines like *Res, Wallpaper* and *Dazed and Confused*.

Notes

1. The film is discussed in Malcolm Le Grice, *Abstract Film and Beyond* (London: Studio Vista, 1977), Chapter 3.
2. *24 Hour Psycho* was also shown as a single projection on a translucent screen at *Spellbound,* a show held at the Hayward Gallery, London, in 1996, in which a group of artists showed cinematically inspired and related works. The screen was placed in such

a way that the film was viewable from behind as well as in front. For the critic Amy Taubin, writing on the work in her catalogue essay, the resulting laterally inverted image 'suggests a metaphor for Norman's psychotic confusion of his sexuality and his inability to separate his own identity from that of his mother'. Amy Taubin, 'Douglas Gordon', in Ian Christie and Philip Dodd (eds), *Spellbound* (London: Hayward Gallery, 1996), p. 75. However, it is unclear whether Gordon intended the work to be viewable from behind. Given its original single-screen form, it seems just as likely that this possibility arose inadvertently, simply because the screen's position allowed movement around it. As Taubin implies, the metaphor is at best tentative, and in any case, the theme of inversion is not peculiar to *Psycho.*

Bibliography

Bachelor, David, *Chromophobia* (London: Reaktion Books, 2000).

Beeton, Isabella, *Cookery and Household Management*, 11th edn (London: Ward Lock Ltd, 1971).

Benjamin, Walter, *One Way Street* (London: New Left Books, 1979).

Brakhage, Stan, *Essential Brakhage* (New York: McPherson and Company, 2001).

Cage, John, *Silence* (Hanover, NH: Wesleyan University Press, 1973).

Chion, Michel, *Audio-Vision* (New York: Columbia University Press, 1994).

Compton, Michael and Sylvester, David, *Robert Morris* (exhibition catalogue) (London: Tate Gallery, 1971).

Cork, Richard (ed.), *Studio International*, special issue on avant-garde film in England and Europe, vol. 190 no. 978, November–December 1975.

Cornwell, Regina, *Snow Seen* (Toronto: Peter Martin Associates, 1981).

Cubitt, Sean, *Videography: Video Media as Art and Culture* (Basingstoke: Macmillan, 1993).

Cunningham, David, *Grey Scale,* sleeve notes to vinyl album (London: Piano, 1977).

Curtis, David, *Experimental Cinema* (London: Studio Vista, 1971).

Deleuze, Gilles, *Cinema 1: The Movement Image* (London: Athlone Press, 1992).

Dodd, Philip (ed.), *Spellbound: Art and Film* (London: Hayward Gallery/BFI, 1996).

Dusinberre, Deke (ed.), Festival of Expanded Cinema exhibition catalogue (London: Institute of Contemporary Arts, 1976).

Field, Simon (ed.), *Afterimage* no. 11, special issue devoted to Michael Snow's films, functioning as the catalogue to his retrospective at Canada House (London: Afterimage Publishing, 1982).

Foster, Hal and Hughes, Gordon, *Richard Serra* (Cambridge, MA: MIT Press, 2000).

Fried, Michael, *Art and Objecthood* (Chicago, IL: Chicago University Press, 1998).

Gidal, Peter (ed.), *Structural Film Anthology*, 2nd edn (London: BFI, 1978).

Gidal, Peter, *Materialist Film* (London: Routledge, 1989).

Heath, Stephen, *Questions of Cinema* (Basingstoke: Macmillan, 1981).

Knight, Julia, *Diverse Practices* (Luton: University of Luton/John Libby Press, 1996).

Kracauer, Siegfried, *Theory of Film* (Princeton, NJ: Princeton University Press, 1997).

Krauss, Rosalind and Bois, Yves-Alain, *Formless: A Users Guide* (New York: Zone Books, 1997).

Lane, Giles (ed.), *Coil* 9–10 (London: Proboscis, 2000).

Le Grice, Malcolm, *Abstract Film and Beyond* (London: Studio Vista, 1977).

Le Grice, Malcolm, *Experimental Cinema in the Digital Age* (London: BFI, 2001).

McDonald, Scott, *Conversations with Film-makers*, vol. 3 (Berkeley: University of California Press, 1998).

Michelson, Annette and O'Brien, Kevin (eds), *Kino-Eye: The Writings of Dziga Vertov* (London: Pluto Press, 1984).

Morris, Robert, *Continuous Project Altered Daily* (Cambridge, MA: MIT, 1993).

Mulvey, Laura and McCabe, Colin, *Godard: Images, Sounds, Politics* (London: BFI, 1980).

O'Pray, Michael (ed.), *Andy Warhol Film Factory* (London: BFI, 1989).

O'Pray, Michael (ed.), *British Avant-Garde Film, 1926–1995* (Luton: University of Luton/John Libby Press, 1996).

Rees, A. L., *A History of Experimental Film and Video* (London: BFI, 2000).

Richter, Gerhard, *The Daily Practice of Painting* (London: Thames and Hudson, 1995).

Rohdie, Sam, *Antonioni* (London: BFI, 1990).

Roud, Richard (ed.), *Cinema: A Critical Dictionary*, vol. 1 (London: Secker and Warburg, 1980).

Sitney, P. Adams, *Visionary Film*, 2nd edn (Oxford: Oxford University Press, 1979).

Sitney, P. Adams, *Visionary Film*, 3rd edn (Oxford: Oxford University Press, 2003).

Sontag, Susan, *Against Interpretation* (New York: Delta Books, 1966).

Various, *John Smith Film and Video Work 1972–2002* (Bristol: Watershed/Picture This Publications, 2002).

Various, *Michael Snow Almost Cover to Cover* (London: Black Dog Publishing Ltd, 2001).

Wade, Nicholas J. and Swanston, Michael T., *Visual Perception: An Introduction*, 2nd edn (Hove: Psychology Press, 2001).

Wees, William C., *Light Moving in Time* (California: University of California Press, 1992).

Wollen, Peter, *Arrows of Desire* (catalogue) (London: ICA, 1992).

Works Cited

Actor, David Hall and Tony Sinden, 16mm, colour, sound, 11 minutes, 1972.

Adebar, Peter Kubelka, 35mm, colour, sound, 1 minute 30 seconds, 1956.

Against the Steady Stare, Steve Farrer, 35mm, colour, film installation, 1988.

All My Life, Bruce Baillie, 16mm, colour, sound, 3 minutes, 1966.

Alphaville, Jean-Luc Godard, 35mm, B&W, sound, 98 minutes, 1965.

Angles of Incidence, William Raban, 16mm, colour, silent, 8 minutes, single or double screen, 1973.

Anju, Annabel Nicolson, 16mm, colour, silent, 10 minutes, twin screen, 1970.

Anticipation of the Night, Stan Brakhage, 16mm, colour, silent, 43 minutes, 1958.

Apocalypse Now, Francis Ford Coppola, 35mm, colour, sound, 138 minutes, 1979.

Arbitrary Logic, Malcolm Le Grice, live manipulation of computer graphics, colour, live music, variable duration, 1988.

Arnulf Rainer, Peter Kubelka, 35mm, B&W, sound, 7 minutes, 1960.

Back and Forth, Michael Snow, 16mm, colour, sound, 52 minutes, 1969.

Beauty No. 2, Andy Warhol, 16mm, B&W, sound, 70 minutes, 1965.

Berlin Horse, Malcolm Le Grice, 16mm, colour, sound, single or double screen, 8 minutes, 1970.

Between, David Hall and Tony Sinden, 16mm, colour, sound, 16 minutes, 1972–3.

Black & Light Movie, Neil Henderson, Super 8, B&W, silent, 10 minutes, 50 projectors, 2001.

Black and White, Simon Payne, video, B&W, silent, 10 minutes, 2002.

Black, Green and Red, Neil Henderson, Super 8, colour, silent, 9 projectors, variable duration, 1997–8.

The Black Tower, John Smith, 16mm, colour, sound, 24 minutes, 1985–87.

Blight, John Smith, 16mm, colour, sound, 15 minutes, 1994–6.

Blowup, Michelangelo Antonioni, 35mm, colour, sound, 110 minutes, 1966.

Breath, William Raban, 16mm, colour, sound, 15 minutes, 1974.

Brighton, Joe Read, Super 8/digital video, colour, silent, installation for 9 monitors, 2001.

British Sounds, Jean-Luc Godard, 16mm, colour, sound, 52 minutes, 1969.

Canon, Guy Sherwin, 16mm, B&W, sound, 3 minutes, 2001

Castle One, Malcolm Le Grice, 16mm, B&W, sound, light bulb, 20 minutes, 1966.

Champ Provençal, Rose Lowder, 16mm, colour, silent, 9 minutes, 1979.

Chumlum, Ron Rice, 16mm, colour, sound, 24 minutes, 1964.

A Cold Draft, Lis Rhodes, video, colour, sound, 30 minutes, 1988.

Condition of Illusion, Peter Gidal, 16mm, colour, silent, 30 minutes, 1975.

Confessions, William Raban, 16mm, colour, sound, 1 minute, 2001.

Corrigan, *Having Recovered*, Tim Bruce, 16mm, colour, sound, multi-screen projection, 26 minutes, 1979.

C/CU/CUT OFF/FF/F, Lis Rhodes and Ian Kerr, two 100-foot 16mm loops, B&W, and photocopier, indefinite, 1976.

Cycle (from the Short Film Series), Guy Sherwin, 16mm, B&W, silent, 3 minutes, 1980.

Cycles 1 (a.k.a *Dot Cycle*), Guy Sherwin, 16mm, B&W, sound, 5 minutes, 1972/77.

Deadline, Lis Rhodes, video, colour, sound, 12 minutes, 1992.

Dear Diary, Nanni Moretti, 35mm, colour, sound, 100 minutes, 1993.

Il deserto rosso, Michelangelo Antonioni, 35mm, colour, sound, 116 minutes, 1964.

Distancing, Rob Gawthrop, 16mm, colour, silent, 15 minutes, 1979.

Drive, Simon Oxlee, video, colour, sound, 8 minutes, 1994.

Eat, Andy Warhol, 16mm, B&W, silent, 45 minutes, 1963.

L'eclisse, Michelangelo Antonioni, 35mm, colour, sound, 125 minutes, 1962.

Edge, David Hall and Tony Sinden, 16mm, colour, sound, 10 minutes, 1972–3.

EETC, David Larcher, 16mm/video, 70 minutes, 1986.

Emak Bakia, Man Ray, 35mm, B&W, silent, 18 minutes, 1926.

Eye of the Projector, Rob Gawthrop, 16mm, colour, sound, 3-projector event, 1976.

Extract, Jo Pearson, 16mm, B&W, sound, 8 minutes, 1993.

Eye of the Projector, Rob Gawthrop, 16mm, colour, sound, 3-projector event, 1976.

Film No. 1, Jennifer Nightingale, 16mm, B&W (negative), silent, 3 minutes, 2001.

Film No. 2, Jennifer Nightingale, Super 8, colour pinhole cartridge, silent, 4 minutes, 2001.

Film No. 3, Jennifer Nightingale, Super 8, B&W, pinhole cartridge, silent, 4 minutes, 2001.

Film No. 4, Jennifer Nightingale, Super 8, B&W pinhole cartridge, silent, 4 minutes, 2001.

Flaming Creatures, Jack Smith, 16mm, B&W, sound, 43 minutes, 1963.

The Flicker, Tony Conrad, 16mm, B&W, silent, 30 minutes, 1966.

Flight, Guy Sherwin, 16mm, B&W, sound, 4 minutes, 1998.

Floor Film, Tony Hill, 16mm, colour, sound, floor projection, 1975.

4 X LOOPS, Nicky Hamlyn, 16mm, B&W, silent, 4 projectors, variable duration, 1974.

4th Wall, Peter Gidal, 16mm, colour, silent, 45 minutes, 1978.

Free Radicals, Len Lye, 16mm, B&W (hand scratched), sound, 4 minutes, 1958.

Glass Ground, Nicky Hamlyn, 16mm, B&W, silent, installation, 2001.

Grey Scale, David Cunningham, 12 inch vinyl LP record, 1977.

Heavens, Joe Read, video, colour, silent, installation, 2001.

Helspitflexion, Stan Brakhage, 16mm, colour, silent, 50 seconds, 1983.

Henry Geldzahler, Andy Warhol, 16mm, B&W, silent, 100 minutes, 1964.

Holding the Viewer, Tony Hill, 16mm, colour, sound, 1 minute, 1993.

Home Suite, John Smith, video, colour, sound, 90 minutes, 1993–4.

Horse, Andy Warhol, 16mm, B&W, sound, 99 minutes, 1965.

Ich Tank, David Larcher, video, colour, sound, 30 minutes, 1997.

Inlets, John Cage, three performers with water-filled conch shells, variable duration, 1977.

Interactive Feedback No. 1, Elliott Ashton, video, sound, installation, 1995.

Interactive Room 12, Espen Jensen, two microphones and electronics, installation, 1 week, 2001.

Jack Hammer, Denise Hawrysio, Super 8, B&W, silent, 4 minutes, 1985.

Lady Dog, Ron Haselden, 16mm, B&W, film and frame enlargements, event, 1975.

The Lady in the Lake, Robert Montgomery, 35mm, B&W, sound, 104 minutes, 1946.

Lamp Light, Gerhard Omsted, video, colour, sound, 10 minutes, 2001.

Line Describing a Cone, Anthony McCall, 16mm, B&W, silent, interactive projection, 30 minutes, 1973.

The Lord of the Rings: The Fellowship of the Ring, Peter Jackson, 35mm, colour, sound, 171 minutes, 2001.

Machine of Eden, Stan Brakhage, 16mm, colour, silent, 12 minutes 30 seconds, 1970.

Mare's Tail, David Larcher, 16mm, colour, sound, 150 minutes, 1969.

Mean Streets, Martin Scorsese, 35mm, colour, sound, 110 minutes, 1973.

MFV Maureen, Ron Haselden, 16mm, B&W, silent, 5-screen loop projection, 1975.

Monkey's Birthday, David Larcher, 16mm, colour, sound, 360 minutes, 1973–5.

Mothlight, Stan Brakhage, 16mm, colour, silent, 4 minutes, 1963.

My Hustler, Andy Warhol, 16mm, B&W, sound, 70 minutes, 1965.

Naughts, Stan Brakhage, 16mm, colour, silent, hand-painted, 5 minutes 30 seconds, 1994.

Night Music, Stan Brakhage, 16mm, colour, silent, hand-painted, 30 seconds, 1986.

Night Train, Guy Sherwin, 16mm, B&W, sound, 2 minutes, 1979.

Nil by Mouth, Gary Oldman, 35mm, colour, sound, 128 minutes, 1998.

Nine for Black and Red, Neil Henderson, Super 8 colour, silent, 9 screens, variable duration, 1996.

1998 Frames, Dryden Goodwin, 16mm, colour, silent, installation, 1998.

Non Places, Karen Mirza and Brad Butler, 16mm, B&W, sound, 14 minutes, 1999.

Normal Love, Jack Smith, colour, sound, 80 minutes, 1963.

La notte, Michelangelo Antonioni, 35mm, B&W, sound, 122 minutes, 1960.

On and Off/Monitor, Simon Payne, video, colour, silent, 3 minutes, 2002.

One Hundred and One TVs, David Hall and Tony Sinden, 101 TV sets, B&W, sound, installation, 1975.

One plus One/Sympathy for the Devil, Jean-Luc Godard, 35mm, colour, sound, 99 minutes, 1968.

ORIFSO, Lis Rhodes, video, colour, sound, 12 minutes, 1998.

Particles in Space, Len Lye, 16mm, B&W, hand-scratched, sound, 4 minutes, 1966.

Pasht, Stan Brakhage, 16mm, colour, silent, 6 minutes, 1965.

The Passing, Bill Viola, video, colour, sound, 54 minutes, 1991.

Peace Mandala End War, Paul Sharits, 16mm, colour, silent, 5 minutes, 1966.

Pierrot le fou, Jean-Luc Godard, 35mm, colour, sound, 112 minutes, 1965.

Poor Little Rich Girl, Andy Warhol, 16mm, B&W, sound, 70 minutes, 1965.

Post Office Tower Retowered, Ian Kerr, 16mm, colour, sound, variable duration, 1977–8.

Psycho, Alfred Hitchcock, 35mm, B&W, sound, 109 minutes, 1960.

Ray Gun Virus, Paul Sharits, 16mm, colour, silent, 16 minutes, 1966.

Red Shift, Emily Richardson, 16mm, colour, silent, 4 minutes, 2001.

Reel Time, Annabel Nicolson, 16mm, colour, silent, 8 minutes, 1973.

La Région centrale, Michael Snow, 16mm, colour, sound, 210 minutes, 1970.

Return to Reason, Man Ray, B&W, silent, 3 minutes, 1923.

Revolution 1, Simon Oxlee, video, colour, sound, 7 minutes, 1994.

Revolution 2, Simon Oxlee, video, colour, sound, 8 minutes, 1994.

Rhythm 1, Nicky Hamlyn, 16mm (unsplit Standard 8), B&W, sound, 4 minutes, 1974.

Rhythmus 23, Hans Richter, 35mm, B&W, silent, 3 minutes, 1923.

Riddle of Lumen, Stan Brakhage, 16mm, colour, silent, 12 minutes, 1972.

Robinson in Space, Patrick Keiller, 35mm, colour, sound, 70 minutes, 1997.

Roman Numeral Series, Stan Brakhage, 16mm, colour, silent, 1–8 minutes, 1979–80.

Romeo and Juliet, Franco Zeffirelli, 35mm, colour, sound, 152 minutes, 1968.

Room Film 1973, Peter Gidal, 16mm, colour, silent, 50 minutes, 1973.

Rue des Teinturiers, Rose Lowder, 16mm, colour, silent, 31 minutes, 1979.

Running Light, Lis Rhodes, video, B&W, 13 minutes, sound, 1996.

The Sadist Beats the Unquestionably Innocent, Margaret Raspe, Super 8, colour, silent, 6 minutes, 1971.

Sanday, Nick Collins, 16mm, colour, sound, 16 minutes, 1988.

Der Sandmann, Stan Douglas, 16mm, B&W, double-screen installation, 1999.

Sculptures for a Windless Space, Barbara Meter, Super 8/16mm, colour, sound, 10 minutes, 1995.

The Searchers, John Ford, 35mm, B&W, sound, 114 minutes, 1956.

Serene Velocity, Ernie Gehr, 16mm, colour, silent, 23 minutes, 1970.

Seven TV Pieces, David Hall, 16mm/video, B&W, sound, 21 minutes, 1971.

Shepherd's Delight, John Smith, 16mm, colour, sound, 35 minutes, 1980–84.

Short Film Series, Guy Sherwin, 16mm, B&W, silent, 3 minutes each, 1975–present

A Short History of the Wheel, Tony Hill, 16mm, colour, sound, 1 minute, 1992.

Side/Walk/Shuttle, Ernie Gehr, 16mm, colour, silent, 40 minutes, 1991.

A Situation Envisaged: The Rite II, David Hall, video, colour, sound, installation, 1988–90.

Sixty TV Sets, David Hall and Tony Sinden, 60 TV sets, B&W, sound, installation, 1972.

Slides, Annabel Nicolson, 16mm, colour, 16 minutes, 1971.

Slow Glass, John Smith, 16mm, colour, sound, 50 minutes, 1988–91.

Snake, Richard Serra, three rolled steel plates, each 104 foot x 13 foot, 1997.

Snow Shovel, Denise Hawrysio, Super 8, B&W, silent, 4 minutes, 1987.

Sortie de l'usine, Louis and Auguste Lumière, 35mm, B&W, silent, 50 seconds, 1895.

Soubresauts, Simon Popper, modified 16mm projector, installation, 2000.

The Sound Recordist Walks Away, Alone; The End, Colin Crockatt, video, colour, sound, 8 minutes, 2001.

Spellbound, Alfred Hitchcock, 35mm, B&W, sound, 111 minutes, 1945.

Sticks for the Dog, Ron Haselden, 16mm, colour, sound, 3 back-projected film loops and transparent frame enlargements, installation, 1976.

Stooky Bill TV, David Hall, video, colour, sound, 4 minutes, 1990.

Synch Sound, Mike Dunford, 16mm colour, sound, 10 minutes, 1974.

Tar Kettle, Denise Hawrysio, Super 8, B&W, silent, 4 minutes, 1987.

Ten Drawings, Steve Farrer, 16mm, B&W, sound, 20 minutes, 1976.

Text of Light, Stan Brakhage, 16mm, colour, silent, 70 minutes, 1974.

Third Party, Sam Taylor-Wood, 16mm/DVD, colour, sound, 7-screen installation, 1999.

Thirty Six Working Projectors, Neil Henderson, Super 8, colour, silent, 36 projectors, 10 minutes, 2000.

This is a Television Receiver, David Hall, video, colour, sound, 8 minutes, 1975.

This Surface, David Hall and Tony Sinden, 12 minutes, 1972–3.

Three Colours Blue, Krzysztof Kieslowski, 35mm, colour, sound, 100 minutes, 1993.

Titanic, James Cameron, 35mm, colour, sound, 194 minutes, 1997.

Tomorrow and Tomorrow Let Them Swing, Margaret Raspe, Super 8, colour, silent, 20 minutes, 1974.

Les Tournesols, Rose Lowder, 16mm, colour, silent, 3 minutes, 1982.

Tree Reflection (from the Short Film Series), Guy Sherwin, 16mm, B&W, silent, 3 minutes, 1998.

Twelve for Black, Green and Red, Neil Henderson, Super 8, colour, silent, 12 projectors, variable duration, 1997–8.

Twelve for Black with Splice Marks, Neil Henderson, Super 8, B&W, silent, variable duration, 12 projectors, 1996

24 Hour Psycho, Douglas Gordon, video, B&W, silent, installation, 1993.

Two Sides to Every Story, Michael Snow, 16mm, colour, sound, 30 minutes, double-sided screen, 1974.

Une Femme est une femme, Jean-Luc Godard, 35mm, colour, sound, 84 minutes, 1961.

Unschlitt/Tallow, Joseph Beuys, wax and tallow, 195 x 306 x 955cm, 1977.

Unsere Afrikareise, Peter Kubelka, 16mm, colour, sound, 12 minutes 30 seconds, 1970.

Untitled, William English, 16mm, colour, sound, 12 minutes, twin screen, 1990–present.

Untitled, Michael Maziere, 16mm, B&W, silent, 18 minutes, 1980.

Video Tape with Bicycle Sound, Colin Crockatt, video, colour, sound, 8 minutes, 2001.

Videovøid, David Larcher, video, colour, sound, 30 minutes, 1993.

View, David Hall and Tony Sinden, 16mm, colour, sound, 9 minutes, 1972.

Wavelength, Michael Snow, 16mm, colour, sound, 45 minutes, 1967.

Week End, Jean-Luc Godard, 35mm, colour, sound, 95 minutes, 1967.

Whistle Blower, James Allen, video, colour, sound, 5 minutes, 1994.

White Light, Nicky Hamlyn, 16mm, colour and B&W, silent, 22 minutes, 1996.

Word Movie/Flux Film 29, Paul Sharits, 16mm, B&W, silent, 1966.

Yellow, Arran Crabbe, video, colour, sound, 3 minutes, 1996.

Yes No Maybe Maybe Not, Malcolm Le Grice, 16mm, B&W, silent, 8 minutes, single or double screen, 1967.

Zabriskie Point, Michelangelo Antonioni, 35mm, colour, sound, 110 minutes, 1969.

Zazie dans le Metro, Louis Malle, 35mm, colour, sound, 92 minutes, 1960.

Index

Note: Page numbers *in italics* refer to illustrations. Colour plates are indicated by *pl.* and the plate number *in italics*.